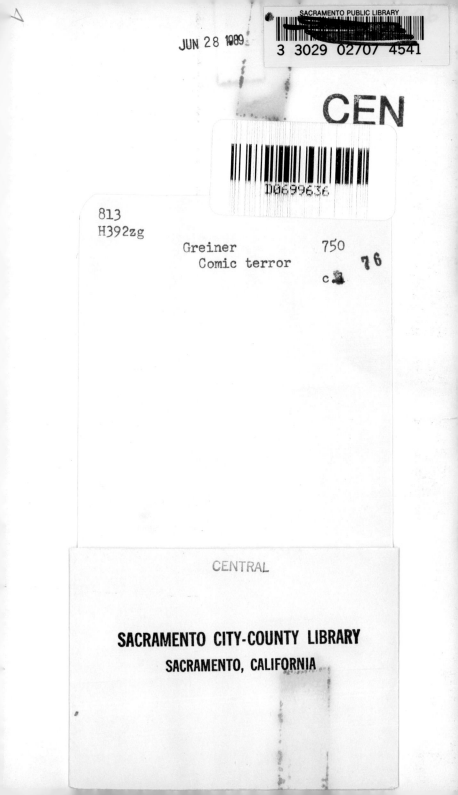

COMIC TERROR

Comic Terror:

The Novels of John Hawkes

Donald J. Greiner

MEMPHIS STATE UNIVERSITY PRESS

This book is for Ellen

Library of Congress catalog card number: 73-81555
ISBN 0-87870-017-X

Acknowledgments

ACKNOWLEDGMENTS are a pleasure to write. To begin, this work was supported in part by a grant from the University of South Carolina Research and Productive Scholarship Fund. I am also grateful to the Department of English of the University of South Carolina for various summer grants. More specifically, I thank Professor Jack Russell of the University of Maryland and Professor John Kimmey of the University of South Carolina for their willingness to read short portions of the manuscript when I was just beginning to write this book. My greatest debt is to Professor Calhoun Winton, Head of the Department of English at the University of South Carolina, not only for his cheerful readiness to engage in the time-consuming task of reading the entire manuscript-in-progress, but also for his sympathy, encouragement, and ability to bolster the confidence of the struggling author. Finally I want to thank my students in English 428 and 751, who began reading John Hawkes with straight faces, but who eventually joined me in the laughter.

I would like to take this opportunity to thank the editors of *Southwest Review* and *Contemporary Literature* for permission to reprint from articles originally published in those journals which appear in revised form in this book. Specifically, part of Chapter One appeared in *Southwest Review* (Autumn 1971), and part of Chapter Six in *Contemporary Literature* (Summer 1970): "The Thematic Use of Color in John Hawkes' *Second Skin*," Volume 11, Number 3 (© 1970 by the Regents of the University of Wisconsin), pp. 389–400.

I would also like to thank the editors of the following journals for permission to publish short passages from material which was first published in their magazines: "Flannery O'Connor's Devil" was first published in *The Sewanee Review*, 70 (Summer 1962), © 1962 by The University of the South; "Notes on the Wild Goose Chase" was first published in *The Massachusetts Review*, 3 (Summer 1962), as was "John Hawkes on His Novels: An Interview with John Graham," 7 (Summer 1966), © 1962, 1966 by The Massachusetts Review, Inc.; "John Hawkes: An Interview" was first published in *Contemporary Literature*, 6 (Summer 1965), © 1965 by the Regents of the University of Wisconsin.

Contents

Preface xi

Chapter One. Technique and Comedy in Hawkes' Novels 1

Chapter Two. Innovative Threesome: *Charivari,*
The Goose on the Grave, The Owl 29

Chapter Three. Casualties of History: *The Cannibal* 67

Chapter Four. Nightmarish Western: *The Beetle Leg* 97

Chapter Five. Small, Yet Beyond Elimination:
The Lime Twig 125

Chapter Six. Love at Last: *Second Skin* 159

Chapter Seven. Memoirs of a Sex-Singer:
The Blood Oranges 201

A Few Remarks and Conclusions 241

Selected Checklist of John Hawkes 249

Index 255

Preface

JOHN Hawkes occupies a peculiar place in contemporary American fiction. He is one of the few truly gifted writers in the so-called black humor movement which has flourished since 1950, but he lacks the renown enjoyed by less talented authors. In the years since World War II innovative American fiction has turned from the documentation of social forms and the use of realistic technique to an evocation of nightmare and fear. The feeling of disruption left from the war, the specter of atomic catastrophe so vividly objectified at Hiroshima, the tensions of the cold war, and the spread of random violence in everyday life have all contributed to the conviction that chaos rather than order dominates day to day living.

The most exciting of today's novelists reflect this sense of the fractured life in their fiction, but, significantly, the prevailing tone in most of their work is not the gloomy pessimism which might be expected but a shocking sense of humor. Shocking because it encourages laughter at events which are, more often than not, horribly violent, the modern comic novel often meets the general feel-

ing of doom with humor. We need only recall Kurt Vonnegut's
Bokonon thumbing his nose at You Know Who while the world
around him solidifies into ice (*Cat's Cradle*) or Joseph Heller's
Yossarian walking naked around the air base because Snowden's
guts spilled on his uniform (*Catch–22*) to understand how a different kind of humor, often grotesque and violent, comments on the
world's absurdities.

Some readers may protest the use of the term "black humor,"
claiming that it is either a cliché or a catch-all phrase which attempts to accommodate too many diverse literary works. The
sheer terror which accompanies Hawkes' comic episodes, for example, seems unrelated to the humanity of Vonnegut's comedy
or the antics of J. P. Donleavy's Ginger Man. For this reason a
variety of descriptive terms has been proposed. Robert Scholes
calls some of these novelists "fabulators." [1] Richard Poirier, in
A World Elsewhere, speaks of "comic-apocalyptic writers," while
Conrad Knickerbocker suggests "humor with a mortal sting." Perhaps we should settle for Richard Kostelanetz's more conventional
phrase, "American absurd novel." [2] It makes little difference what
we call this recent movement in American fiction—I am content
with "the modern American comic novel." The point, of course, is
not the relative blackness of the comedy, but rather the general
vision which most of these authors share. Whether or not a novelist is a black humorist depends upon one's definition. Vance
Bourjaily, for instance, denies Kurt Vonnegut's association with
black humor when he tries to distinguish between it and gallows
humor.[3] If the comedy's intention is "pure kindness," writes Bourjaily, then it must be gallows humor. Bruce Jay Friedman, on the
other hand, dismisses attempts to pin a definition on these novels:
"It is called 'Black Humor' and I think I would have more luck

1. Robert Scholes, *The Fabulators* (New York: Oxford University
Press, 1967).
2. Knickerbocker's article, "Humor with a Mortal Sting," and Kostelanetz's, "The American Absurd Novel," are included in *The World of
Black Humor*, ed. Douglas M. Davis (New York: E. P. Dutton, 1967).
3. Vance Bourjaily, "What Vonnegut Is and Isn't," *New York Times
Book Review*, 13 August 1972, p. 3.

defining an elbow or a corned-beef sandwich. I am not, for one thing, even sure it is black. It might be fuchsia or eggshell." [4] One suspects that the author of *Stern* and *The Dick* knows what he is talking about.

The comparable blackness of a particular writer's humor is indeed secondary—all are black, but some are blacker, and funnier, than others. More important is the attempt to decide what the presence of so many modern American comic novelists means. Taken together, the novels of Hawkes, Vonnegut, Heller, John Barth, Donleavy, Friedman, Thomas Pynchon, Ken Kesey, James Purdy, and others suggest a type of fiction so refreshingly different from the conventional novel that one suspects the prophets of the novel's death to be wrong. What these authors do have in common is a vision of their world as chaotic and fractured. How can one affirm order in a world which is fragmented—and violently so? But though the disoriented quality of modern life prevents the black humorist from celebrating order, it does not propel him to nihilism. The fact that *Catch–22*, *Giles Goat-Boy*, and *Second Skin* have been written, published, and read suggests the authors' hope for meaningful communication at the very least. Thus a modern comic novelist like John Barth can insist that art is "exhausted" and yet show how alive the "literature of exhaustion" is.

In much of Barth's work, and in that of other black humorists, the need to respond to the social issues of a chaotic world is subordinated to the demands of art, whereas in the fiction of an earlier comic novelist, Nathanael West, the social questions are significant. Yet both writers seem to celebrate art as a means of coping with the complexity of contemporary reality. Aesthetic expression acts momentarily to control the chaos. The result is that, in many modern fictions, form dominates content; technique is more important than social or moral commentary. And when the demands of structure are considered superior to the matters to be expressed, the pattern of fiction assumes primary significance. Hawkes has this problem in mind when he declares plot, character, setting,

4. Bruce Jay Friedman, ed. *Black Humor* (New York: Bantam, 1965), p. vii.

and theme to be the novel's enemies. The subordination of these traditional features encourages the author's concern with pattern and structure. If my remarks have merit, then a lot of us are going to have to change our customary criteria for judging a novel: by the validity of the moral vision it communicates, or by the proximity to felt life it reveals. The modern American comic novelist is not sure that a verifiable moral vision exists, or that life can be ordered long enough to approximate it. At the risk of oversimplification, I suggest that these authors refuse to verify a moral code because verification would allude to order and sanity in a world which they see as fractured and absurd. Thus these writers underplay the traditional interests of the novelist. Their common concern is not with morality or reality but with technique.

No one would argue that the black humorist is unusual because he laughs at man's absurdity. Many writers of the past have couched their awareness of their time's chaos in shocking, grotesque images. In the English tradition alone one need think only of Pope, Swift, and Sterne. The ancestor of the modern American comic novel is satire. If we must look for literary antecedents, we should heed Robert Scholes' conclusion in *The Fabulators* that these authors have a closer affinity with the great satirists of the eighteenth century than with the giants of several generations ago, Faulkner, Fitzgerald, and Hemingway. And yet, as any student of modern comedy knows, black humor cannot be defined as satire. Hawkes and his contemporaries show an irreverence, ranging from playfulness to the most sardonic criticism, toward traditionally venerated norms like science, religion, and patriotism. But unlike the traditional satirist—and the distinction is crucial—most black humorists reject the satirist's faith in the ability of satirical laughter to reform man's follies. Even the most elaborate definition of satire must emphasize the author's use of laughter not so much to tear down as to encourage a rebuilding. The black humorist dismisses reformation and ethical certainties to place his faith in what Professor Scholes calls "the humanizing value of laughter." He desires not so much a turn about from folly but an exposé of the absurd. The traditional satirist and the contemporary comic novelist meet primarily in their shared confidence in the value of laughter, but each puts laughter to work differently. For the modern humorist, the ridiculous joke called life must be laughed at if sanity is to be maintained. Most of these novelists show a love of humanity instead of the scorn often found in standard satire.

Black humor is not a conscious rejection of satire as much as a matter of simply not writing it. If modern comic fiction has a literary target, it is realism. Too many readers continue to associate fiction with realism—we have all heard the exclamation that a particular novel was enjoyed because it was "so real." In realism, representation of life is more important than art. But in black humor, with its emphasis on technique, the use of words to explore and express the imagination outstrips the description of things. This is why Scholes finds in fabulation a return to a more "verbal" or "fictional" kind of novel, by which he means a less realistic, but more artistic narrative—more evocative, more concerned with ideas instead of things—in short, a turn away from realism. To appreciate what Hawkes is doing with fiction, we must slough off our traditional notions of what makes a novel. Popular opinion to the contrary, realism is not the sole way of looking at life truthfully. It is no more than another literary device, an outdated one at that. Given the fragmentation of the twentieth century, realistic depiction of it does us little good. We already know that things are bad. Life cannot be made to seem reasonable if it is ridiculous. The more important question posed by a black humorist is how to live with one's self and with others in a fractured world. Laughter may not save the world, but it can help us live our lives. Conrad Knickerbocker distinguishes modern comedy from "normal" fiction by arguing that conventional novelists "prefer to seduce the reader with clever mixtures of the probable and the derived," whereas black humorists "prefer rape." Normal fiction is explained in normal fashion, but black humor "savages" the reader's traditional beliefs in "big cars, families and fancy restaurants." [5] When reading Hawkes it must be remem-

5. Knickerbocker, p. 301.

bered that his characters do not discover absurdity or chaos or
meaninglessness. Rather, these qualities are the given factors. His
novels *begin* with the probability that Michael Banks, or Margaret, or Skipper will meet defeat; whereas traditional fiction usually
details the process of the protagonist discovering the possibility of
defeat and death. Finding out that life is cruel is often the crucial experience for the characters in conventional novels—think of
What Maisie Knew, say, or *A Farewell to Arms*—but Skipper or
Yossarian or the Ginger Man expects cruelty. Their problem is not
how to avoid defeat but how to live with its probability.

John Hawkes is very much a part of this trend in recent American fiction, but when placed beside his colleagues, he is undoubt-
edly the least known. If it were not for the fact that Hawkes' fiction
is of such high merit, his lack of readers would not be deplorable.
But because Hawkes is one of the two or three most talented of all
American writers who have matured since 1950, his obscure reputation is a cause for concern. Incredibly, readers who pride themselves on a knowledgeable awareness of recent trends in fiction
either dismiss his work as too difficult or ignore his comic vision
to stress his truly grotesque horrors. In most cases, however, he remains unknown and unread. He is, as Leslie Fiedler calls him in
the preface to *The Lime Twig*, "perhaps . . . the least read novelist
of substantial merit in the United States." Answering the question
of who reads John Hawkes, Fiedler continues: "Only a few of us,
I fear, tempted to pride by our fewness, and ready in that pride
to believe that the recalcitrant rest of the world doesn't deserve
Hawkes, that we would do well to keep his pleasures our little
secret."

Although Fiedler's comments illustrate a growing body of criticism favorable to Hawkes' fiction, many of the reviews which have
greeted his novels reveal ignorance about both his work as a whole
and his experiments with comedy, violence, and technique. In a
review of *Second Skin*, for example, Paul Levine admits that the
novel is "verbally exciting," but he finally dismisses Hawkes as a
"novelist of virtuosic originality," one whose "tolerance for bi-

zarre effects remains a defect of his imagination." [6] John Wain also rejects the nightmarish episodes, wondering why a gifted writer like Hawkes "should go to such lengths to make his work virtually unreadable." [7] Tom Bishop, on the other hand, accepts the grotesque distortions as meaningful, but he, unlike Levine, laments that Hawkes' style, while lovely, fails "to attach itself more to life." [8]

Criticizing Hawkes' novels for avoiding verisimilitude seems perhaps unreasonable, since one of his announced goals is to disrupt the claims of conventional fiction in the hope of making the novel a more "pleasurable" experience. Yet this is what Jonathan Baumbach does in *The Landscape of Nightmare: Studies in the Contemporary American Novel* (New York: New York University Press, 1965). One would think that a discussion of nightmare in recent American fiction would have to treat Hawkes in some depth, but Baumbach limits his comment on Hawkes' achievement to a footnote. What is puzzling is that he agrees with Hawkes that the novels of manners and of social protest, so significant in the 1930s, have been about written out. As Baumbach notes, social wrongs may still be an issue in the contemporary American novel, but the problem of righting those wrongs is no longer the point. Thus, he celebrates the modern novel of nightmare with its "highly developed awareness of form, a generally impressive technical sophistication." Arguing that the American novel since 1945 has largely abandoned naturalism and the social scene, he devotes his book to a study of those writers who, he feels, explore the "underside of consciousness" and the ways the world accommodates evil to the extent that the surrounding landscape seems to be a nightmare. Yet he dismisses Hawkes' fiction as a "game." Though recognizing that Hawkes' world is deliberately out of focus, very close to "an

6. Paul Levine, "Individualism and the Traditional Talent," *Hudson Review*, 17 (Autumn 1964), 476.

7. John Wain, "The Very Thing," *New York Review of Books*, 26 February 1970, p. 37.

8. Tom Bishop, review of *Lunar Landscapes*, *Saturday Review*, 9 August 1969, p. 31.

actual nightmare," he does not discuss it. I suspect that he avoids Hawkes, despite the emphasis suggested by his book's title, because he looks for an approximation of real life in the novel. For all his appreciation of the use of nightmare in modern fiction, Baumbach continues to call for verisimilitude, for novels which can be believed literally. For example, he admires Truman Capote's command of style in *Other Voices, Other Rooms,* but he finally excludes it from his study on the grounds that "Capote's magical stagelike world . . . is not to be believed." His demand for a sense of felt life in the novel is made clear when he writes, "However, if *real* life is not the final stuff of the novel, it is at least the first stuff." This is precisely the kind of comment which Hawkes would dispute. Since his fiction is closer to nightmare than that of any other contemporary American novelist, it necessarily rejects "real life." But this rejection convinces Baumbach to dismiss it as a game: "His work is prescriptively contemporary, related on the one hand to the nightmare world of Flannery O'Connor and on the other to the antinovels of Sarraute and Robbe-Grillet; for all of the brilliance of Hawkes's style, the novels seem so many eccentric exercises—an extraordinary game superbly played, but a game nevertheless." [9]

So the controversy concerning Hawkes' achievement continues. When he is read at all, his fiction excites both high praise and strongly worded negative criticism in nearly equal amounts. It is not my goal in this study to disprove the charges of his detractors—indeed I do not hope to prove or disprove anything. Yet it seems to me that many of the adverse evaluations and misreadings result from both ignorance about Hawkes' aims and misunderstanding of his often militant experimentation with humor, narrative voice, and structure. What I do hope to accomplish in the following pages is a clarification of Hawkes' technique and comedy, and a study of each novel which will offer suggestions about many of the more troublesome passages and image patterns. The first chap-

9. Jonathan Baumbach, *Landscape of Nightmare: Studies in the Contemporary American Novel* (New York: New York University Press, 1965), p. 5.

ter is an examination of technique and comedy in which I draw upon most of his published interviews and literary criticism. Detailed analysis and illustration of his theories are reserved for the later chapters. The discussion of humor calls attention to what nearly every commentator underplays—his use of comic episodes. Hawkes considers himself foremost a comic novelist, but evaluations of his fiction typically concentrate upon the nightmarish events, failing to discuss how the consistent use of humor affects the terror. Examining traditional theories of comedy, especially those of George Meredith and Henri Bergson, I hope to place Hawkes' humor in perspective and, thus, show why it is apparently so strange. The remaining chapters offer detailed discussions of the three novellas and five novels as a means of illustrating and analyzing his theories in practice and of suggesting possible readings of an extremely difficult body of fiction. Whether or not my comments and analyses successfully challenge Hawkes' negative critics is not the point. But I do hope that what I have to say will encourage more serious readers to pick up his novels. A writer of Hawkes' genius deserves a wider hearing.

COMIC TERROR

1

Technique and Comedy in Hawkes' Novels

JOHN Hawkes has been publishing significant fiction since 1949, but after more than two decades of publication his work continues to be labeled underground or *avant-garde*. The labels themselves are not harmful until the novels to which they are applied are dismissed as willfully unreadable or as no more than vehicles for esoteric experiments with technique. When this kind of distortion determines reputation, fiction which deserves a reading finds itself talked about but largely unread. Unquestionably Hawkes' novels are hard to read, but a degree of difficulty has never stood in the way of serious readers. His writing is also experimental, but he plans his experiments to break new ground for fiction and not to bewilder with deliberately obscure prose.

Contemporary experimental comic fiction—the black humor of such authors as Kurt Vonnegut, John Barth, and John Hawkes—may be called underground, but when applied to these writers this term means more than the standard suggestion of a novelist appealing to a comparatively small circle of dedicated readers. Because these novelists are so openly experimental as they probe the inner recesses of the mind, the term "underground" has come to describe not just reputation but also subject matter and technique. Sensing modern life's fragmentation, and knowing that traditional literary realism is unequipped to handle it, Hawkes and his contemporaries utilize fantasy and absurdity to grapple with the chaos of our age. This underground comic fiction is so consciously experimental, so intense in its need to communicate fear, and so sensitive to the pain and illogic of our circumstances that many readers hesitate to accept as humorous the reading experience which these new novelists offer. These fictions are underground because they explore the unconscious, that part of ourselves about which we know the least and thus fear the most. A discussion of Hawkes' experimental technique and of his special brand of comedy should help us as we investigate his fiction.

Confrontation with our dreamlike states and nightmarish fantasies bothers most of us because we have little control over what we are meeting. Although the experience can be illuminating, it can also be unpleasant. A similar reluctance is, apparently, the excuse of those readers who ignore today's comic writing. Lacking understanding of what these authors are doing and why, otherwise sophisticated readers avoid a valid artistic experience which, while certainly revealing terror, will just as surely enlighten them about the dark side of their lives. Obviously anticipating the problem, Hawkes has gone out of his way to grant interviews and to publish first-rate literary criticism, all of which aids the reader. He has not set down his ideas in a collection of formal essays, nor has he conducted a far-reaching campaign aimed at educating an audience. But his published remarks on fiction and poetry constitute a significant statement about his methods which offers insights into both his own work and contemporary experimental writing as a whole. So far as I know, only Robert Scholes, in *The Fabulators*, has examined Hawkes' literary creed in some detail. Choosing parts of one published interview for analysis, Professor Scholes investigates the question of plot versus structure and the process by which Hawkes works consciously on visions freed from the unconscious.[1] I should like to look at the problem from another point of view, discussing Hawkes' comments on innovation in order to show how his fiction shuns the technique of realism while it borrows from experimental poetry.

Hawkes' efforts to avoid the limitations of realism permit him to exchange the conventional documentation of reality for the created vision of imagination. The controlled vision plays a key role in his theory of fiction because for him a primary pitfall is our traditional notion of the novel which, he feels, constricts both the artistic process and the reading experience. When joined by a language capable of expressing the inner life of man in such a way as to arouse the feelings of pleasure and pain, this imaginative vision becomes more than uncontrolled hallucination or dream writing. In the following statement Hawkes describes the kind of fiction which attracts him and which he writes: "The constructed vision, the excitement of the undersea life of the inner man, a language appropriate to the delicate malicious knowledge of us all as poor, forked, corruptible, the feeling of pleasure and pain that comes when something pure and contemptible lodges in the imagination—I believe in the 'singular and terrible attraction' of all this." [2]

If the modern comic novelist hopes to write of the underground life of the inner man, his first problem is freedom for himself and his readers from what Hawkes calls "the security of constraining realism." [3] Offering security because it deals with only what is known, with life's surfaces, realism also limits the writer because it prevents him from crossing the fine line between wakefulness and sleep, surface experience and underground dream, conscious and unconscious states. One way to break away from realism is to manipulate sympathetic and critical impulses and responses to

1. Robert Scholes, *The Fabulators* (New York: Oxford University Press, 1967), pp. 59–94.
2. John Hawkes, "Notes on the Wild Goose Chase," *The Massachusetts Review*, 3 (Summer 1962), 788.
3. John Hawkes, "Flannery O'Connor's Devil," *Sewanee Review*, 70 (Summer 1962), 407.

pleasure and pain in such a way that the author is liberated from the reader's expectations. Hawkes cites Nathanael West and Flannery O'Connor as two other comic novelists who consistently violate anticipated probability so that their constructed visions rest solely on their own authority as creators. When much of the landscape of Hawkes' novels is privately created, the product of an intensely imagined vision, the reader finds himself stripped of a familiar body of reference by which he can gain his bearings. Hawkes has no desire to render his novels unreadable or his fictional settings unrecognizable, but he does hope to startle us into an awareness of something new about ourselves. The desired result is not the smugness we traditionally feel when we "understand" a work of art, but the lack of security which can force us to a reexamination of our own situation. Reading John Hawkes and his contemporaries, we are stranded in a kind of no-man's land which does not provide ready signposts to what Hawkes, referring to West and O'Connor, terms "these horrifying and brightly imagined worlds." [4]

Thus, a conscious goal of the new comic fiction is disruption of the conventional forms of the novel. Not only forcing us to confront a totally new reading experience, this disruption also enables Hawkes to reflect what he considers to be ruptures in the order of everyday affairs. He has said that he began writing fiction with the assumption that the real enemies of the novel were "plot, character, setting and theme," though this is not to say that his novels completely dismiss these conventions. What he means is that his fictions are not held together nor developed by the traditional methods of plot movement, character portrayal, recognizable setting, or realistic theme. It is true that these familiar ways of approaching the novel may appear in his work, but they are not the primary means of control nor the major aim of the writer. Hawkes has hit on a relatively new way to give the novel coherence, one which depends upon a totality of vision or structure. He writes, "And structure—verbal and psychological coherence—is still my largest concern as a writer. Related or corresponding

4. Ibid., p. 399.

event, recurring image and recurring action, these constitute the essential substance or meaningful density of my writing." [5] His novels avoid conventional ordering devices in favor of coherence based on verbal patterns, parallel images, and cross-references. In *The Cannibal*, for example, the Germany of 1945 is meant to re- call the Germany of 1914, but neither era has more emphasis than the other. Hawkes' detachment allows the events of each Germany to rest side by side and mirror one another. Although 1914 occurs earlier than 1945 in chronological time, the two years are juxta- posed in such a way that the images and events of one Germany recall or foreshadow those of the other. In 1914, for instance, Stella loves the "white prancing horses" which symbolize the mili- taristic state. In 1915 the horse turns black because Germany is plunged into war, and in 1918 "the old horse is dead." Thus, in 1945 when Zizendorf begins his coup to reestablish Germany's militarism, one of his first plans is to restore "the old horse statue back on its feet. Young couples would make love beneath it on summer nights." [6] The reference to love is ironic, for we know that the war cycle is about to begin again. Hawkes makes no effort to stress the relationship between the horse images. None of them has a climactic effect, and all can be missed by the careless reader. We must sift through patterns which lack chronological sequence, keeping in mind recurring image and action, if we hope to follow the complex structure.

In his efforts to liberate fiction from the limits of realism, Hawkes looks for innovation that will give new life to the novel. Speaking generally about experimental fiction, he describes his own goals: "Every fiction of any value has about it something new. At any rate, the function of the true innovator or specifically ex- perimental writer is to keep prose alive and constantly to test in the sharpest way possible the range of our human sympathies and constantly to destroy mere surface morality." [7] His goals as an in-

5. "John Hawkes: An Interview," *Wisconsin Studies in Contempo- rary Literature*, 6 (Summer 1965), 149.

6. John Hawkes, *The Cannibal* (New York: New Directions, 1962), p. 183.

7. "John Hawkes: An Interview," p. 143.

novator are twofold and reflect the underground writer's concern
with both technique and subject: to keep the novel from stifling
in traditional forms which have lost their vigor and to engage the
reader in an experience which will make him face himself. These
aims are not new, of course, but they give direction to Hawkes'
fiction. Given a world of chaos and absurdity, he hopes to use fiction to reveal our potential for evil and violence. The novels may
"expose, ridicule, and attack," but the fictional process is always
positive by the very fact that it is creative. Commenting on his own
concept of the *avant-garde*, which has its roots in a long tradition
from the early picaresque writers to today's black humor, Hawkes
writes:

> This constant is a quality of coldness, detachment, ruthless de-
> termination to face up to the enormities of ugliness and poten-
> tial failure within ourselves and in the world around us, and to
> bring to this exposure a savage or saving comic spirit and the
> saving beauties of language. The need is to maintain the truth
> of the fractured picture; to expose, ridicule, attack, but always
> to create and to throw into new light our potential for violence
> and absurdity as well as for graceful action. I don't like soft,
> loose prose or fiction which tries to cope too directly with life
> itself or is based indulgently on personal experience.[8]

The experimentation necessary to maintain "the truth of the
fractured picture" is obviously not gratuitous, nor is it a hin-
drance to Hawkes' potential for change. From the early *Charivari*
(1949) to *Second Skin* (1964), the direction of his fiction has been
a move away from extreme experimentation to what resembles the
conventional novel. Professor Scholes calls *Charivari* "militantly
avant-garde," and, indeed, its surrealistic images and narrative
line shock the unprepared reader. *Second Skin*, on the other hand,
is more easily accessible, not as aggressive in its innovations as the
earlier work. But this does not mean that it is a typical novel or
that it makes use of those traditional novelistic conventions which
Hawkes has generally avoided. Without sacrificing his role as innovator, he has moved from the fiction of pure vision to that which

8. Ibid., pp. 143–144.

experiments with the conventions under the guise of using them traditionally. He admits that he has become "increasingly interested in the conventions of the novel and in novelistic method," and that at the conception of *Second Skin* he planned to use the traditional fictional method of the first-person narrator.[9]

But even as he begins to accept traditional devices, Hawkes remains an experimenter, maintaining his faith in the duty of the modern novelist to do something new in order to keep prose alive. He has taken steps away from aggressive innovation primarily because of an "increasing need to parody the conventional novel."[10] Thus, his later novels appear more traditional only on the surface, for he parodies the conventions in such a way as to violate both novelistic "rules" and the reader's expectations. These encroachments on anticipated probability negate the security which the average reader feels in the presence of a conventional novel. *The Beetle Leg*, for example, makes fun of the American western while *The Lime Twig* parodies the hardboiled detective thriller. These two novels mock subjects which have a long history in American fiction and which we normally expect to adhere to certain rules of the particular genre. In *Second Skin* Hawkes' primary target for parody is not a form but a long revered technique—the first-person narrator—and the outcome is a novel so comic that even the dullest reader cannot miss the humor despite the atmosphere of terror.

Writing his "naked history," Skipper, the narrator of *Second Skin*, knows what has happened to him, but he has trouble evaluating his experience. He is so close to most of his material, having just finished the "history" following "last night's spectacle," that he darts here and there in chronological time searching for the right perspective. He refers to his narrative technique as "the erratic flight of the hummingbird," an apt description, for the novel follows not the chronological development of the usual first-person history but Skipper's demands as a story-teller. In his efforts to judge his experience and to find motives for the terrible pain he

9. "John Hawkes on His Novels: An Interview with John Graham," *The Massachusetts Review*, 7 (Summer 1966), 459.
10. "John Hawkes: An Interview," p. 149.

has suffered, he becomes a first-person narrator as much in search
for the clues to his life as we are. Hawkes' comic parody of this
narrative technique creates a first-person narrator who is not quite
sure what he is talking about: "High lights of helplessness? Mere
trivial record of collapse? Say, rather, that it is the chronicle of recovery, the history of courage, the dead reckoning of my romance,
the art of memory, the dance of shadows." [11]

Hawkes describes his decision to experiment with the first-
person narrator as the result of a "series of semi-conscious impulses
and sheer accidents." [12] He wrote *The Cannibal*, for example, in
the third person, but in revision he found himself wishing to be
identified with Zizendorf, the unsympathetic spokesman for the
terrifying neo-Nazi rebellion. The change from third to first-
person pronouns was conventional enough, but he then decided
to violate the traditional limitation of the first person by leaving
Zizendorf with omniscience. "The result was interesting, I think,
not because *The Cannibal* became a genuine example of first-
person fiction, but because its 'narrator' naturally possesses an
unusual omniscience, while the authorial consciousness was given
specific definition, definition in terms of humor and 'black' intelligence." [13] Hawkes' first attempt to create an actual human
voice in the first person is the short prologue to *The Beetle Leg*.
An afterthought, the prologue is spoken in the foolish sheriff's
voice, thus contrasting with the novel proper which is in the third
person. Neither Zizendorf nor the sheriff is meant to be fully developed. It is their voices that count, their distorted, comic points
of view, not their characters. Hawkes' initial sustained effort with
the first-person narrator is Hencher's long prologue to *The Lime
Twig*, which he also terms an afterthought. Describing Hencher's
narration as "a fully created voice that dramatized a character
conceived in a certain depth," Hawkes places Hencher in the fore-
front of the comic action. Yet innovation remains a prime motive,

11. John Hawkes, *Second Skin* (New York: New Directions, 1964), p.
162. All subsequent references will be in parentheses.
12. "John Hawkes: An Interview," pp. 149–150.
13. Ibid., p. 150.

for he challenges the reader's expectations. Not only do many of Hencher's observations turn out to be wrong; he is also killed less than a third of the way through the novel. The remainder of *The Lime Twig* is third-person narration, and we never do know the exact reasons for Hencher's death. Only in *Second Skin* and *The Blood Oranges* is the first-person voice sustained throughout, and the parody of technique revolves around Skipper's and Cyril's bumbling efforts to narrate what has happened to them and why.

Whatever use Hawkes may make of traditional fictional methods, he insists that he takes "literally rather than figuratively the cliché about breaking new ground." [14] The creative imagination should always discover new worlds, and the experimental writer who truly believes in the possibilities of fiction will make these private landscapes, originally unearthed in the artist's unconscious, visible to the reader. But these constructed visions, these alien landscapes, are more than a product of the innovative process. They also serve the artist by protecting him from the "dangers of familiarity" and by helping him maintain the absolute detachment necessary for comedy. With these settings he is able to avoid autobiographical fiction and to sustain distance between himself and his materials. Hawkes writes, "I want to try to create a world, not represent it. And of course I believe that the creation ought to be more significant than the representation." [15]

The key to this created world is the visual sense, the image-making ability which resides in the unconscious. Commenting that he is never aware of "story" when he begins to write, he explains that his novels have as their germs the "mere flickerings" in the imagination. Narrative materials and specific characters are secondary matters until the imagined landscape takes shape as an intensely visual construction. These images may be sparked by an idea, but they are literally seen just as we are able to see the "pictures" in our dreams. He names *The Cannibal* as his clearest example of a patterned vision, a novel which began with a series of pictures and which developed into a "kind of absolute coher-

14. Ibid., p. 154.
15. Ibid.

ence of vision." As the novel is being conceived, even the meaning of the images remains secondary to their visual sense: "It is perfectly true that I don't know what they mean, but I feel and know that they have meaning. . . . Yes, it is visual, it's compulsive, and a conscious knowledge of exactly what it means is not always there." [16] This kind of comment disturbs readers used to traditional fiction which ties together the various narrative strands so that coherence based on meaning is maintained. Modern comic fiction often baffles conventional readers because they have been taught to look for a beginning, middle, and end to the development of meaning. Such fiction presupposes orderly processes in reality. But in a world full of events which are absurd and inexplicable, meaning cannot always be determined. For Hawkes the modern novelist must have a feeling for the chaos, an understanding that rational answers to complex problems are not readily available. In its attempt to reflect the contemporary world, today's experimental writing eschews completely developed meaning and other traditional ordering devices and relies on the visual sense to sustain coherence. Thus, many events in Hawkes' novels remain motiveless: the Duke's cannibalism in *The Cannibal*, Monica's murder in *The Lime Twig*, Kate's iguana in *Second Skin*.

In fiction which depends upon coherent visions, imaginative processes are more important than the action of the rational mind. But once the imagined underworld surfaces from the unconscious, Hawkes consciously uses his skills to mold the visions into a tightly controlled whole. His emphasis is always on the structured vision, not on the kind of free flow we associate with dream writing. The relationship between conscious art and reliance on materials which are unconsciously liberated is not as paradoxical as it seems. Conscious art gives shape to unconsciously discovered visions so that the darkest recesses of our minds may be exposed and, it is hoped, confronted. To do this Hawkes must suppress his ego so that the unconscious can direct the creative imagination. Once the visions are freed the artistic consciousness, fully aware of what it is

16. "John Hawkes on His Novels," p. 452.

doing, takes over and gives the invented image patterns coherent, carefully constructed shape. Discussion of this method of composition makes it sound more planned than it is. Professor Scholes correctly notes that Hawkes' method involves "discovery and creation simultaneously." It is unplanned, dependent upon image correspondences and verbal patterns rather than on plot chronology or character development.

The ideal reader does not resist the pull of these dreamlike visions; he yields to the novel's invented setting and enters it, much like Alice stepping through the looking glass. Once inside he may encounter a topsy-turvy world, abounding with cruelties and brutal humor, a world that inverts normal expectations, but he will also discover meaningful truths about reality. Confrontation with dark distortions makes us face up to the possibility that the same things, though reduced, can happen in our daily lives. As Hawkes presents it, we either challenge the darkness or succumb to it. In *The Lime Twig*, for example, Michael Banks tangles with his dreams, but his willingness to face them comes too late. The concrete manifestation of the dream—the race horse—destroys him.

Dismissal of traditional literary realism is indeed a significant characteristic in today's comic fiction. But just as important is the close relationship between these innovative novels and contemporary poetry. Aware of this affinity, Hawkes notes, "I'm trying to hold in balance poetic and novelistic impulses in order to make the novel a more valid and pleasurable experience." [17] In other words the novelist's use of certain techniques, especially in matters of structure and language normally assigned to the poet, helps to keep prose alive. This relationship between the contemporary poem and the experimental novel is not so much an alliance, as Hawkes notes, "as merely the sharing of a birthmark: both come from the same place and are equally disfigured at the start." [18] Both art forms belong to what he suggests is a larger genre, experimental writing, and both rely on the imagination's use of uncon-

17. "John Hawkes: An Interview," p. 149.
18. John Hawkes, "Notes on Violence," *Audience*, 7 (Spring 1960), 60.

sciously discovered visions. For Hawkes describes the contemporary poem as "the experimental effort in a short form." [19] What counts is the author's innovation; the form it assumes, poem or novel, depends upon him and his material.

Hawkes grants that, generally speaking, we do not find the "precise use of language" and the sheer joy of newly discovered worlds as readily in the conventional novel as in poetry, but experimental fiction is another matter. Always struggling to free the novel from realism, Hawkes writes the kind of prose which joins the poem in its delight with expressing the author's private purposes. He is one of the new fiction writers who, in his words, hopes "for more in the novel than trying to build brick walls of brick." [20] Distinguishing this kind of writing is what he terms "the prophetic role in reverse," a process by which we face up to the darkness of the "imagination's nursery." [21] This role opens up demonic images, the fears and repressions which we have stored away, so that we can meet our forgotten side. Novels such as *The Cannibal* or Djuna Barnes' *Nightwood*, those comic fictions which explore the ancestral fears of our racial memories, are examples of the kind of "prophetic" writing which interests Hawkes and which, simultaneously, baffles many readers. As we have noted, *The Cannibal* examines Germany in the middle 1940s in order to suggest a cycle of history which will eventually cause another major war in Europe. But rather than look ahead in its prophecy, the novel turns back to the Germany of 1914. In other words, the reversed prophetic role describes a future catastrophe by confronting us with the innate martial instincts from the past. Defining the relationship between his own work and poetry, Hawkes writes:

> Like the poem, the experimental fiction is an exclamation of psychic materials which come to the writer all readily distorted, prefigured in that nightly inner schism between the rational and the absurd. . . . A comic sense of the dream, the presumption of a newly envisioned world, absolute fastness, firmness, insistence upon the creation of that other landscape where the

19. "Notes on the Wild Goose Chase," p. 785.
20. Ibid.
21. "Notes on Violence," p. 60.

> moon hangs like a sac loaded with water . . . this unchallenge-
> able elevation of impulse and sudden poetic outspokenness
> drifts also through the climate of what we may still think of as
> *avant-garde* prose.[22]

This kind of experimentation enjoys paradox and antithesis, not only in its subject matter, but also in its effect on the reader. Celebrating writing which can both harrow and solace, Hawkes combines his comic spirit with a vision and language full of death. A combination so paradoxical is meant to startle us, yet Hawkes insists that it is highly moral. In a review of Edwin Honig's poetry, he praises Honig's art for revealing a poetic spirit which is "often winkingly comic" but which is also "unsettlingly omnivorous," constantly recalling "the ultimate thunderclap." [23] Although describing another artist, this review discloses a good deal about Hawkes so that much of what is said can be applied to his own work. This is certainly true with regard to his observation about the paradoxical spirits which writing full of the comic and the "omnivorous" employ. Both his novels and Honig's poems deny the reader the usual props so as to surprise him with antithetical subjects. But the reader's experience is also paradoxical, for as he is shaken he is simultaneously soothed by a new awareness. Thus for Hawkes the writing is moral in a dual sense: in its use of antithetical universalities such as birth and death, and in its ability to provoke paradoxical responses which jolt our complacent attitudes toward these subjects. Commenting on Honig's poetry, Hawkes indirectly describes some of his own works:

> A highly moral poetry, true enough: but very nearly all of these
> poems construct a kind of ghostly and biting double exposure,
> or hold in some mercurial suspension, suasion, the two deplor-
> able and astounding processes—that of dying and that of birth-
> ing. Hence the felt morality, the moral judgment, the eternal
> moral prescience, is most often lodged in soft anxiety-provoking
> antithesis or jocular paradox.[24]

22. "Notes on the Wild Goose Chase," p. 786.
23. John Hawkes, "The Voice of Edwin Honig," *Voices: A Journal of Poetry*, No. 174 (January–April 1961), 39.
24. Ibid., pp. 40–41.

Hawkes' efforts to explore the kinship between the poem and
the experimental novel can be illustrated by his pleasure with the
apparently inappropriate word or phrase. By virtue of its concentration, poetry must make the most of the positioning of each
word, and it often enjoys its best effects from word placement. In
his concern to control his unconsciously liberated visions, Hawkes
borrows from poetry and employs a word or phrase which often
seems paradoxical to the whole. This device, of course, is not entirely new in fiction. He cites Flannery O'Connor's *The Violent
Bear It Away* as an example. But more than his contemporaries
Hawkes takes special delight in the comically placed word as part
of the pleasure he finds in the problem of structure. In *Second
Skin* Skipper calls the belly bumping contest in which the fat "begins to fly" an "obscene tournament." The word *tournament* excites laughter because it suggests all of the fair play and gallantry
which Skipper may wish to apply but which is certainly absent.
Tournament also calls to mind the shining knight fighting to preserve the damsel's virginity—an image which Skipper often has of
himself and Cassandra—but nothing is further from the truth. He
and Uncle Billy are no more than one of "eight pairs of bump-
ers"—a far cry from the heroes of chivalric romances. But while
tournament is used comically, it paradoxically pains the reader,
for it underscores again the sad discrepancy between Skipper's sin-
cere hopes and the crude realities which negate them. Although
he wins the tournament and is awarded a gold crucifix, he suffers
another defeat. Cassandra has used the excitement of this modern
jousting match to sneak off to her orgy. Thus *tournament*, not
obscene, becomes the most painful word in the description even
though the vision it suggests of fat, balding Skipper jousting to
save his wayward daughter is laughable. The careful use of the
word supports the poetic injustice of the novel, for Hawkes magnifies Skipper's calamities until they become a metaphor for a
twisted universe in which normal expectations of good and evil
with their traditional rewards are comically inverted.

A final example of Hawkes' efforts to use certain techniques
usually thought of as poetic is his skill with alliteration and asso-

nance. These devices are obvious, but specific illustrations should be given here because of the pleasure he takes in the sound of his prose. We should listen to the words if they were poetry, and indeed many passages in his novels demand to be read aloud for us to experience the full effect. The use of sound is part of his concern for the totality of the constructed vision, for it is often the medium by which the vision is given us. In other words, we must not only imagine as we read but also hear the words on the printed page if we hope to enter his fictional landscape. Two examples from *Second Skin* must suffice. "Brass bugle blown in the desert, a little spit shaken out on the bugler's sleeve" (p. 38). "Wet hands on the flaking white sill. Sudden shock in the nose, chin, cheeks, sensation of the cold glass against the whole of my inquisitive face. Kerosene stove breathing into the seat of my woolen pants" (p. 73). The poetry of Skipper's two observations belies his analysis of the scenes as he reports them to us. The first passage refers to the experience with the AWOL soldiers whom Skipper fears will rape Cassandra. But nothing happens. The second illustration describes his activities just prior to the dance in the high school gym at which the belly bumping contest occurs. The assonance and alliteration suggest the beauty he feels which lulls him into the mistaken belief that he has nothing to be afraid of at the dance. But again he is wrong—Cassandra is successfully seduced. Both passages point to the kind of paradox which fascinates Hawkes, for their poetic beauties mask the terrors of the scenes which they describe. The reader takes pleasure in the "saving" grace of the language while he feels pain for the violence of Skipper's situations. The poetic effects not only describe Skipper's circumstances; they also engage the reader in a process of purification through the exposure to art: "The changing elusive contour of the poetic self is only something to be heard. So for us there is the listening, then, and the being cut clean by the sound. Because certainly it is safe to say that this listening is, finally, a kind of purification." [25]

While the novels of John Hawkes seem shadowy and dreamlike, not easily accessible to the unwilling reader, they are extraordi-

25. "The Voice of Edwin Honig," p. 17.

nary constructions so tightly knit that complete concentration is necessary if we hope to encounter the full effect of the created vision. Professor Scholes is surely correct when he suggests that one of the delights we discover when experiencing a Hawkes novel is the beauty of its form. The control with which he orders his rich store of materials adds to the satisfaction we feel when we surface from a Hawkes vision. We need only keep in mind that his fiction is highly innovative, divorced from the conventions of realism, and in many ways closer to poetry than to the type of novel we are used to. This kind of experimentation applies not only to Hawkes but to black humor in general. What finally makes these underground fictions so exciting is the union of experimental technique with nightmarish fantasy to create a comic effect.

Yet comedy in Hawkes' fiction is so different that it often forms an additional stumbling block for those readers who are unfamiliar with what is commonly meant by black humor. Since the acceptance of black humor and the theater of the absurd, comedy and fantasy—man's ability to laugh and dream—have become subjects of popular investigation. What do we laugh at, and why, are questions which now interest not only the theorists of comedy but also the mass circulation magazines. Reading Hawkes' comic novels today, we realize that the traditional causes for laughter, which seemed only modified in the 1960s, have experienced an even greater alteration than we first suspected. We are undergoing a crisis in comedy, a change in the reasons why we laugh and fantasize, which has been gradually developing but which is now easily recognizable.

Time magazine, for example, devotes a *"Time* Essay" to an article by Melvin Maddocks: "We Are Not Amused—And Why." [26] Commenting that the absence of laughter today is deafening, Maddocks wonders if we are victims of cataplexy, a "disease" which renders its victims physically unable to laugh though they want to. He notes the change from Sinclair Lewis's *Babbitt* to Kurt Vonnegut's *Mother Night*, from John Kennedy's "Yankee salt" to

26. Melvin Maddocks, "We Are Not Amused—And Why," *Time*, 20 July 1970, pp. 30–31.

Richard Nixon's "wit," and from *Some Like It Hot* to *M*A*S*H*, and he wonders why our laughter has changed to the extent that we rarely laugh at all. Suggesting—with Freud—that anxiety and laughter have a causal relationship, Maddocks speculates that a chief source of American anxiety, puritanism, was so successfully challenged in the 1960s that the humor which we created in years of battle with that old curse is no longer adequate in the face of new anxieties. Thus, Maddocks concludes, comedy itself is not dead, but we have yet to produce a new brand of humor to relieve the conditions which American society has produced in the late 60s and early 70s.

Writing in the *Saturday Review*, theologian Harvey Cox investigates the crisis in more depth. He notes that America's present material opulence has been purchased at a frightful price, and he wonders what will become of a people who have lost their "capacity to dance and dream." [27] Our lives are impoverished because we are losing two vital elements: festivity—"the capacity for genuine revelry and joyous celebration"—and fantasy—"the faculty for envisioning radically alternative life situations." As our science-oriented culture expands, our imaginative visions decay to the extent that our revelry is checked by an obsession with facts. The rigidity of factual knowledge inhibits the freedom necessary for true laughter, and the result is an acceptance of televised situation comedies as genuine humor. Cox argues that a shrunken psyche is the effect of our crippled capability for visions, and that Western Man is in danger of losing touch with his "mysterious origin and cosmic destiny."

Unlike Maddocks, Cox sees a revival of fantasy, laughter, and vision already beginning in the arts. But what has been overlooked in discussions of this crisis in humor and festivity is that the so-called black humorists or antirealist authors have been exploring different forms of comedy for some time now. Many of us talk about black humor as if it were a brand new art form, but remarkable examples of this "new" comedy have been part of the modern

27. Harvey Cox, "In Praise of Festivity," *Saturday Review*, 25 October 1969, pp. 25–28.

American novel for nearly forty years. The legacy of Nathanael West's *Miss Lonelyhearts* (1933) and of Djuna Barnes' *Nightwood* (1937) has been inherited by a score of contemporary novelists, with Hawkes as a most difficult but representative example. Acknowledging a change in the causes and results of laughter, I should like to discuss at this point some traditional theories of comedy in the light of Hawkes' comic fiction and comments about comedy so that we may see why and how the laughter of Hawkes is so different and, thus, apparently so strange.

The problem, it seems to me, is not the apparent silence of our laughter but the different reasons for it. The point is that comedy can no longer be limited to a leisurely escape from the pressures of reality or to a means of social correction for the wayward individual. Comedy has been analyzed for centuries, at least since Aristotle, who suggested that the genre was based on a sense of the ridiculous which excites laughter without causing pain. Even in more recent times, theories of comedy have traditionally emphasized the comic imperfection of the ridiculous as a departure from standard behavior and the comic resolution in which laughter acts as social pressure to cure the ridiculous and to heal the rupture it causes in the social norm.

Hawkes, however, belongs to a line of comic practice which includes Cervantes, Swift, and Sterne, and which emphasizes the disjunction between social "reality" and the individual's inner life. He dismisses the concept of a benevolent social norm, with the result that traditional comedy's aim of using laughter as a utilitarian means for social correction is meaningless to him. Lacking a widely accepted standard of behavior, comedy seems strange, and this is one reason why Hawkes' novels are so difficult to read as comic fiction. He daringly mixes horror with humor, the grotesque with the heroic, creating a complex tone which some readers find hard to accept. To ignore this complexity is to render his fiction simply an exploitation of terror, for the dire events are too obvious to be missed, whatever difficulties the reader has with the humor. Even the reader who sees that Hawkes' fiction concerns itself with comedy is likely to find the novels rough going. Sensing the humor, he may wonder if his horrified response to the action is inappropriate, or, recognizing the terror, he may doubt his original intimations that the novels are indeed comic. When this and similar difficulties appear in the theater, cinema, and other arts at the same time, a crisis takes shape. It is not that humor is dead, but that the traditional forms of comedy have been altered in order to respond more meaningfully to an untraditional world.

An examination of some older theories of comedy verifies this change. The traditional comic process has always used pain, but the wound is more an irritation for the character who is shackled with the ridiculous than a genuine hurt. Rarely does the pain in conventional comedy include the audience. In his "On Comedy and the Uses of the Comic Spirit," George Meredith recognizes the presence of some pain in comedy when he calls the comic spirit "humanely malign." Yet the malicious sense always takes second place to the humane. Defining the capacity for comic perception as the ability to detect the ridiculous in yourself or in those you love without loving either less, he suggests that the test of true comedy is that "it shall awaken thoughtful laughter." To accept this definition, we must concur with his belief that the state of society is founded on common sense, that is, a kind of norm against which deviations can be measured. Meredith's humanely malign laughter is malicious only insofar as it exposes distortion to evoke thoughtful laughter. In this traditional comedy, the general atmosphere of the comic spirit is benign, constantly reassuring the reader that common sense will, in the end, prevail.

Stressing the appeal to malice more than Aristotle or Meredith do, Louis Kronenberger writes that comedy excites laughter, which is often partly malicious, because it is concerned with human imperfection.[28] Noting, with other critics, that the concept of tragedy is implicit in comedy, Kronenberger suggests that the tragic possibility is negated in the comic resolution when the wayward character regains the self-awareness necessary to reenter normal so-

28. Louis Kronenberger, "Some Prefatory Words on Comedy," in *Comedy*, ed. Marvin Felheim (New York: Harcourt, Brace and World, 1962), pp. 194–198.

ciety. But while he insists on the presence of malice or melancholy in the highest forms of comedy, he remains a traditionalist. He sees laughter as an enemy of hypocrisy and pretense and thus as a social corrective with the assurance that an ideal standard of behavior exists. This spirit of reconciliation between the ridiculous individual and the social norm is the key to conventional comedy.

Jane Austen's *Emma* is a prime example. For all of Emma's innate goodness, beauty, and social position, she misunderstands herself and thus creates misunderstanding in those about her. The results of her meddling are not always wildly comic; indeed, they are often painful and embarrassing both to Emma and to the other characters. But if Emma wavers between good behavior and bad, the social norm remains stable, and the happy ending prevails despite the pain caused while reaching the benevolent conclusion. Emma returns to the fold of acceptable social behavior, just as we know all along she will. The novel is comic not simply because it exposes her mistakes but also because it shows these errors in the process of correction. This is traditional comedy at its best—the kind we are used to—in which the humanely malign is brought to a benign close.

Probably the most influential discussion of comedy is Henri Bergson's "Laughter." Bergson mentions lack of awareness and rigidity of action as prime causes of laughter when he notes that a character is comic in proportion to his ignorance about himself. Like most traditional theorists of laughter, he sees comedy as a means of pointing out defects which often appear ridiculous in order to modify them. In this way laughter "pursues a utilitarian aim of general improvement." Humor, as a corrective measure, becomes a "social gesture" which can "repress a special kind of absentmindedness" in humanity. But Bergson expands the traditional definitions of comedy when he argues that emotion is the chief enemy of laughter. Indifference serves as the natural environment for humor, for comedy "demands something like a momentary anesthesia of the heart. Its appeal is to intelligence, pure and simple." We may laugh at someone who inspires in us affection and pity, but to do so we must, for the moment, negate those emotions.

Generally speaking, then, traditional comedy posits a kind of uniformity among the people of a particular era. Kronenberger writes, "Comedy is always jarring us with the evidence that we are no better than other people, and always comforting us with the knowledge that most other people are no better than we are." But in an age of blanket standardization, automation, and worship of scientific precision, the "evidence" which Kronenberger mentions remains jarring without the possibility of comfort. The point is that most traditional comedy of the past, including especially the most popular form of higher comedy, the comedy of manners, bases its laughter either on personal ignorance or on unawareness of a social standard of action. This kind of comedy is indeed positive criticism, and it has led in the past to personal or social enlightenment. But at the heart of the kind of comedy we are used to resides the stable standard against which the participants are measured. Thus, while traditional comedy can use melancholy or sardonic criticism if it wishes, it must treat the mistakes of its characters, the deviations from the norm, with a benevolent spirit. The happy ending prevails, not because traditional comedy is blandly optimistic, but because its aim of social correction automatically assumes that such improvement is possible. But this kind of assumption is possible only in a stable, ordered world, one in which norms, ideals, and standards remain fairly constant for a particular era.

Hawkes' experimental comic fiction suggests at least two reasons why he repudiates traditional comedy's acceptance of a social standard. First, the concept of a standard applicable to a particular society implies stability, an easily accessible norm. But Hawkes and his contemporaries see the world as fractured, chaotic, and lacking stability because of universal violence which can strike at any man without warning. Secondly, the ideal of a social norm suggests a standardization of manners and behavior which is desirable. Kronenberger has this kind of uniformity in mind when he comments that comedy comforts us with the knowledge that "most other people are no better than we are." But this concept causes Hawkes to demur, for standardization to this degree strengthens the already rampant automation of modern society while, at the same time, it negates individuality.

Despite Hawkes' dismissal of traditional comedy, Meredith's definition of the comic spirit as humanely malign remains appropriate to the modern comic novelist. We need only recognize that Meredith, using humor as a utilitarian means for social correction, stresses the humane side of laughter, while Hawkes, writing about a fractured world in which correction seems impossible, emphasizes the malignant quality of comedy to point out the pain and absurdity of reality. Meredith would pronounce as "harsh" all laughter not caused by his definition of the comic spirit, but this is exactly the kind of laughter Hawkes feels is necessary to startle us into an awareness of the chaos.

Another reason why contemporary humor seems so strange is our traditional acceptance of Bergson's separation of comedy and emotion. Arguing that laughter demands a momentary "anesthesia" of the heart, he insists that we cannot simultaneously laugh at and feel pity or affection for a character. Hawkes violates this long accepted rule of comedy, thus upsetting the response of readers who have been trained to react in a traditional way to a humorous situation. For we cannot laugh at his characters without feeling at the same time pity for their painful circumstances. In most comic situations typical of Hawkes' fiction, our intelligence and emotions react with equal force. The heart is not anesthetized, and the result is a laughter which also causes pain. We are horrified while we laugh at the Duke slicing up Jutta's boy (*The Cannibal*), or at Margaret's acceptance of a beating which will kill her (*The Lime Twig*) because these characters, while they perform ridiculous acts and reveal absurd personal defects in the manner of traditional comedy, rarely discover their faults in time so as to be safely re-established with society.

Hawkes' characters are not stoics. They respond to their predicaments, but their responses are usually at odds with what the reader expects. In many ways his novels are comedies of the inappropriate response. We laugh, as in traditional comedy, because of a deviation from a standard, but Hawkes knows that the standard resides in the reader's expectations and not in the novelist's created world. Thus, the reader often experiences horror as he laughs because the humor fails in its traditional role as a measure for correction. Hawkes might accept Northrop Frye's observation that comedy is not designed to condemn evil, but he would not agree that comedy's primary object of ridicule is the lack of self-knowledge. His comedy is a product of the contemporary world with all of its potential for violence. Self-awareness in the world of his fiction is usually ineffectual because the terrifying, destructive events remain beyond the character's control whether he realizes what is happening to him or not.

Writing about an era which has denied God and nature as moral forces and which has destroyed man's sense of traditional order and community, Hawkes isolates his lonely characters so that they must order their own lives. The chaos of reality leaves them with perhaps the only sense of order remaining: private, irrational, comic, often violent fantasies. In such a dreamlike world what appears to be abnormal to the reader with traditional notions of humor is real and normal to Hawkes' protagonists. Many times the reader is divorced enough from these characters so that the comedy of the inappropriate response prompts him to laugh *at* them even though he may pity them, as for example when the Duke cuts up the boy to make a soup he will serve to the boy's aunt. But just as often Hawkes uses comedy for defense. Humor then allows the character to reduce an overwhelming problem to something he hopes he can manage. When Skipper (*Second Skin*) laughs at his "victory" over Miranda, the reader is so closely identified with the character that he joins in the celebration and laughs *with* Skipper.

Second Skin is probably the best Hawkes novel for illustration of his comedy of nightmare. Using first-person narration, he places Skipper in the predicament of trying to save his daughter from seduction and suicide even though she welcomes both. Cassandra sides with those who would help her to either calamity, leaving Skipper as one man against all. But Skipper is no Horatius at the bridge. Nor is he the skipper of his own fate, for in his passion to do good he refuses to believe that the others, including Cassandra,

would take advantage of his naiveté. We despise the enormous
weaknesses in this fat, balding fifty-nine year old man because we
see so plainly the things which blind him. But while we are frustrated because of his blindness, we like him because of his capacity
for love. The first-person narration narrows the distance between
reader and character so that we feel the pain which wounds him
even though the painful situations are often hilarious.

For example, in the following passage Skipper momentarily
leaves a dance at which he is the unwanted chaperon and steps
outside to a snow-covered cemetery. We intuitively suspect some
disaster, for the dancers have been insulting him as a kill-joy. A
trap has been set, and good-natured, loving Skipper walks into a
deluge of iced snowballs which massacre his face. But note his inappropriate reaction:

> But I stopped. Listened. Because the air seemed to be filled with
> low-flying invisible birds. Large or small I could not tell, but
> fast, fast and out of their senses, skimming past me from every
> direction on terrified steel wings and silent except for the un-
> accountable sharp noise of the flight itself. One dove into the
> snow at my feet . . . and I stepped back from it. . . . Escaped hom-
> ing pigeons? A covey of tiny ducks driven beserk in the cold?
> Eaglets?   (pp. 86–87)

Seeing his blood begin to spot the snow, he shields his eyes. Perhaps, we think, he has finally realized his predicament and will now
begin to fight back instead of continuing to believe snowballs to be
vengeful birds. But no; he accepts the evidence only after he has
failed to find "the ice-crusted body of a small bird" by crawling
around in the snow as the snowballs continue to wreck his face.
Now we expect action. Yet to our frustration his response is comically inadequate, for rather than feel anger he is relieved: "I knew
that this time at least I had nothing to fear from any unnatural
vengefulness of wild birds." What can we do but laugh at his ridiculous reaction. Even his description excites laughter, for the
words "this time at least" tell us that he seriously believes vengeful birds could attack him "next" time. Yet because of our identi-

fication with Skipper we also feel his pain, just as we are horrified at the hit and run tactics of his enemies.

We want to kick Skipper into action at the same time that we wish to lash out at those who hurt him, and all the while we are laughing at the ridiculousness of the scene. Hawkes is aware that his untraditional comic fiction has contributed to the crisis in humor, for he notes that a typical reader response is to stress his diabolical elements at the expense of the comic. "I have always thought that my fictions, no matter how diabolical, were comic. I wanted to be very comic—but they have not been treated as comedy. They have been called 'black, obscene visions of the horror of life' and sometimes rejected as such, sometimes highly praised as such." [29] He names Djuna Barnes, Nathanael West, Flannery O'Connor, and Joseph Heller as other comic writers who use extreme violence, and he argues that the good reader, when faced with the cruel joke he finds in these writers, can feel the idealism, "the need for innocence and purity, truth, strength" behind the desperate humor.[30] Yet the mixture of the grotesque and the ideal, of horror and humor, confuses most readers precisely because it succeeds in its goal of using truly terrifying events which nevertheless excite us to laughter.

Hawkes insists that comedy focuses a different light on the nightmarish qualities of his work. But his comic spirit is not used in the traditional sense of comic relief. Never once does he suggest that the role of humor is to soften the shock of the grotesque. Rather he uses comedy to force the reader to a recognition of the nightmare:

> Of course I don't mean to apologize for the disturbing nature of my fiction by calling it comic, and certainly don't mean to minimize the terror with which this writing confronts the reader— my aim has always been the opposite, never to let the reader (or myself) off the hook, so to speak, never to let him think that the picture is any less black than it is or that there is any easy way out of the nightmare of human existence.[31]

29. "John Hawkes on His Novels," p. 459.
30. Ibid., p. 461.
31. "John Hawkes: An Interview," p. 145.

Describing Edwin Honig's poetry, Hawkes writes of a literature which harrows the reader, yet which has the counter ability to solace him.[32] This description obviously fits Hawkes' own work, for his images and themes are "thick with death" while his creative spirit is highly comic. Part of the difficulty for the reader is the acceptance of a comic spirit which also forces a recognition of the terrifying gulfs within man and between men. The comic scenes constantly recall death as the ultimate loneliness, and the reader is unsettled because Hawkes' grotesque visions deny him the familiar frames of reference.

Meaningful fiction today is, in Hawkes' words, "hard, ruthless, comic," the kind of writing which shows both humor and fear in everyday affairs. Its purpose is to objectify the terrifying similarities between "the unconscious desires of the solitary man and the disruptive needs of the visible world." [33] Naming characteristics which he deems necessary for contemporary comedy and which he finds in the comic novels of Barnes, West, and O'Connor, Hawkes points to wit, the humorous treatment of violence, and extreme detachment. The key to modern comedy is detachment toward violence, for detachment encourages sympathy. Terrifying incidents and grotesque images are meaningless without sympathy for both the instigators and the victims. "The writer who maintains most successfully a consistent cold detachment toward physical violence ... is likely to generate the deepest novelistic sympathy of all, a sympathy which is a humbling before the terrible and a quickening in the presence of degradation." [34] In *Second Skin*, for example, we sympathize with Skipper because of his violent defeats, but Hawkes, as author, remains detached, objectively telling the story with little regard for Skipper or us. We are emotionally caught up in the processes of violence because these artists seem to remain uninvolved; the extreme fictive detachment of today's comedy is kin to literary understatement.

32. "The Voice of Edwin Honig," p. 39.
33. "Notes on the Wild Goose Chase," p. 787.
34. Ibid.

What finally confounds the reader and adds to the crisis in humor is modern comedy's ability to suggest hope in the midst of the violence. Laughter, for Hawkes, is as it has been through the ages, a "saving" attitude, and it is this mutual emphasis on futurity which most unites black humor with traditional comedy. For while contemporary humor denies the reality of a stable social standard of behavior, it maintains faith in the invulnerability of basic values: love, communication, sympathy. Given a world of fragmentation, self-destruction, and absurdity, Hawkes tries to meet the terrors with a saving attitude of laughter so as to defend and celebrate these permanent values. Thus, modern comedy also functions to expose evil, not the kind of human inadequacy which in traditional comedy is a deviation from a norm, but the very real evil which generates violence and which threatens to annihilate those eternal verities so treasured by Hawkes. In summation of his comic method, Hawkes describes what he hopes his humor achieves:

> . . . on the one hand it serves to create sympathy, compassion, and on the other it's a means of judging human failings as severely as possible; it's a way of exposing evil (one of the pure words I mean to preserve) and of course comic distortion tells us that anything is possible and hence expands the limits of our imaginations.[35]

Today's crisis in comedy is certainly real, but not because humor is fatally ill. Nor can we blame the modern comedians for failure to develop a humor which reflects the times. In many ways the crisis is our own fault, the result of ignorance about the ways the new comedy functions. For we have tried to hold onto traditional theories of laughter which presuppose an ordered world. Suspecting this stability to be shattered, but unaware that traditional comedy is no longer relevant, we experience a dilemma: should we laugh or cry when faced with a violent society that can obliterate us without blinking an eye. We should do both, says the author of *The Cannibal* and *Second Skin*. Rather than rely solely

35. "John Hawkes: An Interview," p. 146.

on the intellect, contemporary comedy like Hawkes' calls for the involvement of both our intellects and our emotions. The result is a different brand of comedy which reflects how totally immersed we are, not in a particular social norm but in the chaotic world as a whole. As we examine Hawkes' fiction in the following chapters we should keep in mind the experimental technique and the comic spirit which he uses to create his vision of the violent world.

2

Innovative Threesome: *Charivari*, *The Goose on the Grave*, *The Owl*

HAWKES' three novelettes, *Charivari* (1949), *The Goose on the Grave* (1954), and *The Owl* (1954), are his most aggressively experimental fictions.[1] Averaging only seventy-five pages each, these three short novels not only present us with surrealistic, often inexplicable events, but they also challenge us to follow the narrative line. In other words, we are first summoned to find out what happens, a discovery which is rarely completely successful with one reading, before we can begin to decipher the various grotesque images and actions. Not everything in these novels is meant to fall into place. Many of the passages remain motiveless and unexplained, contributing not to a rational plot summation which ties up all of the loose ends but to a particular atmosphere which permeates each tale's mixture of comedy and horror. Only one of the three, *The Owl*, seems to me to be totally successful, but all

1. References to all three novels will be to John Hawkes, *Lunar Landscapes* (New York: New Directions, 1969). *Charivari* was first published in *New Directions Anthology*, 11 (1949); *The Goose on the Grave* and *The Owl* were published together by New Directions in 1954.

have their merits and are quick to reward us if we are willing to grapple with their complexities.

CHARIVARI

The first published of Hawkes' major works, *Charivari* presents formidable problems primarily because it is so obviously intended to shock the complacent reader. Novelistic conventions such as plot and character are thrown aside to make room for a fiction full of purposely flat characters, disjointed narrative line, and dream-like sequences. Robert Scholes comments, "*Charivari* is militantly *avant-garde*, not in the philosophical sense employed by Hawkes in speaking of a perpetual avant-gardism, but in the more trivial sense of formally shocking." He suggests that it is "more aggressive and more tentative" than *The Cannibal*, "more certain of what it is not, less certain of what it is." [2]

Our problems begin with the title, an uncommon word in any vocabulary. "Charivari" means a mock serenade, usually for a newly married couple, performed with pans, horns, and kettles, the raucous noise often signaling the serenaders' disapproval of the wedding. The celebration in this case is for the marriage or anniversary of a forty year–old couple, Henry and Emily, and the boisterous serenade takes place at a weekend houseparty attended by loud, comic guests. Neither Henry nor Emily seems to be in love in the conventional sense, and they rarely speak to each other during the party in their honor. The chief complication is Emily's pregnancy, a fact which has not been announced at the beginning of the novel but which assumes more importance in their minds than the imminent celebration. Both Henry and Emily are unaware of how to handle a marriage, much less a baby, and the novel's narrative line focuses on how they solve the problem.

If "plot" suggests movement from a beginning to an ending, then *Charivari* has plot in this simple sense—the pregnancy crisis is finally resolved. But the progress from beginning to end is so fragmented in this novel that an account of the "plot" is war-

2. Robert Scholes, *The Fabulators* (New York: Oxford University Press, 1967), pp. 74–75.

ranted. Divided into four parts, "Courtship," "The Bachelors," "The Wedding," and "Rhythm," *Charivari* begins with Henry and Emily asleep in separate rooms while a huge dog patrols the intervening space. Henry dreams that he is cleaning a stable while a woman, probably Emily, makes love to the stable boy. A baby appears in the woman's arms, and Henry is instructed by the "Expositor" of the dream to drown it. Fearing the baby will bite him, Henry tries to run away—the dream continues all night.

This grotesque dream sets the violent tone for the rest of the novel. Henry and Emily meet for breakfast, he with "spiteful" eyes, she with "strained pleasure," and they begin the "negative contemplation of each other." They then stand in a receiving line to welcome a series of weekend guests with names such as "a ruddy monster from South America," "determined unnamed adventuress in green," "an ungracious daughter," and "vicious little Noel" (p. 55). Following a grotesquely described lunch, the adventuress in green fails in her attempt to seduce Henry—he offers her instead a piece of celery and a glass of tomato juice. Emily, meanwhile, sits with the guests, preoccupied with guarding her stomach from Noel's undisguised explorations of her clothes and her "flat smooth surfaces." The afternoon wanes while Emily rests placidly and while Noel fidgets and flares. Describing the guests, Hawkes suggests the comic ridiculousness of the houseparty: "One by one the audience disappeared: one to the stables because he liked the smell of hay, another crawling down the stairs because he couldn't walk, another with his tail between his teeth, the ungracious daughter back to the lavender retreat" (p. 62).

The scene shifts to the two sets of parents: Henry's, a meek woman named Beady and a vain parson who "never appeared before a group of less than three hundred. All of his choir boys had his initials stitched on the collars of their gowns" (p. 105); and Emily's, a seven-foot general and a lean woman who carries a swagger stick, speaks in the clipped tone of a sergeant major, and presents cards inscribed "General and Generaless Soris Smithson Valentine." Already upset by Henry's continuous losses in business speculations, they are soon shocked by Emily's "strained" announcement that she is pregnant. Henry escapes to the cellar with his friend Gaylor, leaving behind "a sudden burst of chattering voices and the drastic sobs" (p. 68). Sitting beneath the basement steps, drinking with Gaylor, Henry explains his bewilderment: "I simply don't understand . . . I feel as if there were a hundred persuasions, attachments, curried and combed asses, all tangling themselves about my neck, all people I have never seen before, but there is nothing I can put my finger on" (p. 69). There are suggestions of Gaylor's homosexuality, but Henry has time for neither Gaylor nor Emily—he writes a letter to Emily and leaves the house.

Henry flags a bus and journeys to a seacoast town, all the while intrigued by a woman on the bus who wears a black hat and who resembles Emily. Taking a room on the top floor of a boarding house (which he reaches by climbing a ladder), he accepts it as his bridal chamber. But when he looks through the window and sees the mysterious woman again, "still wearing the little black hat, a phantom bride-elect," he walks out to meet her. Instead he loses his nerve though he still suspects the woman to be Emily, and he enters a seaman's tavern. Inside he finds warmth and fellowship which contrasts with the charivari at home, but the peace he enjoys is shattered by the news that the girl in the black hat has drowned near the docks: "The stag party for the groom-to-be was robed with black, but none of them seemed bereaved" (p. 91). Henry decides to go home, and his father turns up to carry him back, his rebellion crushed:

> "I've come to take you back, Henry."
> "Yes, sir." There was nothing he could do.   (p. 93)

Hawkes never tells us who the woman is or how the parson knows where to find Henry.

The rest of the novel nearly abandons plot to depend upon a series of hallucinatory scenes which describe the wedding and its aftermath. Emily commissions a collier's wife to make her gown, but the seamstress seems more preoccupied with kicking a cat that talks and with stabbing the bust of the wedding dress following a pin-prick than with making the gown. The wedding itself is a fiasco: "In the middle of the procession, the flower girl's shoe came undone. While her mother left her pew and stooped to tie it, the organist repeated two notes over and over again.... Wind blew through the cold chancellery and the candles jumped. The flowers were numb, ears red" (p. 109). The drunken houseparty continues while Emily puts the baby in her pocket, and while the adventuress in green loses "her green." Terrified more than ever of the pregnancy, Emily suffers a horrifying vision which merges with Henry's trip to the seacoast town, for she dreams that she is "a cute little thing with a plain white face and a little black hat cocked on one side of her head" (p. 121). This dream suggests that the mysterious woman drowned herself because she was pregnant, and that Henry identifies Emily with her because of that fact, but we are never sure. The generaless finally takes Emily for a medical examination which she envisions as sheer torture. Imagining herself a prisoner, she transforms the doctor's probing into a violation by a riveter's gun while the doctor strops a scalpel. The scene shifts abruptly to the next morning and to the guests playing croquet. Shaving, Henry daydreams that he is both too old and incapable of fathering a child, yet the Expositor tells him that it is all his fault. He goes out to meet Emily and sees her running happily across the lawn, "hair loose and flying, colored skirt whirling about her knees" (p. 136). Realizing, as she laughs, that she is not going to have a baby, he thinks:

> "My goodness . . . she *does* look young." She ran quickly towards him. Gaylor blew loudly on his whistle. "All right," he called, "it's time to play."   (p. 136)

These are the last words of the novel, and the key is Henry's observation of Emily's "youth." The point is that this forty year–old couple fears adulthood, and pregnancy is one sure sign that they are no longer children despite their ages. Hawkes never tells us whether the pregnancy is hysterical or aborted—what matters is that Henry and Emily now feel free to continue their fun and games. They reenter their childish world as Gaylor blows the whistle for the croquet to begin again—the charivari goes on.

In spite of this relatively simple narrative line, the novel is extremely difficult to read. It is highly comic, and its fun develops from the guests' repartee, the parents' boorishness, and the ingenious hallucination scenes, all of which contribute to an atmosphere that carries much more significance than the plot. The narrative line seems no more than a vehicle for the various parts, but this is not a negative observation. Hawkes obviously hopes to disrupt the conventional forms of the novel and to make a break from traditional realism. The horrifying hallucinations and the comic scenes are not meant to be explained logically but are to be enjoyed and understood as a means of supporting the total vision. Although *Charivari* is a work of youth, it is significant because it represents an early example of black humor as well as Hawkes' first extended attempt to work with themes and techniques, especially the role of dreams and the paradoxical mixture of terror and comedy, which are developed more skillfully in the full length novels.

Henry and Emily are purposely presented as flat characters. They do not "live" in the conventional sense because Hawkes is more interested in their immediate fears and repressions. We know very little about them beyond what we discern from their reactions during the houseparty, and we have no idea how the resolution of the pregnancy crisis will affect them in the future. Hawkes even withholds possible motives for their predicaments, events from their pasts which might offer clues as to why they are so panicked at the thought of marriage and children. The one explanation we have for Henry's situation is in his conversation with Gaylor in the cellar when he complains of being weighed down by a hundred "attachments," but nothing he can put his finger on. He does not understand how he always manages to allow himself "to be talked *to*" (p. 67). Similarly, Emily's problems seem to stem from over-attached and domineering parents. During Noel's "explorations," for example, she suddenly remembers "her mother's words, 'Don't ever let a man do *that* to you!' The generaless had looked very stern" (p. 63). But Hawkes leaves the source of her repressions equally as vague as Henry's—there is nothing she can put her finger on. In a hilarious summation of her problems, Hawkes satirizes her bewilderment and her sterility:

> The lack of genes, the lack of a ganglion, the lack of a seed; the moon was not right, or the baby was dropped, or the chemist was wrong, or the teacher untaught, or the night air bad, or the witch was around, but something concocted these discreditable results; something gave the little woman a bad temper, made her lonely and kept her eyes open in the darkness.   (p. 74)

This is really all we know about the main characters. But if Henry and Emily do not live in the traditional sense of literary verisimilitude, their fears and longings leap with life. The point is that Hawkes downplays the kind of life which we would recognize to stress the subconscious reality. *Charivari* satirizes a middle-aged romance made grotesque by fear, and it attacks the supposed security that the family unit traditionally offers. The subconscious tensions of the various family members have surfaced so often that they have become reality. Especially ludicrous, the two sets of parents provide a reasonable hint to the kind of couple Henry and Emily will become:

> All of them are elders, bawdy old-folks, clustered around the water hole. In succession they peer down milk-white shoulders to seek and relish the sight of younger elders. . . . They ride in *petit* leather saddles to the hunt and are entirely harmless. Though they peek. And they worry. Beneath all of their eyes, beneath indifference, and fish and wine, is a humorless apathy.
> (p. 63)

The key to this description of the parents is that they consider Henry and Emily to be younger "elders," for the children, at age forty, have yet to grow up. They are old babies, just as humorless and apathetic as their parents, reflecting the same tensions and fears. Emily's parents, for example, do not communicate with each other except when the generaless prods the general with her swagger stick or orders him to avoid "terms of affection" like "dear" when addressing her. And Henry's father reveals his feelings about Beady when he places a picture of Christ on his desk while he keeps one of Beady face down in the drawer.

Having lived so long with these subconscious tensions, the parents now accept them as reality. Life is humorless and apathetic because they are so solemn. Henry and Emily seem doomed to the same fate. Although their minds are full of feelings which need expression, they rarely speak. In a pathetically comic scene immediately before he leaves the party for the seaside town, Henry writes a letter to Emily though she is in the next room. He complains that he has lost his parents, Gaylor's understanding, and closeness to her, and he wonders why the family disregards him. But underneath this confession is his fear of fatherhood. Calling the pregnancy "charming but frightening news," he undercuts the seriousness of this attempted communication by asking a question which renders the entire scene comic: "Why don't they come and change my pants" (p. 71). This is the kind of unexpected humor which shocks and surprises us. Henry realizes that once the child is born he is no longer the baby of his family.

Willful distortions, such as Henry's comic remark, give *Charivari* its peculiar atmosphere. The nightmares and suppressed fears surface during the pregnancy crisis. Only when Emily and Henry are assured that the nightmares are indeed illusions—when the pregnancy is either aborted or termed false—can they be soothed. But Hawkes' irony suggests that once freed from the nightmare they will sink back into the sterility of their everyday lives. They seem faced with a choice between horrifying dreams and arid reality; the one stirs them to frantic undirected action while the other lulls them to lethargy. In either case they are grimly comic figures, for their reactions to their situations are usually inappropriate and unpredictable. Lacking a fruitful life in reality, they are unable to deal with the possibilities of their dreams. Their dreams degenerate into hallucinations full of violence and cruelty, visions which reveal the other side of their bland lives. The dreams are mystifying, cannot be dealt with, because Henry and Emily have spent forty years avoiding the meaningful experiences which might have provided clues to their subconscious selves. They are grotesquely unpleasant people caught by their own emptiness in uneventful situations. Afraid to exert their personalities and live, they also fear to liberate their subconscious instincts and dream. At the end of the novel all they can do is heed Gaylor's whistle and return to their games.

In addition to providing comment on the role of the subconscious, *Charivari* is also significant for its mixture of comedy and violence. This novel represents Hawkes' initial attempt to experiment in an extended fiction with what has later come to be known as black humor. The mixture of humor and horror is established early in *Charivari* when, in the midst of the hilariously described luncheon, the narrator says, "And have you heard, or do you think we are likely to hear what very private shames and resentments and misgivings these people are harboring? May we be cruel enough?" (p. 55). This statement is about as direct as Hawkes ever gets, and in the course of the novel the "very private shames and resentments and misgivings" are indeed cruelly, but humorously, exposed. Two key sequences illustrate his use of brutal humor: the mysterious woman in the black hat and Emily's trip to the hospital.

The woman with the little hat is referred to throughout the novel's last half, and thus references to her constitute a recurring image which helps to unify *Charivari*. Interestingly enough, Henry's reactions to this stranger reveal the mixed feelings about Emily which he has repressed. Thinking that the woman resembles Emily, he links her to his terrifying dream at the beginning of the novel when he imagines that the woman's little black hat sits "above the pointed skull of a Jezebel." The merger of the unfaithful woman in the stable, the woman with the hat, Jezebel, and Emily suggests what we already suspect, that Henry cannot accept his role in Emily's pregnancy. But his tendency to think that Emily has been made pregnant by some other man is complicated by his counter identification of the woman with Emily the faithful bride. Thus, the woman with the black hat is also described in Henry's illusion as "a bartered, mythical bride, vaporous Emily" and as "a phantom bride-elect" (pp. 80, 82). Not knowing whether to accept Emily as Jezebel or bride, Henry's dilemma is solved for him when the mysterious woman drowns and when his father returns him to the houseparty. Her drowning refers back to Henry's dream in which the Expositor orders him to drown the newborn baby, but by this point lethargy has recaptured him. A short time later he "tried to remember something about a seacoast town but could not" (p. 117).

But Hawkes is not finished with this delusion. In a brutally comic twist, he lifts the mysterious woman out of Henry's hallucination and places her in Emily's. Now married, Emily's fears have magnified to the extent that she imagines the baby already born. It has sideburns and demands, "You better give me another kiss!" (p. 112). In the midst of this hallucination the woman with the black hat appears and a few minutes later Emily overhears Dr. Smith talking about a woman with a little black hat who needed an abortion. The comedy stems from the wildly incongruous relationship between what we know about the woman's fate, Henry's and Emily's delusions about her, and Dr. Smith's off-the-cuff remark. Smith's comic comment about unwanted pregnancies, which Emily overhears, foreshadows the novel's end:

> Well . . . that's the way they get stung, stuck and undeceived. They lose it, drop it, throw it away before it's big enough to name or be a bastard in the family circle. . . . Sometimes, though, . . . it's all a mistake, a dream and there isn't any roe at all; and they end up just as dry as ever.   (p. 122)

This extended hallucination is indeed a cruel exposure of the private shames and resentments which people harbor, and the reader is caught between a tendency to laugh at the ridiculousness of the scene and an urge to cry out at the suffering. Smith's comment is the first substantial hint that Emily may not be pregnant after all. Thus laughter is the result of the disparity between the unverified facts and the exaggerated, inappropriate responses. Emily's hallucination becomes even more grotesque in the hospital sequence. In the midst of his description of the mysterious woman, which he considers a lewd joke, Dr. Smith says that he solved the problem by sending "her over to a classmate of mine who hadn't made the grade. Give him a hatchet and he was happy" (p. 121). The horror of abortion obviously crowds out the possibility that she may not be pregnant, for Emily's vision immediately shifts from the hatchet reference to her trip to the hospital.

A prisoner in a car which travels as if it were first a train and then an airplane, Emily is suddenly metamorphosed into the woman with the black hat:

> Emily, in the middle, felt gusts of cold air climbing up her back, bent her head to escape the wind that swept through the cracks in the celluloid windshield. She wanted to scratch her nose beneath the veil, but each of her wrists was pinioned at her side by firm unrelaxing fingers. The blindfold pressed into her eyes and the little ribbons in her hair were squashed down under the black hat.   (pp. 123–124)

This surrealistic description is expanded when she reaches a hospital complete with smokestacks, blinking lights, mountains of ice, and "tar-covered tugs and wrecked bridges" in a river which runs along the "lower face of the hospital" (p. 126). Her examination is pure delusion, conveying pain through its description of violence and exciting laughter from the ludicrousness of Emily's grotesque responses. But because of her hallucination our suspicions are confirmed: Emily fears not only pregnancy but sex. When Dr. Smith asks "to take a look," she clamps her hands over her skirt. The prenatal examination becomes in her mind a rape by a riveter:

> With a violent effort he heaved her onto the table and Emily felt the broad flat straps falling over her body, needles jabbing into her arms.
> "Drive the damn thing in," screamed the riveter.
> The examination began.   (p. 132)

Sexual sterility, as one of the secondary themes, is indirectly referred to in other suggestive metaphors. A seamstress, for example, literally attacks Emily's bridal gown with a hatpin. Rice, traditional symbol of fertility at weddings, falls short of the couple. The hallucination of Emily's physical examination is balanced by a surrealistic scene in which Henry imagines an operation for emasculation. And when the Expositor of his dream blames him for the pregnancy, Henry insists, "I never was capable." These are pitiful people, leading empty lives, and their fear of healthy sexuality illustrates how incapable they are of regeneration. They deserve the charivari. Most of these outrageous sequences are horribly violent, but their exaggeration makes them comic. Reading *Charivari* is like watching a ghost movie purposely turn into a comedy due to the presence of one too many chain-rattling skeletons. The word "purposely" should be stressed here, for Hawkes maintains full control. Without the comic effects, the novel would degenerate into gratuitous violence.

Despite the care with which Hawkes manipulates the tension between comedy and terror, *Charivari* lacks the kind of internal coherence so skillfully developed in the later novels, especially *The Lime Twig* and *Second Skin*. Closer to *The Goose on the Grave* with its picaresque structure, this early novel tends toward the isolated action or scene, such as the hospital sequence, to provide coherence rather than toward complex patterns of recurring action and parallel image. Henry and Emily experience a series of events, each a contained whole and each contributing to the plotline. But the experiences tend to be separated in the sense that once they are completed Hawkes seldom refers to them again. The strange woman in the black hat remains one of the few images that interlocks several of these events. Yet this characteristic of *Charivari* is not a flaw but the natural result of Hawkes' decision to experiment with hallucinatory scenes. Recognizing the privacy of the subconscious, he structures the novel with a succession of these individual delusions so that it necessarily is reminiscent of the picaresque form. The mysterious woman is a particularly fortunate stroke, for by placing her in both Henry's and Emily's visions, Hawkes illustrates the mutuality of their fears. Yet in many ways *Charivari*'s external form is conventional for a Hawkes fiction, if convention is possible in a work so aggressively innovative, because the traditional unities of time, setting, and dramatic focus are maintained. The action occurs at a party, during one weekend, and while Henry and Emily make brief ventures from the celebration, the central object of concern remains always the pregnancy. The poetic effects which unify the later novels are here often isolated set pieces. Reading them we are puzzled, horrified, amused, and outraged, but the effects are controlled and restrained, accessible to the willing reader. And like all of Hawkes' fiction, *Charivari* pulls the reader into the action without the traditional novel's convenient conventions of exposition or introduction. Backgrounds are not explained and characters are not developed—we open the book, and things begin to happen. Hawkes makes no effort to prepare us for Henry's terrifying dream on the first page, yet while reading we are able to piece together his sad relationship with Emily.

Most of the isolated hallucinatory effects occur in the last two sections, "The Wedding" and "Rhythm." Emily's trip to the hospital, for example, takes place in "Rhythm," and the first part of the section contains a series of comic surrealistic scenes in which the revelers speak. Emily talks to "the baby," the generaless feeds a cat, the adventuress in green loses "her green," and Dr. Smith flirts with the ungracious daughter. But as isolated as these scenes are, they are unified by the refrain of "kiss." Peering over the bassinette, Emily hears the imagined baby say, "You better give me another kiss!" (p. 112). She slams the door with the words "kiss, kiss, kiss" echoing in her ears. At the same time Dr. Smith says to the room full of guests, "Everybody wants to kiss, kiss, kiss." He then directs his remarks to the ungracious daughter: "You better give me another kiss." The windows rattle with the music, and "a kiss in the dark" floats along the ceiling (p. 114). And later, while feeding the cat, the generaless says to either the general or the cat (we are not sure which), "You better give me a kiss" (p. 117). This recurring refrain satirizes the notion of love which these people have, making them even more grotesque, but the refrain is also significant as a device to hold together a series of separate scenes. Because of the repeated words, the scenes reflect the novel's concern with modern romance. But while these fragments are never developed, the refrain suggests a unity among them which in turn helps to structure the novel.

These fragmented scenes also keep us in touch with the actions and whereabouts of the many secondary characters. Grotesquely humorous like Henry and Emily, the minor characters are necessary to sustain the party atmosphere. The games, the repartee, and the descent into drunkenness provide the raucous noise which is usually associated with a charivari. Henry and Emily worry about pregnancy while the wedding celebration goes on unconcerned. To control the numerous secondary characters, Hawkes often uses a short series of direct statements which survey and describe an entire scene. For example, immediately following Emily's dream of her grandmother's funeral, the actions of the guests are summarized:

> The adventuress in green, on the monster's back, thought she was riding a dromedary over the sand. . . .
> Dr. Smith had cornered the ungracious daughter, who was sleepy but frightened. He was talking of sutures and instruments, and an oval abdomen.
> The Burgesses were drinking beer, remarkably content.
> Mr. and Mrs. Young looked at photographs.
> Mrs. Wheeling Rice slept soundly on the sofa, her gown undone.
> They carried bamboo sticks and cellophane to build their nests.   (p. 76)

Although these guests' names appear periodically, we know even less about them than about Henry and Emily. Hawkes makes no effort to develop them or to keep up with their antics during the celebration. He mentions them only to tell us where they are or what they are doing, allowing them to drift in and out of the more fully developed visionary scenes so that he can sustain the party background. The technique not only orders the various characters but also contributes to the comic tone. Close to understatement, this kind of structural device permits Hawkes to maintain the detachment necessary for laughter. The last sentence of the quotation is never explained, but it suggests how irrational and ludicrous the party has become. This method of description is the novelist's answer to the clown's deadpan expression—the characters' ridiculous actions are reported without comment.

But despite *Charivari*'s experimental structure and successful blend of comedy and terror, the novel encourages a curious attitude in us toward the characters. Hawkes' later novels suggest that we harbor similar fantasies and fears within ourselves, thus establishing sympathy between reader and fictional victim. But we are so detached from the characters in *Charivari* that our laughter is never tempered with sympathetic concern. Commenting on the problem, Professor Scholes writes, "a sense is established of reader and narrator conniving to expose 'them'." [3] The problem may be that these people are too simple a target for Hawkes' genius. On the one hand the characters are so sterile that we have trouble sympathizing with their problems. Thus, the narrator's "cruel" exposure of their "private shames and resentments and misgivings" fails to bother us. On the other hand the narrator chooses to have us on his side rather than the characters' so that the partygoers become strawmen—they are so easy to blow down that victory over them seems slight.

Comic detachment without sympathetic concern negates the attraction-repulsion antithesis which gives Hawkes' later work its complex tone. Although we laugh, our laughter is directed *at* Henry and Emily. *Charivari* lacks the kind of reader sympathy which allows us to laugh *with*, say, Skipper in *Second Skin*, even though many of his bumbling actions are as disgusting as Henry's. The point is that we learn so little about ourselves in *Charivari*. The characters exist in another world which we do not enter— rather we stand outside and judge. Because we are so detached, their hallucinations and potential for violence seem to remain their own fault, the special effects of their pitifully sterile lives. Unlike the later novels, *Charivari* does not implicate us too as we explore the unconsciousness of these terrified people. Instead its particular successes are Hawkes' controlled handling of the nightmare sequence and the tension between comedy and fear.

THE GOOSE ON THE GRAVE

The Goose on the Grave experiments with loose form even more than *Charivari* does. Highly picaresque, it sidesteps the unity

3. Ibid., p. 78.

which *Charivari* gains from the focus on Emily's pregnancy and reactions to it. Some readers might argue that *The Goose on the Grave* has no form at all, for the episodic structure is held together only by the presence of the main character Adeppi. But one of the innovative qualities of this novel is its formlessness, in the sense that it avoids traditional patterns of structure. There is no definite dramatic event similar to the pregnancy crisis which links the violent incidents. Rather Adeppi, an orphan in an unexplained war, encounters various rogues and villains with the result that the novel exposes a society rendered sterile by its adherence to outmoded traditions and meaningless rituals. The unity of *The Goose on the Grave* is primarily derived from sustained themes, particularly Adeppi's search for a protector with the corresponding violation of his innocence, and the sterility of the present which looks back to the past without understanding it because of reliance on empty ritual.

Although *The Goose on the Grave* is set in Italy, Hawkes renders the events universal and timeless so that it makes no difference where they occur. Nothing is to be gained by trying to pinpoint the specific location or time of Adeppi's adventures. Reading *The Goose on the Grave* we must, for the while, dismiss our traditional notions of the novel and enter a fictional landscape which Hawkes names "Italy." In an early review Jerome Stone summarizes the experience which the unprepared reader faces: "Hardly a scene will be comprehensible to the reasonable-minded reader, yet the whole thing reverberates with overtones and after-images, inexplicable, unresolved, but oddly affecting, even to those who will accuse him of pointless obscurity." [4] The traditional laws and religion which these characters observe are now ineffective for two reasons. On the more simple level war has destroyed the order and sanity which are necessary for the rational state. But more importantly, traditions have degenerated to empty observances which have form but no meaning. And caught in this wasteland is the orphan Adeppi, "one of Italy's covey of fragile doves" (p. 201).

4. Jerome Stone, "Surrealistic Threesome," *Saturday Review*, 24 July 1954, p. 36.

The unexplained events begin on the first page. Three priests on three white donkeys descend from the mountains, enter Adeppi's house, walk to his mother, and "cross, lift, and carry her off" (p. 201). We are never told why, and no further reference is made to this mysterious action until the very end. There the priests Dolce and Bolo arrive at a convent and thrust Adeppi's mother into a pile of flaming wood. Hawkes never explains, and the only hint he gives us is the mother's name, Theresa. But this possible reference to the Spanish saint Theresa of Ávila seems more like a false lead to trap the unwary reader who might also try to form a pattern out of the fact that there are three priests and three white donkeys. All we can be sure of is that religious overtones permeate the two violent acts, kidnapping and human sacrifice, which frame Adeppi's search for a protector. The mysticism associated with priestly orders and centuries of religious heritage intensifies the novel's grotesqueness and adds to the sense of tradition which permeates the narrative.

Left alone despite the presence of brothers and sisters, Adeppi stations himself between a bakery and a hospital which treats battle casualties. Hawkes comically contrasts the pain of the war wounded with fingers burned by hot bread: "Adeppi had come into the world's platoon of broken lances and even while he smelled the iodine, he heard the far-off cries of women as the hot crusts burned their palms" (p. 203). Pain is pain, and Adeppi learns a good deal about it in the course of his adventures. The first adult to adopt him is Nino, a wounded soldier who tries to teach the boy to sing. A kind of happy-go-lucky rogue, Nino steals cotton wads for his injured neck and "borrows" Edouard's guitar to woo Maria. But Nino is a shadowy figure, living on the edge of more serious crimes. There are hints of pimping and of sexual deviations, and Nino's affection for Adeppi often wavers. Only when he is ready to return to war does his violent nature surface. Running straight to Adeppi, he confronts the boy with a pistol:

> The soldier did not touch him, did not put a hand on his arm, but placed the muzzle against the boy's temple. The gun was steady.... The pistol was pressing against Adeppi's ear, he

> stared ahead shamefully, bewildered. Still aiming the gun, deli-
> cate, menacing, Nino began to rub his flat jaw. Absently, he
> opened the tunic. . . . Then, as if trying to remember, Nino laid
> the pistol on the well rim beside the boy.   (p. 211)

Completely detached, Hawkes presents this chilling scene without comment. As with the sacrifice of Adeppi's mother, we never know the motive for Nino's act, nor do we learn why he fails to pull the trigger. Lack of motivation makes the event more startling because it points up the random violence which can strike so unexpectedly and which thus nullifies Adeppi's search for an ordered life. But what magnifies the terror is Hawkes' suggestion that Adeppi's murder, had it occurred, would have passed unnoticed. In a tone of comic understatement, Hawkes describes merely the physical results if the shooting had taken place. There would be a flash, a recoil of the pistol, a sharp noise, and then the eventual disappearance of the echo, but no authority would investigate the shot and no one would miss Adeppi:

> Had the short scarred finger pulled the trigger, there would
> have been a flash, a leaping of the silver gun in the air, and a
> sharp noise echoing away among the ruins. The shot would
> have crossed the ancient tiles and disappeared. . . . a man so ex
> cited in the early morning, clad only partially in a uniform,
> could have killed and not disturbed the early puttering of the
> old peasants in their yards.   (p. 211)

Later, following another comic scene in which Nino snaps a farewell photograph of Maria as she exposes her unclad hips, he shakes hands with Adeppi and says goodbye. But the experiences with the soldier have tarnished Adeppi's innocence: "thereafter, while he counted upon the return of his companion, he was armed" (p. 213).

  Nino is a comic character, a gangling, unstable man whose outbursts of violence never explode into destruction. Hawkes hints that Nino later shoots himself; at the end of the novel the soldier is cold, alone, and dreaming "despite the presence across the valley of the enemy." His mistreatment of the boy is regrettable but harmless by itself. But Adeppi's loneliness is serious, a fact which

Hawkes stresses by a description of the town's madonna immediately after Nino's departure. Unusually small, the madonna is carved of wood, its colors faded, its extended arms empty. The woodcarver has suggested its traditional symbol of maternity by sculpturing the madonna "still with child." Yet whatever significance this religious symbol had in the past, it is now meaningless, All it can do is look "down on this square of small boys," unable to offer solace or to promise hope.

With his mother kidnapped, Nino gone to war, and the madonna impotent, Adeppi turns to a series of protectors: Edouard, Jacopo, Arsella, and the priest Dolce. None are able to comfort him. Edouard and Jacopo, for example, are aging homosexuals, and Adeppi's initiation to sexual aberration begins with Edouard. In keeping with the mysterious atmosphere of the novel, Hawkes never makes the deviation explicit. But the experience is obviously planned, for Edouard waits for Adeppi before completing the act. He leads the boy to Nino who is "helpless," dressed in only a short army tunic which fails to cover his waist. Although an audience of women pleads with Edouard to "cover him up," he involves Adeppi and Maria in the undefined ritual and then pays Adeppi with a Florentine florin. Hawkes carefully avoids any statement that might decipher this degrading act, but with this incident he establishes a series of episodes which involves a mixture of sex and violence.

Now forced to sing in Edouard's cheap restaurant, Adeppi meets Jacopo, the accordion player. Jacopo and Edouard have had a long history together, traveling the continent as lovers and partners, obviously wealthy at one time. Now they are without fortune, and Jacopo is left with his dreams, as he plays, of "Edouard's face, Edouard standing with cane and straw hat, Edouard throwing him a coin in Il Valentino" (p. 216). Jacopo, however, is more than another sexual deviant. Describing him in terms of two traditional figures, the strolling violinist playing for lovers and the pied piper, Hawkes establishes Jacopo's part in the theme of sterile ritual. Jacopo, as an artist figure, remembers his music and role, but he has outlived his ability to create. Either the tables are empty or the customers talk, and all Jacopo can do is press the accordion keys and remember his past. "Alone, hair faded at the temples, Jacopo was central Europe's aged violinist among empty tables. He was not of the crowd—thinking, plotting, remembering behind the smoke and the beckoning of the instrument—a worn, thinned, narrow-eyed renderer of wine-cellar music" (p. 217). Similarly, his association with the archetypal pied piper is no longer relevant. Time has passed Jacopo by—he goes through the forms, but all meaning has disappeared: "He is unshaved. Each day he has crossed at the same time, followed by no children or rats, approaching from the west one day, the east the next" (p. 225).

Yet for all their sterility and willingness to take advantage of Adeppi, Jacopo and Edouard are also comic characters. As with most Hawkes comedy, there is a grotesque blend of violence and humor with the result that the comedy makes the scenes bizarre. In one incident Jacopo grabs Edouard's tie and begins to choke him. Edouard gags and coughs, pleading with Jacopo to use discretion because the restaurant patrons are watching. Hawkes, however, is interested not in the results of the attack or the motives for it but in the inappropriate responses. As he fights for breath, Edouard notices that the accordion is out of tune, and it, in turn, becomes personified, "conscious only of its own chromatic preoccupation, its blinded chords." With eyes watering and face turning pale, Edouard makes the attack ridiculous with his desperate, choked whisper, "You will . . . wrinkle my tie" (p. 218). Although Jacopo throws Edouard aside in disgust at that remark, he is not through. A few minutes later he knocks Edouard unconscious in the flooded outdoor lavatory. With a hilarious response (which looks forward to Skipper's relief in *Second Skin* that the snowballs are not vengeful birds), Edouard takes heart because the ringing in his head flashes beautiful colors to his eyes:

> He concluded after some minutes—vaguely the thoughts rattled about inside his head—that since Jacopo hit him with the upperside rather than the underside of the hand, it was the nails he felt on his cheek and their stinging that remained when the arm

swept each time to the end of its half circle in the dark. It was
true, his eyes did flash, and at one of the more painful blows—it
glazed his eyelids—he took heart because he loved color.

(p. 222)

As Adeppi's third substitute parent figure, Jacopo is the link between the themes of sexual violence and religious aberration. He
takes the boy for a walk to see a train, and in a sudden switch of
scene, Adeppi finds himself with Arsella and her family. Asleep
between the cow's front legs in Arsella's barn, Adeppi and the cow
mock "the nativity of the crèche" (p. 236). But Adeppi's mockery
is innocent while that of Arsella's family is crass. Arsella's mother,
for example, wears a hair shirt because she thinks that the hair belonged to the disciples. Except for some itching, no punishment
remains in it, but she continues to go through the form of suffering. Similarly, Arsella's bedroom has only one decoration, a grotesque painting of a bleeding heart with mustard green thorns
thrust deep into bright red arteries. It displays "the frightening
inaccuracies of the imagination," yet Arsella kisses it every morning. When Adeppi declares that he does not believe it, she piously
answers, "God the father . . . anything is possible." Hawkes undercuts this ridiculous religiosity with Adeppi's comic question. Having pondered the bleeding heart for some time, he asks, "Arsella,
did he eat the brambles?" (p. 237).

Arsella earns money by selling religious ornaments, which her
blind husband Pipistrello makes, to the priest Brother Bolo, who
in turn sells them for profit to the churches. It is on such a trip to
Bolo's that Adeppi meets Dolce, his final inept protector. Unlike
the other religious people in Adeppi's life, Dolce has the potential
for genuine worship. But he is obsessed with the pain in Christ's
face, with the agony itself. In other words, he worships pain and
is, thus, no better than Arsella's mother with her hairshirt or Arsella herself with the bleeding heart. For Dolce imitation of Christ
means imitation of the suffering face: "Dolce carried this exact
expression where he went, showing to strangers only his own insignificant suspicion, a trembling chin, meanly concealing the im-

ages of wind-beating locks and thorns" (p. 243). Dolce further perverts religion by his exaggeration of personal chastisement. He fasts, prays, confesses, and prostrates himself, all the while fearing an unknown "they." He is afraid of the sudden shout, of "them" bursting in on him while he prays. He, too, has his share of the ridiculous. Going to bed, he sleeps with his hand "raised above the head and cupped defensively as if to catch some weight hurled out of the heavens through the roof" (p. 247).

Dolce is, however, the most violent of Adeppi's caretakers. Not only responsible for the kidnapping and burning of the boy's mother, he is also to blame for Arsella's mother's hairshirt. Hawkes never makes the connection with the mother explicit, but he does describe this act of cruelty in such a way as to suggest the possibility. An old woman begs Dolce and Bolo, both novices at the time, for aid and chastisement, but they try to ignore her. On the "day of visible ascension," they finally lose patience and fulfill her wish. Stripping her to the waist, they stitch together a shirt of uncured rat skins. Dolce piously tells us that though the swing of the needle was awkward, "the old woman was not pierced." This is the kind of perversion—be it sexual or religious—which Adeppi encounters during his picaresque journey, and it is all climaxed when Dolce permits the boy to witness the burning of his mother. Hawkes remains uninvolved; neither he nor Adeppi seems particularly bothered by the incident: Dolce strips Adeppi and then petitions the saints to forgive the child's transgressions, while Adeppi humorously observes that he did not know there were so many saints. The mother seems forgotten.

This blend of humor and horror is consistent, but it is not the point of the novel. The comedy of these rascals is part of the picaresque tradition, serving as a means of satirizing Adeppi's world. Usually brutal and terrifying, the humor gains its power from Hawkes' authorial detachment while he exposes a series of foibles ranging from twisted neckties to human sacrifices. *The Goose on the Grave*, however, is not just a modern picaresque novel. Hawkes' primary interest is the contrast between the overly ritualized past and the present fragmented by war. Symbolized by madonnas, hairshirts, and meaningless art forms, the past has lost its ability to nourish the present. Its storehouse of tradition and sustaining forms of action has long been depleted. Caught in a present characterized by war, orphans, and hunger, Adeppi cannot possibly find stability because the adults who should offer it rely upon the sterile past for guidance.

Hawkes' choice of Italy for his setting calls attention to the long heritage of religion and art. The sense of history is suggested by Adeppi's trip to the ancient aqueduct, but we know that the skills which fashioned this genuine engineering feat are no longer fertile. Creativity has come to a standstill. Just as there has been a prostitution of religion, so there has been a degeneration of art. Jacopo, Pipistrello, Dolce and even Adeppi are artist figures who now lack inspiration and skill. Jacopo, the aging pied piper, no longer has listeners or children to follow him. Pipistrello's religious pottery is no more than cheap angels which Bolo will resell at outrageous prices. Dolce longs to give a sign to the people, to perform a ritual, but while the crowd waits, he offers nothing except the words "Patience, patience, temperance, patience" (p. 274). And Adeppi, in his role as street singer, finds himself "isolated in a glaze of medieval lyricism." Struggling with his songs, "he forces himself to voice those ecstatic melodies to which so many countesses have met and sinned, so many wolfhounds bayed" (p. 206). That this degeneration is widespread is suggested by the grim image of the rats which now occupy the aqueduct.

Hawkes' point is that the heritage of the past is lost. Michelangelo's sculpture becomes Pipistrello's pottery, and the country stumbles along without "the activity of shoot or sprout, without shadow." "The vendors continue to hawk china molded on the thumbs of Michelangelo over the mountain where the renaissance has failed" (p. 232). Form without content rules the present, but the people cannot break with a past which no longer offers meaningful direction. Thus while an undefined war rages, religious relics are sold, the Sforza family is "all but dead," the Grand Hotel burns, and rats own the aqueduct. Hawkes suggests that this deterioration of history is endless. The process of life becomes a sur-

vival of "the least fit" so that those capable of regenerating the
present find their actions stultifying in ritualized patterns. With
a pessimistic look to the future, one of the novel's few comments
on the future, a dying Edouard prophesies the final triumph of
sterility:

> And Edouard thought of the centuries to come with a drop of
> blood shared by a hundred, and the generations it would take
> for the sports to appear, when men would be dwarfed and with-
> ered of limb, when the weak, the sickest, and the abandoned
> would steal the figs from the archbishop's tree and inherit the
> plains wherever the wind blew.   (p. 273)

For Hawkes the worst result of this process is the violation of
innocence and youth. Recalling Selvaggia's corruption in *The
Cannibal* and foreshadowing Monica's destruction in *The Lime
Twig*, Adeppi finds himself a victim of history. No matter where
he goes or to whom he turns, he is alone, cut off from life: "Adeppi
expects every traveler to know him. He waits to be recognized,
holds his hands over his head against the sun and is disappointed"
(p. 232). Only he sees the crow, the herald of death, flying across
the crowd assembled at the end of the novel to await Dolce's sign.
Religion, like war and art, becomes simply one more means by
which man expresses himself, one more unstable human institution. All degenerate because of the present's failure of imagination
and spirit and because of its inability to spark new life in old in-
stitutions. The renaissance has failed. The forms of past greatness
remain whole—the aqueduct still stands and the madonna continues to look down on the square, but rats live in one while deranged
priests take advantage of the other. The content which could give
meaning to the forms is gone. Having paid homage to the concrete
reality of their heritage, to the *fact* of the aqueduct, or to the
statue of the madonna, for so long, the people have lost sight of
the spiritual truths needed to sustain the life of these ancient relics.
The ingenuity which built the aqueduct is lost, as is the purity of
Mary, with the result that the concrete representations of ingenuity and purity have come to stand for the abstractions themselves. Thus the failure of the renaissance engulfs perverse and

innocent alike. The potential for regenerative art and revitalized ritual withers—the geese are dancing upon the grave.

Much of the novel's grotesqueness is the result of what Earl Rovit has named the victim theme in Hawkes' fiction.[5] The desires of victim and victimizer merge until both are satisfied with the masochistic-sadistic union. In general terms, the people of Adeppi's world seem willing to submit to the degeneration of tradition while they simultaneously destroy it. This fusion of victim and victimizer becomes explicit in the violent scenes involving Jacopo's beating of Edouard or the priests' chastisement of the old woman. Dolce and Bolo, for example, receive as much pleasure from providing the hairshirt as the old lady does from her supposed privilege of wearing it. She leaves the monastery with a radiant face, as if the priests had "pronounced that henceforward her children's children would go free of sin." The priests in turn agree that "more like her should wear the shirt" (p. 250). Parallel urges of masochism and sadism join, with both victim and victimizer finding perverse meaning in the patterns of pain and violence. This union reaches its ultimate climax when the victim becomes indistinguishable from his torturer. Rovit suggests that "they are both victims of their desires and victimizers of the puny human agencies which serve to actualize their yearnings." In many ways this union is a key theme in *The Goose on the Grave*. A reciprocal relationship exists between a people made ineffectual by the sterility of past rituals and the dissipated traditions which the masses insist on following. The result is a circle which spins away to meaninglessness.

The Goose on the Grave is an extremely difficult novel to read, and Hawkes does not make the process any easier when he withholds information which we are used to having. This is not a violation of the so-called moral obligation of the author to supply necessary facts for the reader, for nowhere in the novel is Hawkes unreliable. We have no reason to suspect that the impersonal narrator lies when he tells us, for instance, that Adeppi's mother

5. Earl Rovit, "The Fiction of John Hawkes: An Introductory View," *Modern Fiction Studies*, 11 (Summer 1964), 150–162.

burns, but Hawkes declines to drop a single hint which would reveal why she is sacrificed. The facts are there for us to read, but
he refuses to spell out motives or meanings. In doing so he forces
us to plunge into the imagined landscape, to participate with the
characters who are denied the same information we are. For the
reader who is at ease with only realistic fiction, the absence of motive or meaning is often infuriating. He finds himself struggling
to put together a complete pattern, refusing to grant Hawkes the
right to hold back the pieces which he must omit. Desiring traditional plotline rather than Hawkes's term—vision—the unprepared
reader works so hard to fill in "missing" information that he ne-
glects the truly significant points. Hawkes' technique creates the
effect of dream, nightmare, and fragmented history, all of which
are vital to the shadowy atmosphere.

Why, for example, do we have the four paragraphs describing
the locust fight? Fascinated with these colonies of two-headed insects, Adeppi watches them turn against themselves. They have
"forgotten how to denude the olive trees and their afternoons were
confined to scaling the terraces" (p. 252). Similarly, the hounds
which chase through the night remain unexplained. Hawkes tells
us that the dogs can climb the aqueduct, and that they are not
harmful: "No mastiffs these, but the inbred packs whose prey,
when run to the ground, came to no harm" (p. 253). Yet he also
describes them as like "flesh-eating sheep" and as "the dogs of un-
rest," and men take to the trees when the dogs are loose. Thus, we
can never be sure just how harmless these dogs really are. They
seem more like harbingers of random violence, recalling the roving
dogpacks in *The Cannibal*. One explanation for these bizarre images comes from their relationship to ritual. The locusts, for example, go through the forms of devouring all that stands in their
way, but they have forgotten how to "denude the olive trees."
Turning on each other, the timeless pattern is maintained, but
the result is perverse—they become their own victims. The dogs
also represent the venerable rite of the hunt; they lead riders
clothed in "ancient velveteen, their épées electrified." But the
form of the hunt is now meaningless, lost in a more violent cycle

in which men kill each other in war or chastise fellow sufferers in the name of religion. Other examples of unexplained violence abound: Pipistrello being crushed by a boulder or Adeppi's discovery of a dead shepherd. The point is that we should not be distracted by our inability to decipher exact meanings. Hawkes has no desire to render his grotesque effects logically explicable. To do so would not only suggest a rational world, a possibility which he dismisses; it would also destroy the dreamlike atmosphere.

Very little hope is present at the end of *The Goose on the Grave*, and nothing implies a positive future for Adeppi. Yet the novel is finally a comic fiction despite the predominance of violence. Peopled with characters who will not acknowledge anything that does not touch them directly, this novel gains its sense of humor from the incongruity between the ridiculous way the characters act and the seriousness of what is happening to them. They are comic people because they go about their daily business unaware of their spiritual and artistic decline, unable to see how they fail to measure up to their once great heritage, and unwilling to take the blame for the chaos. And the humor is particularly black since Hawkes suggests that they could not remedy the situation even if they knew what was happening. Even the war, the general symbol of their predicament, goes unnoticed. The reader sympathy that is missing in *Charivari* is here for Adeppi. We care about what happens to him, and we are pained when he suffers. But Hawkes encourages no hope that Adeppi can halt the trend or blossom into the genuine artist figure needed to reverse the failure of the renaissance.

THE OWL

By far the most horrifying of Hawkes' three short novels, *The Owl* is also the most successful. The terrifying incidents, the blend of violence and humor, all used to good advantage in *Charivari* and in *The Goose on the Grave*, are here kept under tighter control. The result is a sharper focus, a dovetailing of theme, character, and action into a highly imaginative gothic comedy. Like *The Goose on the Grave*, *The Owl* explores the weight of the tradition-ridden past on the present, and it makes use of some similar images—geese, madonnas, even a hunchback living in a dark mountain fortress—to round out the bizarre events. But by avoiding the picaresque form of *The Goose on the Grave*, Hawkes directs all of his special effects to support his theme. *The Owl* has no extraneous matter—each character and event contributes to the whole.

Once again Hawkes creates another complex novel around a simple narrative line. The background is an undefined war. All of the young men are either dead or fighting, a situation which panics the older fathers who now lack potential husbands for their strictly raised daughters. The only available male in Sasso Fetore, the hangman, known as Il Gufo (the Owl), is traditionally off limits because he is bound to the gallows, the dark lady. But the war has made matters so desperate that the fathers begin to waver: "Not one had thought to put his daughter's hand into mine or expected mine to fall on hers. Now they were tempted" (p. 137). A prisoner is captured, and the fathers fall into a comedy of frantic action as they rush to the mountain fortress begging Il Gufo to spare the prisoner for marriage to one of the daughters. Signor Barabo, father of the most desirable virgin, Antonina, is the most vocal of the pleaders, a comic character who forever carries with him "some item intimate to the nuptial, the garter, the soldi the bride tucks against her bosom, some aphrodisiac trinket he had spirited from Antonina's seven-year store" (p. 143). But Il Gufo refuses their pleas. It is not that the hangman is a personification of evil, though he is far from charitable; tradition dominates him, too, despite his absolute power over the population. His duty, proclaimed for centuries and symbolized by an escutcheon showing an owl destroying a rodent, is to hang prisoners. Any deviation from the ritual would suggest dereliction:

> To the hangman went the souls of death's peasants, to him were bonded the lineage of a few artisans and not least the clarity of such a high place, a long firm line of rule. If there was decay, it was only in the walls falling away from proclamations hundreds of years old, still readable, still clear and binding.   (p. 138)

This quotation illustrates the present's homage to the past. Any rule or tradition which once carried power remains to this day a binding force. There is no such thing as reinterpretation of the law in Sasso Fetore. The remaining action is quite simple. The prisoner escapes on wings made from gander feathers; Il Gufo seduces Antonina; the prisoner is recaptured, tortured, and hanged; and the ritual goes on.

But as with all Hawkes novels, the plot is mainly a vehicle for the visual impact of a brilliantly imagined fictional world. What counts is the constructed vision. The atmosphere is developed to give a sense of stultifying rituals and rigid codes which govern every pattern of life. The prisoner belongs to the hangman; the fortress is property willed to the hangman, and no one dares to think otherwise. Another renaissance has failed. History loses the strength to replenish itself, and history becomes the true villain of the novel when it degenerates into stale tradition, abdicating its role as a storehouse of model action. Il Gufo tells us that in Sasso Fetore the "air of longevity was strong," and that "the immense king's evil of history lay over the territory" (pp. 169, 176). Describing the view from the fortress, he reveals the sterility: "The earth looked like the mud holes of rice flats, it stretched away only to provide a surface in which to hide excrement" (p. 153). The power of the past blocks all human effort to create something positive and forward looking because the urge to honor the past outweighs the desire for change. Even a desperate man like Barabo stops short of crossing Il Gufo. Creating a purveyor of death as the god figure of Sasso Fetore, Hawkes suggests the inevitable end of a people bound to the decrees of their forefathers.

Hawkes takes pains at the beginning of *The Owl* to give us a feeling for Sasso Fetore's isolation and for the rigid life patterns. The town itself, for example, is completely cut off, dominated by the towers of the hangman's fortress. It is possible to find the sea if one looks in the right direction, but the townspeople prefer their own limited horizon: "If any in Sasso Fetore saw out there a Venetian sail, they pretended it was a dream" (p. 138). Avoiding the rest of the world, these people have nothing to turn to but history. Il Gufo's escutcheon takes its decoration from a decree "dating to the Council of Bishops and Gaolers." The city's "virginal design" has not changed since its builders first constructed the plans; it remains "intact as it was, echoing, beset with the constant fall of the rain, unviolated and dark as in the Holy Day curfew of the year twelve hundred" (p. 141). Hawkes describes the town as "a judgment passed upon the lava, long out of date ... the more intolerant and severe" (p. 141). Even the hangman is aware of this eerie atmosphere. Walking in the high tower, he experiences "that curious feeling in the fortress of half human, half mildew of history" (p. 144). The hangman's size and dress follow traditional patterns handed down for centuries. Laws dictate the manner in which a hanging occurs or the way a prisoner is paraded to the fortress. The entire world of Sasso Fetore is a pageant, a stylized play in which virgins are condemned to read *Laws of the Young Women Not Yet Released to Marriage,* and in which the people observe "the regimen set down for the citizens."

Such a ritualized life leads inevitably to stagnation, for the form soon becomes more valuable than the content for which the formal patterns are created. Significance gives way to style. The unwed virgins who are denied a truly meaningful rite, the marriage ceremony, act as Hawkes' primary symbol of this sterility. When the prisoner arrives, the daughters are bathed, bosoms are pressed to the windows, food is thrust upon the guards, and fathers plead with the hangman, but tradition cannot be broken. War slaughters the young men, execution destroys the prisoners, and the women are left with their dowries. *The Owl* would be unbearably bleak were it not for the bumbling efforts of the fathers. Apparently unaware that Sasso Fetore is being destroyed by its adherence to ancient laws, the fathers are much more concerned with the marriages for ritual's sake than for the infusion of new blood wedlock might provide. Hawkes suggests that "the end of existence" hovers close by. Yet note the comic reference to potentially dead crabgrass that is placed incongruously in the middle of this dire prediction:

> Hardly a woman or girl was left behind in the thin black streets
> of Sasso Fetore, vacated as they would be at the end of existence.

> But the field below was filled with the noise of feet that would
> kill the crabgrass, and I saw how few childbearers remained for
> all the pleasure they seemed to be taking and despite their de-
> mands for husbands.   (pp. 178–179)

The life cycle has been stylized out of productivity. Movements
are made and social gestures observed, but they all lack meaning.
Death, in the person of Il Gufo, is ritualized and worshipped so
that reproduction no longer counts. The people share a kind of
civic pride in their ability to withstand change: "They approached
the gate that was proud only of its immunity after a past of doges,
conservatories, learning and brotheldom—the Renaissance driven
from our garrets and streets" (p. 154). Hawkes creates two key sustained scenes to illustrate in detail: the hangman's synod with his
twelve Mongers and Pucento's dance with the trained dog. Described with great imagination and vigor, the synod serves as a red
herring for those readers inclined to religious interpretations. If
the scene has any ecclesiastical significance, it is a parody of the
Last Supper as Il Gufo and his twelve disciples sit at a judgment
dinner during which the "cuisine of justice" is served while the
Mongers and the hangman decide the prisoner's fate. In reality,
though, the prisoner's sentence is automatic, passed centuries ago.
Thus, the synod is no more than an opportunity to "perpetuate
the feast of the law body which preceded Sasso Fetore's original
compulsory execution." Custom dictates the meal of fish, down to
the last detail of how the dinner is served and the method by which
the fish is eaten: Il Gufo with fork, Mongers with fingers. Even
the clothes are rigidly prescribed with hardly a variation from the
shirt and headgear of a "primitive monastic order." The entire
celebration reads like a story out of *Grimm's Fairy Tales*, complete
with a hunchback waiter, an overseeing owl, and a roaring fire.
An extended quotation is necessary to suggest Hawkes' successful
creation of the fairy tale atmosphere:

> I rapped my knife on the table and passed it twice sharply in
> front of my face, blade toward the lips. . . . The hunchback went
> down the left side then the right, taking the plate from each as
> he was supposed—assuming the familiarity that might be ex-
> pected from the serfs with their rock plows or from the wine

presses—tapped each councilman on the shoulder so that the
citizen should be represented and their fraternal feelings, like
the tipping of a hat or the offering of swine for mercy, should be
expressed. But he did not touch the hangman. When he took my
plate, setting down the tall stack of the rest, he pulled a crust
from his pocket and rubbed it in the remnants of the fish oil.
Then ate the crust.   (pp. 165–166)

This incredible and highly imagined scene is what Hawkes means
by constructed vision or fictional landscape. We are hypnotized as
we read, drawn into this grotesque synod until it seems as if we
are hovering in the shadows by the fire, the unwelcome witnesses
of an ancient initiation rite. When Barabo suddenly rises to rip
open his shirt and expose his now stuffed belly—the traditional
sign that he wishes to address Il Gufo—we laugh, but our laughter
is part of a horrified response.

The irony is that the hangman is more than an executioner, the
taker of life. Because of his absolute rule, he also has the power
to grant life, to spare prisoners who would, in turn, contribute to
the town's regenerative process. But Il Gufo is a product of this
atmosphere, and, thus, he is a victim of his own code. Although
Sasso Fetore is slowly destroyed, a challenge to tradition never
enters the hangman's mind. With a sure comic touch, Hawkes
makes us laugh at Il Gufo's longing for the good old days "in the
time when there were men to hang and those to spare, with clem-
ency for neither" (p. 180). Because of the war, the hanging business is suffering through hard times.

The most grotesque scene which illustrates the power of ritual
is Pucento's participation in a gavotte with a trained dog. A symbol of the "mastery of training over the temptation and distraction
that plagued the low species," the dog has learned from the ancient combat between man and beast to dance slowly on its hind
legs. It is muzzled, and Pucento keeps a thin red leash taut between himself and the animal as they execute the dance pattern.
The last of its kind, this dog, like its breed, has been deprived,
whipped, and painfully trained by the monks. What makes this
scene so striking, coming as it does at the end of the novel, is
Hawkes' decision to parallel it to the plight of Sasso Fetore. The

monks destroyed the bitches of the breed and imposed a kind of virgin's manual on the male dogs by commanding them to be "pure unmercifully." Thus, as the daughters are denied sex and the feminine role, so these dogs are not "permitted the lather, the howl, the reckless male-letting of their species." Desire is relegated to ritual, for the remaining dog's urge to wail and reflex to kill are choked by tradition.

Hawkes skillfully connects the sexual perversion of the town with that of the gavotte, for he suggests a bestial attraction between Pucento and the dog. They are drawn to each other by the sheer force of the dance. But like Il Gufo's victimization by his own code, Pucento unwittingly finds himself a victim of the dance pattern. Rather than fulfill his role as lord and master of the dog, he realizes that the rigidity of this highly stylized dance rules them both. "The dog followed Pucento on the end of the tight rein, a heavy animal, the white coat become tarnished and cream with age. The women could not see how Pucento sweat, himself straining to duplicate the measure, the ruthless footstep of the past" (p. 182). Hawkes stresses the pain of this scene with a carefully understated word. As the dog leaps three times in the air on one leg, its position is simply described as "unnatural." That one word summarizes the entire life style of Sasso Fetore. This closely detailed horror is, however, balanced and "saved" by the humorous climax. For despite Barabo's efforts to protect Antonina, she sneaks off with Il Gufo while the crowd watches the dance. Barabo, the comic dupe, is tricked again. He can neither beg a husband for his daughter nor protect her virginity. Reaching out for Antonina at the conclusion of the gavotte, he clutches only his old wife's waist.

The Owl is a good example of what Leslie Fieldler, writing about *The Lime Twig*, calls the theme of love breeding terror in Hawkes' fiction, for the love relationships degenerate into a victim-victimizer entanglement.[6] Il Gufo's need to desecrate life and productivity in order to celebrate death and sterility matches Antonina's longing for love and fulfillment. Both partners in the love

6. Leslie Fiedler, "The Pleasures of John Hawkes," in John Hawkes' *The Lime Twig* (New York: New Directions, 1961), p. xi.

affair are compelled to complete the union, and both receive some satisfaction. But the results are terrifying, for in gaining fulfillment Antonina, the victim, wastes away, as if by magic, to an old woman doomed to live out her days thumbing through the manual for virgins. The offspring of a union with the hangman is a kind of death, all revealed when we discover that the fearfully mutilated owl has Antonina's purse which is supposed to be kept under her skirts until marriage:

> He was old, scabrous at the window, he regarded the night from his stone and branch and all the night was preoccupied with some stretching of tissue or memory deep within the feathers, while rectifying the vision of the world in his owlish eyes, watching it as he might something that dared not move.... He gripped Antonina's purse in his claw and now and then shook it, already it was ripped and musty as if it had been his forever. At times it fell to the window ledge and he kept near it.
> (p. 188)

Love breeds terror, but the ritual must be completed—gesture is all. Obviously pleased that Il Gufo has chosen his daughter, Barabo struggles to the mountain fortress with half of Antonina's dowry on his shoulders. He would have brought it all, he explains, but he could find no one to help him. But if love breeds terror in a Hawkes novel, then terror encourages comedy. Stumbling to the mountain top with his load of money, Barabo suddenly lowers one shoulder, sways, and drops the cask over the edge, showering the slope with coins. His only comment is "Ah, sfortunato," and he starts down the cliff to retrieve what he can. The comic parallel is drawn: Barabo's bumbling efforts to protect his daughter lead to the owl ripping Antonina's purse and to Barabo himself losing her dowry. Virginity is shattered, but the treasure of marriage gets away.

The courtship of the hangman and Antonina is as mechanical and empty as Pucento's gavotte. Both performances reek of listlessness. The form is perfect, but the perfection lacks meaning because in the world of Sasso Fetore form is all that counts. The final irony, the most terrifying truth to all this, is that Il Gufo,

Antonina, Pucento, and the dog *all* suffer as victims of ceremony. The music stops, the dance is completed until next time, and the ritual itself triumphs over the participants. Il Gufo is as much a victim of the hangman's legacy as Antonina is, and as Pucento and the dog are of the ancient dance. Only the prisoner dares to mock the city's slavery to form. Escaping, he kills the prefect's ganders and then arranges the bodies in a mysterious geometric pattern which has perfect dimensions but which remains inexplicable to the citizens: "The ganders had been felled carefully, symmetrical and clean. The long necks, straight, each perpendicular to the next, were crossed one over the other near the heads, the necks touching and torn, left in their severed lines and with their cold windpipes in this intimate, unnatural pattern" (p. 192). Note that Hawkes describes the dead ganders' positions as "unnatural," recalling his description of the dog's pose in the gavotte. The prisoner knows that extreme attention to detail warps instinct while it inhibits free flow—his design of ganders is as formally perfect as any other pattern in Sasso Fetore, and as meaningless.

Hawkes suggests mythic references to Icarus and Daedalus when he describes the prisoner's escape on feathered wings, but the references are more a false lead than a significant parallel. His real interest remains the mixture of comedy and horror that shocks us into an awareness of life's darker sides. The prisoner, for example, decides to escape by flying only because "none before him had thought of it." Hawkes does not comment on the impossibility of this feat. The torture following recapture is pure Hawkes terror. Suspended on hooks, the skin of his belly is later stripped off in one piece to make a drum. A free person who dares to challenge the system, the prisoner later hangs. The severity of the suffering is not lost on Il Gufo, yet he remains a comic character because of his rigidity. In an earlier reference to the torture, the hangman lists a series of inconveniences which he would rather endure than witness the prisoner's fate. But note how Hawkes uses Il Gufo's private fetishes, hardly causes of extreme pain, to reduce the hangman's words to a comic confession. The incongruous relationship between what the prisoner endures and what Il Gufo considers to be excessive discomfort excites laughter when we finally learn of the prisoner's sentence. "But I would sooner my boots pick up fresh dung by the hour, the rain splatter my bald skull, the ice stiffen my red cape, and the dwarf trees lash my shoulders at a run, than sit bent over, afraid to injure my windpipe, studying the silent drops of moisture on the aquiline nose of one being garroted in a cellar thick as a furnace" (pp. 156–157). Is Il Gufo squeamish? We never know, but the possibility contrasts humorously with his foreboding appearance.

The Owl remains one of the best of Hawkes' early fictions to read for the pleasures of language and form. The "saving grace" of language acts as a positive counterbalance to the weight of the purely negative atmosphere by the very fact that language artistically used is creative. Saving the novel from being a completely bleak reading experience, this kind of creativity rewards the reader with its innovative technique while he suffers the nightmarish fantasy. Imaginative uses of language and form balance pessimistic visions. For example Hawkes describes a storm as "green and sudden" to suggest the freshness, and the setting sun as "the windy collapse of the day." Many of these eye-catching images support the novel's dark atmosphere: " . . . and we proceeded through that time of dawn when the werewolf gives up his feasting and the assassin lifts his hands from the jugular vein of history" (p. 190). This particular sentence offers a striking example of Hawkes' control of language and image, for in addition to using references to assassins and werewolves which are appropriate to such a novel, the sentence suggests the irony of Sasso Fetore's predicament. Every twenty-four hours it may pass through "that time of dawn," but the city has long since given in to the past. It no longer has the means or desire to free itself from strangulation by history.

The Owl has a stronger sense of unity than *Charivari* or *The Goose on the Grave*, and thus it offers a better example of what Hawkes means by the totality of the constructed vision. Avoiding the picaresque form of *The Goose on the Grave* and the numerous secondary characters of *Charivari*, the events of *The Owl* revolve around a single dramatic action over a short period of time—the execution of the prisoner. Nothing is extraneous, and the reader feels a definite narrative progression. Always before the reader's eye, the figure of Il Gufo dominates the novel in such a way as to serve as a controlling focal point. Everything that happens is either initiated by or in reaction to the hangman. He maintains as tight a control on the novel's form as he does on the inhabitants of Sasso Fetore, never once relinquishing the spotlight to someone else. Even in the dance scene, Il Gufo usurps Pucento's primary position when we discover that he has used the spectacle of the gavotte to cover up his seduction of Antonina. What makes the novel so remarkable is Hawkes' successful rendition of history, for while reading we feel that we have been in Sasso Fetore for centuries. The atmosphere drips with the past, and we know that the prisoner's fate would have been exactly the same a thousand years ago.

But more than any other one technique, the narrative method gives *The Owl* its eerie quality. Recalling his use of Zizendorf in *The Cannibal*, Hawkes endows his first-person narrator with an unusual omniscience which allows him to move anywhere in time to supply information traditionally unavailable to the first-person narrator. The effect is startling, for the technique seems to give Il Gufo complete freedom from authorial control and thus adds to his aura as supreme master of this damned town. Il Gufo has no way of knowing, for example, the prisoner's thoughts and actions as he escapes and kills the ganders, but the hangman nevertheless reports them to us. Such a calculated violation of verisimilitude supports the novel's form by contributing to Il Gufo's position as the focus of all that occurs. Removed from the conventions of narration and from the limitations of time and cause and effect, he appears all the more diabolical. His hold on the people seems solidified because the narrative technique reenforces his position. But of course he remains a victim of Hawkes' authorial manipulation just as he is victimized by his own supreme situation. In each case his power is an illusion.

Although *The Owl* is completely pessimistic, the exaggeration of the horror and the comic responses of the characters keep it from degenerating into a meaningless experiment in terror. A beautifully written, sustained fiction, it remains the best of the three short novels not only because of its sharply focused form but also because of the success with which Hawkes creates the ghostly atmosphere and then draws us into it. Reading *The Owl* we suffer the feeling of being shut in a dark room—the only light-colored objects in the novel seem to be the ganders which have been grotesquely slaughtered. The novel abounds with blackness and shadows, all dominated by the bleak fortress high on the cliff. The feeling is that of a walled city caught in a plague—no one can escape and no one dares to approach. The population dies slowly, but comically, because it acts as if the crisis were not serious. Despite the dissolution all about them, the people remain more interested in maintaining their allegiance to the forms of the past than in combating the sterility which threatens to annihilate them. *The Goose on the Grave*, though of similar theme, lacks this dire bleakness because it is open-ended. Adeppi can go on to another protector, just as Henry and Emily of *Charivari* can choose to play another game. But the ending of *The Owl* is final. Tradition drowns this brilliantly created landscape, and when we finish reading we know that we have witnessed history's victory over the present.

3

Casualties of History:
The Cannibal

IN *The Goose on the Grave* and *The Owl*, Hawkes defines history primarily as tradition, in the sense of forms of action and states of mind which solidify to the extent that the past dominates the present. The historical process itself is barely touched upon, and no attempt is made to probe the interrelations between people and historical forces. Hawkes' interest remains the effects of tradition upon a populace too enfeebled by war to revitalize itself. Yet neither *The Goose on the Grave* nor *The Owl* can be classified as a war novel, for the vaguely defined wars of these two novels exist merely as background, as a means of indicating the chaotic settings.

In *The Cannibal* (1949), however, Hawkes has written a full-fledged war protest novel which reveals his horrified response to World War II in general and to Nazi Germany in particular. Highly experimental and extremely difficult to read, *The Cannibal* avoids the detailed picture of military life which structures most war protest fiction, say *Three Soldiers* or *The Naked and the Dead*. Hawkes gives us no battle scenes, no accounts of dull army routine, no descriptions of the insensitivity of officers. In truth the particulars of war are rarely mentioned. But by setting the novel in a hallucinated Germany wallowing in total collapse after World War II, Hawkes communicates his fear of war as the ultimate human nightmare.

What makes *The Cannibal* so much more important than the three novelettes is its investigation of history. Hawkes' premise that the events of 1939–1945 were simply the inevitable result of the assassination of Archduke Ferdinand in Sarajevo in 1914 is nothing new, but as a novelist he is not interested in a factual analysis of the century's two major catastrophes. In *The Cannibal* he views history as an ill defined process, a vague but overpowering force which sweeps up humanity and throws it into recurring nightmares. History in the guise of nationalism is the main character. Its cyclical nature is so insistent that it crushes man's efforts to resist, and Hawkes leaves little doubt that the end of World War II means no more than a moment of stasis before the explosion of the next global encounter.

In his introduction to the novel, Albert J. Guerard comments that the "characters are passive somnambulistic victims of the divine or diabolic process (history), yet to a degree are aware of their historic position. ... History is blind, inconsecutive, absurd." [1] This is a shrewd observation, for it suggests that history moves as blindly as the characters who stumble in its wake. The great difference is that history is an active force, able to generate worldwide conflict, while the people remain passive, unable to counter the historical forces. Yet, as Guerard notes, the people are vaguely aware of their place in history. Hawkes uses this awareness to produce some of his most stunning effects. As victims of history, his characters not only parallel historical figures but momentarily assume their identities. The fictional scene in which Ernst chases the carriage of Stella Snow and Cromwell is transformed for an instant to that historical moment in Sarajevo when Gavrilo Princip stalks the Archduke Ferdinand and his duchess, intent upon the assas-

---

1. Albert J. Guerard, "Introduction," in John Hawkes, *The Cannibal* (New York: New Directions, 1962), pp. xii–xiii.

sination which will trigger a new cycle of war. This scene and numerous similar ones suggest the scope of the novel's illogic and distortion. Commenting on Hawkes' fictional vision, Guerard mentions the fine line between fantasy and the creation of another universe "which the best surrealism attempts." Hawkes walks that line successfully in *The Cannibal*, fashioning a microcosm full of macabre humor and horror in which the decayed German town *Spitzen-on-the-Dein* serves as the world caught up in all of its desolation and despair. The characters find themselves trapped in a historical process which transcends them—they have no understanding of it. Once in a while they may be dimly aware of a role they play, as, for example, when Stella says to Cromwell, "If in this hour of crisis, we must ride side by side, I will become, as you wish, your Archduchess for the people, but where your eyes and theirs cannot look, I am arrogant." [2] But this limited awareness remains useless, for no individual understands the overall design. All he can do is play his prescribed role. History cannot be controlled; thus the irony of the American soldier Leevey "overseeing" one-third of occupied Germany or of the neo-Nazi Zizendorf "directing" a new revolution.

In addition to man's helplessness before the unfolding of events, Hawkes also conveys his fear of history's repetitive nature. Guerard notes that history in *The Cannibal* is "inconsecutive," a carefully chosen word to describe the cyclical or repetitive surges which would be predictable if we could see the total span of events. Hawkes insists that history itself is irrational, upsetting us with its constant returns to the past, terrifying us with its sudden departures from what might have been a logical forward progression. At the end of the novel, Germany is indeed renewed, about to rise from the ashes of the war. But ironically the old world is about to begin again, the Germany of 1870, 1914, and 1939 that caused the holocaust which did not end until 1945. Zizendorf's victory over Leevey signals the resurgence of militant nationalism. The insane

2. John Hawkes, *The Cannibal* (New York: New Directions, 1962), p. 55. All other page references will be noted in the text.

asylum reopens its doors, and Zizendorf watches with satisfaction "the long lines that were already filing back into the institution, revived already with the public spirit" (p. 195).

The choice of the reopened asylum as a symbol for the rebirth of German militarism is frighteningly accurate, and it permits Hawkes to end the novel with a thrust toward the future. Once the inmates' (the German people) "public spirit" gathers momentum, the furies of war will again be unleashed. The concluding note is gloomily pessimistic. In an interview Hawkes specifies the future as his primary concern in the novel: "The contemporary part of the novel is dated 1945, but that date is supposed to be taken as something to disregard. The time of that novel is simply in the future." He goes on to note that the juxtaposition of these post–World War II events with the historical period of 1914 is "intended to try to suggest that perhaps we don't move so much in cycles as repetitions or that we have always had these particular problems of violence, destruction, sadism and so on." [3] But his distinction between cyclical and repetitive history ultimately makes little difference. The terrifying truth communicated in *The Cannibal* is that history returns again and again to its catastrophic moments, and that man can do nothing to control it. Those, like Zizendorf, who think that they can direct their destinies find that they are no more than victims of history.

Upon first glance *The Cannibal* seems disjointed and chaotic, full of isolated scenes which attest Hawkes' ability to create terrifying events but which seem to be self-contained, having little relationship to each other. Reader reaction to this novel usually begins with evaluations of the success or failure with which Hawkes controls the horrifying images, grotesque characters, and juxtaposed historical moments. Peter Brooks, for example, admires Hawkes, especially *The Lime Twig* and *Second Skin*. But he argues that the world of *The Cannibal* "is known only in such momentary 'shots,' projected and distorted by an intense illumination, tending towards the status of surrealistic image rather than towards any over-

3. "John Hawkes on His Novels: An Interview with John Graham," *The Massachusetts Review*, 7 (Summer 1966), 450.

all narrative coherence." [4] This comment is a good description of Hawkes' use of surrealistic "shots," but the criticism of the novel's coherence seems more appropriate to the novelettes with their basically picaresque structure. Although an anlysis of *The Cannibal*'s structure will be made later in this chapter, it should be pointed out here that the novel reflects Hawkes' experimentation with narrative patterns and ordering devices, what he calls "recurring image and recurring action." By virtue of consistent juxtaposition of 1914 and 1945, plus several references to the Franco-Prussian War, he suggests a specific historical frame which is supported by interlocking patterns of imagery and by series of parallel events. In other words, the individual moments, often intensely illuminated and surrealistic, so consistently reflect each other that narrative coherence is sustained. *The Cannibal*'s structure is certainly unconventional and perhaps not as well controlled as that of *The Lime Twig* and *Second Skin*, but its unity is better defined than that of *Charivari* or *The Goose on the Grave*.

Both the recurrence of imagery and the verbal patterns suggest a psychic order at work beneath the physical disorder of the novel's surface world. Germany in 1945 is a smashed country, and Hawkes makes us feel the chaos with his dislocated time sequences and intense imagery. But the parallels between the two wars and the recurring narrative patterns reveal the historical process which, be it cyclical or repetitive, enforces unity upon what seem to be directionless incidents. David Littlejohn has suggested that the locale of *The Cannibal* warrants Hawkes' intense personal vision and hallucination because it is based upon a "genuine historical nightmare." The terrifying passages are "justified by the monumental horror of the chosen locale." [5] Apparently isolated scenes such as the rebellion in the asylum or Stella's son's cinema house do not comment directly upon the war, but they do express a horrified reaction to the historical cycle which caused it plus the fear that it may all happen again.

4. Peter Brooks, "John Hawkes," *Encounter*, 26 (June 1966), 70.
5. David Littlejohn, "The Anti-Realists," *Daedalus*, 92 (Spring 1963), 257.

The breakdown of order in the asylum turns into a bad dream which mirrors the greater nightmare of war outside its walls. Fearing "erratic outbursts" and "snarling attacks" by the patients, the nurses exhaust the supply of sedatives, leaving the men "half-subdued" and angry. The only set of keys to the windows is lost so that "the horrible cold swept in and out of the long guarded wings." Doctors disappear, charts are uninspected, shock tubs are left dry, and "the news from the outside was dangerous" (pp. 150, 151). All this may be the normal result of abnormal times, but Hawkes intensifies the scene when the laboratory rats and monkeys die. Thrown out on the main grounds, the bodies quickly freeze in lifelike poses. The patients insist that the monkeys move about at night, for each morning, despite the night's snow, "the monkeys appeared uncovered, exactly the same as the day they were tossed into the yard, wiry, misshapen, clutching in their hands and feet the dead rats" (p. 152). In the midst of this surrealistic vision, Hawkes interjects a detailed account of Stella Snow as she violently rips the heads from chickens. Her hands are still soaked with blood when the Census Taker summons her to help put down the rebellion in the asylum. When they reach the hospital, they find the inmates huddled together near the stack of monkeys: "One of the monkeys seemed to have grown, and frozen, was sitting upright on the bodies of the smaller beasts, tail coiled about his neck, dead eyes staring out through the gates, through the light of early morning as dim and calm as the moon. 'Dark is life, dark, dark is death,' he suddenly screamed as the women charged across the snow" (p. 155). Hawkes does not develop the scene any further—nothing more is made of it in the rest of the novel. Viewed in this limited way, it is indeed an isolated "shot," a momentary vision having little to do with the developing action. In this sense it is no more important than the description of Jutta's encounter with the Mother Superior or of Stella's maimed son with his "stump and steel canes," living with his wife in an abandoned moving picture house, each day showing "the same blurred picture to no audience." What matters, however, is not so much the brilliant individual constructions of nightmare but the accumulative force of these scenes. Taken alone, the asylum rebellion stands by itself as a vivid surrealistic vision of the absurdity of life and death when war dominates both. Fear and terror are much better communicated in this manner than in any realistic description of battle, perhaps because we are conditioned to accept lists of casualties and photos of devastation as so much evening news. But when these individual visions join together in the reading process, the nightmare nearly overwhelms us. This technique is not a mere piling up of horrors. It helps to unify the novel by intensifying the emotional effects, what Earl Rovit has called "the emotional accretions of image and mood which inform *The Cannibal.*" [6] Events and images such as the revolt and the monkeys often seem at first reading irrelevant to the controlling dramatic action, and they may foreshadow nothing in the sense of conventional fiction's use of prefiguration. But while self-defined and apparently isolated, they increase the novel's force by heightening the emotion. The revulsion we feel toward each of these scenes mounts as the number of scenes accumulates until our response to war is as fearful as Hawkes'.

One of the most prevalent unifying motifs is cannibalism in various guises. The Duke, of course, is the novel's literal cannibal as he stalks, dismembers, and cooks Jutta's son. But the children of *Spitzen-on-the-Dein* are in general spiritual victims of adult cannibalism. Hawkes' fictional world allows no room for the standard protection of children as the carriers of innocence and the hope of the future. Although the prospect is frightening, the future of this ravaged country and, Hawkes suggests, of the world will not be found in the children but in the historical repetitions which will lead us to another global war. The children themselves may not be wrapped up in the historical process, but they depend upon the adults who are pawns of history. Stella's maimed son with his rerun film is just one example. Jutta's daughter Selvaggia has widespread eyes which are "always afraid." Herr Snow, Stella's father-in-law, is proud of his boy Ernie because "his other son, a

6. Earl Rovit, "The Fiction of John Hawkes: An Introductory View," *Modern Fiction Studies*, 11 (Summer 1964), 153.

boy of nine, forever wore his head strapped in a brace, and the words that came from the immovable mouth came also from a remote frightening world" (p. 46). Even Stella's twin brothers are spiritually cannibalized, trained and dressed as potential soldiers in a country which glorifies its militarism. Completely isolated in the house, "the boys never saw their parents, since the old man and woman had been the age of deaf grandparents at the time of the brothers' remarkable conception. The brothers ate and lived alone" (p. 65). Since it encourages this attitude toward the young, *Spitzen-on-the-Dein* cannot help but sink deeper in its mire. Renewal through the reeducation of youth is impossible, a truth borne out by Zizendorf's hopes for the new nation which will rise from his revolution. Planning his National Headquarters, he decides to keep Jutta with him, but "of course, the children would have to go" (p. 183). The novel's final scene shows his attitude in action. Crawling back into Jutta's bed following a night of proclaiming the revolution, Zizendorf is interrupted by Selvaggia. She has witnessed Leevey's murder, and she is puzzled. Zizendorf, instead of Jutta, replies to her questions:

> I answered instead of Jutta, without looking up, and my voice was vague and harsh; "Nothing. Draw those blinds and go back to sleep . . ."   (p. 195)

This exchange ends the novel, and it suggests Hawkes' fear that the new historical pattern will do no more than repeat the one which began in 1914 and ended in 1945. Commenting on this exchange, he says that Zizendorf's order to Selvaggia reflects "the idea, more the notion, of the latency of destructive force, rather than the possibility of life-force." [7] In this sense history is the greatest cannibal of all, and the nation, because it is caught up in historical processes, is its own victim as it once again readies itself for the resurgence of nationalism and the resulting catastrophe of war. The inhabitants of Hawkes' Germany may vaguely remember history, but they are doomed to repeat it anyway. One reason is that the potential leaders are all as impotent as their sexual adven-

7. "John Hawkes on his Novels," p. 451.

tures suggest. Zizendorf and the Census Taker maintain a sterile
sexual union with Jutta which parallels Leevey's meaningless sex
with his diseased mistress. Performing with Jutta, Zizendorf enjoys
the old Census Taker watching them from the chair. His victim
Leevey lies beside "a laughing slut who was covered with invisible
red clap" (p. 144). The sex is mechanical, a means to forget the
present and to avoid confrontation with past guilts and fears. Both
conqueror and conquered participate in the history. D. P. Reutlinger notes that leadership and cannibalism are synonymous in
this novel.[8] Immediately following his slaughter of the boy, the
Duke is named by Zizendorf to be the Chancellor of the new nation. The impotent Census Taker will be the Secretary of State.
And Stella Snow, the "Archduchess" in 1914 and the "Queen
Mother" in 1945, remains in Zizendorf's eyes as "the very hangman, the eater, the greatest leader of us all" (p. 131). Stella is indeed both the eater and the greatest leader. Literally she joins the
Duke to taste his "soup," but as the symbol of German history, she
figuratively destroys the country. Once the nation "rises" again, it
will devour itself, filing back into the insane asylum revived with
a new public spirit. The entire community is implicated in the
madness of nationalism.

The victimizers of Miller, Leevey, and the children become victims of their own revolutionary efforts as they succumb to the
repetitions of history. Their positions of leadership are, of course,
ironic. History collapses to cycles of terror, but the present forgets
past sufferings. Stella's and Jutta's father is a good example of a
past leader who is now his own victim. A hero of the Franco-
Prussian War, he vaguely recalls the occasion, but in 1914 neither
he nor the crowd which gathers to hear his wisdom remembers the
lesson that war victimizes its participants. Paris may be encircled,
but only at overwhelming costs:

> *The boy didn't realize what he said, 1870, it would take many
> dead men to encircle Paris, and the responsibility, that's what
> he didn't understand or no one could speak in such a manner,*

8. D. P. Reutlinger, "*The Cannibal:* 'The Reality of Victim'," *Critique*, 6 (Fall 1963), 32.

> *pride on the heights.* "War," her father said, and there was a
> terrible fire in his eye through the ferns. "War," and he leaned
> slightly forward as if to strike her, but his arm only raised part
> way, shivered, and dropped back on the plate.   (p. 67)

Stella's mother has told her that her father grew up the same way
that five generations of German men did, "tall, handsome, dis-
creet and honorable soldiers, all looking exactly alike as brother
eagles" (p. 68). Each generation reflects the one just past so that
history moves in cycles. Thus, while the father has outlived the
rest of his generation, which died young, he remains dead in every
sense except literal because the historical repetitions have passed
by him. Whatever individuality he once may have had has long
been sacrificed to the glories of marital heritage. And in his sterility, he confuses the end of his war in 1870 with the beginning of
World War I. With a sure comic touch, Hawkes places this tottering old man on a balcony in front of a reverently silent crowd.
The father can no longer speak more than one word at a time, but
the people listen anyway. The scene ends with the crowd ridiculously misunderstanding the one word he manages to utter: "All
at once he spoke, and the single word fell upon them hushed and
excited. 'Victory.' For a moment they waited for more, watched,
listened and then broke out in screams of appreciation while the
old man was led back inside the house. They did not realize that
he thought the war, which had just begun, was over, and they took
up the word and sent it flying along the street from one startled
citizen to the next" (p. 70).

This crowd in 1914 ignores the immediate past of 1870 and the
dead at the seige of Paris to celebrate the beginning of World
War I as if it were a holiday. But by the end of World War II,
when the historical cycle momentarily plays itself out, the populace no longer gathers to await the victory cry from an aged hero.
They are now too sterile, too cannibalized by their own nationalism—their humanity is lost. They stumble through each day in a
mechanical routine, and their emptiness is suggested by a comparison between their dances in 1945 and those of 1914. In 1914
Herr Snow's *Sportswelt Brauhaus* is "austere and licensed, patron-

ized and rushed upon." The room is brightly lit, the music is joyfully loud, and the crowds marvel at Stella's songs. Because the war has yet to start, the young officers are undecorated, but they are straight and cordial in the new gray tunics. By 1945, however, the bright beerhall has given way to an unkempt and artificial clapboard storehouse. No orchestra is heard, only a scratching needle on a record while women silently dance with women, men with men. There is nothing to drink, and the crowd is made up largely of refugees: "all were spiritless from the very strangeness of the country and so they crowded themselves, unwanted, into this end of town. All of them slept in the back rooms on hay that should have been fed to the herds" (p. 32).

Given such widespread sterility, Zizendorf easily seizes the role as leader, a "liberator" who will guide them to the next catastrophe. If the aged general only dimly remembers that a measure of spiritual sustenance can be found in victory, Zizendorf has no notion of spiritual life at all. For him "the land is important, not the *Geist*." This is one of the most important lines in the novel, for it calls attention to the narrow nationalism which measures standard of living in square miles rather than in the quality of life. Although he does not realize it, Zizendorf's celebration of land over spirit completes the cycle of cannibalism which is first suggested to Ernst in 1914 during his race down the avenue of heroes: "When he passed the line of statues, each Hero gave him a word to harden his heart: *love, Stella, Ernst, lust, tonight, leader, land*" (pp. 54–55). Hawkes picks up this series of words and uses it for chapter titles as he describes Zizendorf's rising fanaticism. This degenerative cycle from love, be it between persons or for a country, to the blind patriotism which values land over spirit suggests the collapse of history. History turns back in on itself, moving in repetitions, rather than with a forward thrust which would permit a measure of hope that past disasters can be cut free. It is in the chapter entitled "Land" that Zizendorf, fresh from his successful assassination of Leevey, distributes his ironic declaration of independence, "Indictment of the Allied Antagonists, and Proclamation of the German Liberation." Only the land has value. Zizendorf's proclamation is a rallying cry for chauvinism: "The rise of the German people and their reconstruction is no longer question-able—the land, the Teutonic land, gives birth to the strongest of races, the Teutonic race" (p. 176).

Hawkes investigates the historical process in other hallucinated scenes, many as comic as Zizendorf's proclamation. But by far the most startling historical parallel remains the scene in which Stella and Cromwell ride down the avenue of heroes while a comically frustrated Ernst pursues them. These three characters literally act out the assassination at Sarajevo before the actual historical moment occurs, suggesting that the needs of the historical cycle dominate the individual and implicate him whether he is aware of the process or not. In this frightening scene historical parallelism gives way to identification when Hawkes' fictional characters usurp a famous historical moment. It begins with Herr Snow urging Ernst to be more aggressive in his courtship of Stella. Ernst is drunk, and he thinks of other drunks who have floundered in the alley behind the beer parlor, "sprawled like a murdered Archduke, his face in the bile" (p. 53). This forward view into the immediate future snatches his identity away from the beerhall and places it in Sarajevo. Running on the avenue of heroes in pursuit of Stella and Cromwell, Ernst tries to "run his own smallness into something large," and his zig-zag dashing becomes a race "to coincide with Princip in Sarajevo" (p. 54). But in a totally unexpected move, as if we are not startled enough by the scene, Hawkes introduces a comic note. Ernst has drunk too much beer, and he needs to urinate. He knows that any hesitation may cause him to lose Stella and Cromwell, but his belt is about to burst. In desperation he rushes to the bushes, only to fear that his mother will see him. So he pushes in behind the foliage where the branches scratch his fumbling hands, all the while frantic to pursue the carriage. Relieving himself, he thinks, "already the guns were being oiled. And the Belgians, not he, would use that Merchant as a target" (p. 55).

Stella continues her ride while Cromwell predicts that war will break out the following day. What makes the ride so effective for Hawkes' purpose is Cromwell's speech which predicts that this particular cycle of history will not end for fifty years and that the whole "incident" should be viewed as "the loyalty of civilization." In other words German nationalism will cause one war after another:

> It is pleasant, in moments such as these, knowing with certainty an approaching catastrophe, to view the whole incident that will probably extend fifty years, not as the death of politics or the fall of kings and wives, but as the loyalty of civilization, to realize that Krupp, perhaps a barbarian, is more the peg where history hangs than a father who once spoke of honor.   (p. 55)

With this speech Cromwell literally becomes the Archduke Ferdinand, and Stella agrees, if he wishes, to become "your Archduchess for the people." Only now, with the historical identities complete, does Ernst-Princip catch up with the carriage. Cromwell-Ferdinand actually waits "to see the short muzzle of the pistol, to feel his ears enveloped in concussion." By now Stella-Archduchess knows that she is near "her greatest love." Hawkes does not define her love, but the force of the scene points to war as her lover. And as the three characters converge to act out a historical moment, Hawkes transforms fiction to history:

> Francis Ferdinand lay on the seat of the carriage, his light shirt filled with blood, his epaulettes askew and on the floor lay the body of his departed wife, while the assassin, Gavrilo Princip, ran mad through the encircling streets. Obviously the advent of the great war would not throw them all together, make them friends, or even make them enemies; Ernie was ready, even in the throes of love, for a goal of religious fanaticism; Cromwell simply longed, desperately, to fit into the conflict somewhere; and Stella knew only that she was climbing high and would someday lose him.   (p. 56)

Hawkes reorders history in the nightmare of *The Cannibal* so that fictional characters not only assume historical identities, they also foresee historical tragedy. A flaming plane which crashes, comically enough, in "typically English" fashion, kills Stella's mother, and with a look to the future, Stella murmurs, "Gavrilo . . . what have you done?" (p. 79).

The most complex character in the novel, Stella spans the whole cycle. She touches the 1870 war through her father, and she is directly involved in 1914 and 1945. In many ways she represents Germany, the entire sweep of the Teutonic heritage, a kind of earth mother of the tribe. Although Hawkes has not written an allegory, he does suggest that the population of *Spitzen-on-the-Dein* in 1945 reflects the dismal decline of the once vital German race: "Of Nordic stock, they were silent, the tribal cry long dead from their rolling tongues" (p. 14). Note the connection which Hawkes insists upon between 1945 and the distant past. It is as if war were in their blood, an inevitable result of their particular racial consciousness. By 1945 war has exhausted them, and the traditional battle cries fall silent. Yet through the entire cyclical movement, Stella remains the personification of this German Spirit. In 1914, before she designates herself the Archduchess, she is described as a direct result of her barbarous ancestors. Her life span stretches back to the very beginnings of Teutonic war and violence, and this history runs in her blood. Hawkes suggests that this heritage is her life sustenance: "Her ancestors had run beserk, cloaked themselves in animal skins, carved valorous battles on their shields, and several old men, related thinly in blood from a distant past, had jumped from a rock in Norway to their death in the sea. Stella, with such a history running thickly in her veins, caught her breath and flung herself at the feet of her horned and helmeted kinsmen, while the Bavarians schnitzled back and forth in a drunken trio" (p. 43). On the symbolic level, Stella has lived forever, sweeping "through ironclad centuries, a respected crone" (p. 13). The "crossed barbaric swords" which figuratively hang over her head indicate her eminent position in Germany, and we understand why she is addressed as "Queen Mother" in 1945. Significantly, Zizendorf's plans call for the elimination of the old as well as children when the new nation proclaims its independence. Thus, at first he thinks Madam Snow too old to understand—in his opinion she should "wither away and die." But after meeting her, he quickly admits his mistake. Age has nothing to do with her power, for as Germany itself, she will never wither. She is, paradoxically, both cannibal and leader, a historical force who devours them while she tries to inspire them to glory. Zizendorf's description of her is apt: "Here I was wrong, since she was the very hangman, the eater, the greatest leader of us all" (p. 131).

Stella's sister Jutta, on the other hand, is completely cut off from the German heritage. She remains outside of the historical cycle, surviving peace and war because of her spiritual stasis. She exists but does not live. With her entire being limited by her personal narrowness, as opposed to Stella who spans the centuries, Jutta fails to understand the German life: "She had never been quite able to allow a love for her country to intrude within her four walls, had never been loyal, and though she gave herself like segments of a fruit, she never envisioned the loyalty due her State" (p. 25). Totally apart from the historical process, she is the only character free from nightmare. Guilts, fears, and the pangs of racial identity do not affect her, but she is no better off because of her isolation. Following her illness in the convent in 1914, we rarely see her out of the bed to which she welcomes Zizendorf. Emotionless and detached, she exists only in the act of lovemaking. While Stella is a paradoxical earth mother who devours all that she produces, Jutta is a sterile fertility principle. Her son is literally cannibalized, and her daughter Selvaggia is warped by the chaos around her. Jutta's passivity stems from her discovery about life following the illness. Opening her eyes, "she was glad to know, being allowed to wake once more, that life was not miraculous but clear, not right but undeniable" (pp. 120–121). The point is that life wastes away moment by moment, a process which is more inevitable than miraculous. Jutta lacks Stella's connection with the span of history, and she thus settles for the progression of moments. Free from racial memories, she does not suffer the bewilderment of those who are caught up in history and who lack clear insight. Jutta's clarity, of course, exists at the expense of a full life within her heritage, but Hawkes suggests that neither position is enviable. Her knowledge parallels that of Zizendorf, who also decides that life is not miraculous. Garnering his insight from the eternal old horse, Zizendorf decides that "life is not the remarkable, the precious, or the necessary thing we think it is. . . . death is as unimportant as life" (pp. 130, 131). But the crucial difference between them is that Zizendorf regards life as secondary to the state. What counts for him is the struggle, "the piling of bricks" so that the nation might be restored to its former glory. In his feverish compulsion to revitalize Germany, he ignores the lessons of history and succumbs to fanaticism. Jutta's reaction is the opposite. She assumes a silent, cold life in 1914 and does not change for thirty years. Although free from the historical nightmare, she is no better off in 1945 than she was thirty years earlier: "Thirty years is not enough time to measure the complete crystallization of a nation, though partially lost; to measure the greatest advance of communal men, though partially destroyed, and Jutta, far removed from the rise, fall, and eventual rise, was far from being within the thirty years, far from being successful or adored" (p. 25).

Jutta's relationship with Zizendorf is heightened by the presence of the old Census Taker, witness to their sexual performances. The chaotic situation of post-war *Spitzen-on-the-Dein* is nicely rendered by this drunk and uncaring man who never notes the additions to and deletions from the official population. At Stintz's death, for example, the Census Taker murmers that he "won't bother to take him off the roster." His most glaring oversight, however, is his refusal to note the rise in population which the influx of asylum inmates makes. The novel begins with the patients being set free to join the town, but though the institution is now empty, the population does not grow. The headcount which would normally suggest order is neglected—everything is formless as if by official sanction. Ironically described as "ordered," the asylum loses its veneer of calm when the riot shatters the regular routine which is prescribed for the disordered minds of the patients. Only at the end are order and form restored when, following Zizendorf's coup and the resultant rise of nationalism, the inmates file back into the institution. In this chilling scene, Hawkes suggests that the reopening of the asylum parallels the revival of militarism, and that calculated insanity in the form of war is about to become the dominant life form. To the Census Taker, of course, these fluctuations in the population mean nothing—his official position is as sterile as he is. In one of the few statements Zizendorf makes with real insight, he notes that the Census Taker is as "muddled and lopsided as the badge of his marine cap," and that he has stature "only through responsibilities that had gone" (p. 23). But despite this observation of the Census Taker's ridiculousness and of his comic standing in the community, Zizendorf fails to see the irony when he describes him as "my relic-brother, whose actions and despairs, whose humorous awkward positions and dry attempts were similar to mine." He enjoys "the Census Taker watching us from the chair" (p. 23). The irony of these statements escapes Zizendorf, who does not realize that, by naming the Census Taker as his relic-brother, he exposes his own grotesqueness.

The point is, of course, that Zizendorf is as sterile as the town official he makes fun of. He can act, and he can perform sexually with Jutta, but his results are as impotent as the Census Taker's bumbling. Although he sees himself and his cohorts as "primal, unordered, unposted sentries, lounging against the earth without password, rifles or relief," his role as the archetypal guard of freedom is worthless because he lacks memory of the past (p. 129). In naming himself a new fuhrer who is plotting for the common good, he forgets the effect which the last fuhrer had. He is a casualty of history because he has no idea of how the present situation developed, and he thus suffers the delusion that he controls the Teutonic destiny: "In every town there are a few who, though they don't remember how it came about, or how they returned, or when they went away, or what the enemy expects, gather together in the night to rise again, despite the obstacle of their own people or the swarming invader" (p. 126). Zizendorf's celebration of land over *Geist* is about to destroy the country itself, the very thing he wants to preserve. Yet for all the horrors which he represents, Zizendorf remains a comic character. Hawkes leaves little doubt that we are to laugh at his "Indictment of the Allied Antagonist, and Proclamation of the German Liberation" when he composes it in an inflated style full of clichés and misconceptions. Zizendorf truly believes that the assassination of one American soldier, Leevey, will free Germany from the oppressor, and he closes his proclamation with a rhetorical flourish: "From the ruins of Athens rise the spires of Berlin." This is an obvious non sequitur, humorous enough in its conclusion. But Hawkes completely undercuts Zizendorf's victory when, following the proclamation, he has the leader admit, "actually, I had never seen Berlin" (p. 177). Professor Guerard correctly notes the rich humorous irony which Hawkes gains from the interplay between the formal prose of the implied author and the colloquialisms of Zizendorf, the vulgar narrator.[9] The effect makes Zizendorf all the more comic, for his attempts at elevated prose, as in his proclamation, fall far short of Hawkes' mastery of language.

Zizendorf is also responsible for the short prefatory note in which he brags about the town's rise "under my guidance." Hawkes leaves the matter ambiguous, but Zizendorf's statement that he wrote this novel while on a forced leave from the town suggests that he was in the asylum. If this is so, then the novel's controlling consciousness is insane. Hawkes makes the narrative method even more outrageously funny because he gives the first-person narrator omniscience. Although Zizendorf's actions occur in 1945, he also reports the events of 1914 despite the fact that he was not present. To suggest these warped circumstances, Hawkes consciously uses anachronisms, as, for example, when Zizendorf tells us that the patrons of Herr Snow's beerhall sing the *Horst-Wessel Lied* in 1914 though the song was not composed until years later. This omniscience in a supposedly limited point of view makes for much of the humor, especially when Zizendorf dutifully reports the thoughts of the other characters as if he were playing all of the roles. When, for instance, he knocks on Stintz's door, ready to kill him, he switches to Stintz's consciousness to tell us in pious tones, "Oh, he knew it was I all right." Or when he disposes

9. Albert J. Guerard, "The Prose Style of John Hawkes," *Critique*, 6 (Fall 1963), 27.

of Stintz's body, he informs us that Jutta "wished that I would hurry home." We laugh because Hawkes has successfully established the conflict between Zizendorf's obvious limitations and his delusions of total control which his omniscience ironically suggests.

Unlike Zizendorf, Stintz and the Mayor remain troubled by their involvement in the historical cycle. A tuba player and ex-school teacher, Stintz plays the role of the artist figure who tries to shake off the nightmare. His concern for artistic and intellectual matters contrasts sharply with Zizendorf's dismissal of *Geist*. In his struggle to awaken from the nightmare, he longs for the reestablishment of justice as a means to free the present from the cycle in which it is trapped. Stintz gets his chance when he witnesses Zizendorf's murder of Leevey, and he tells the leader, "There's retribution for everyone in this country now, justice, and it doesn't roll along a road where it can be trapped. Someone always *knows*, you really can't get away with anything . . ." (p. 173). But *Spitzen-on-the-Dein* has no room for justice. This confession that he has seen the murder costs him his life, for Zizendorf believes that "the honest man is the traitor to the State. . . . His honesty is a hopeless misgiving" (p. 171). He murders Stintz with the tuba in a highly comic scene which uses humor to call attention to Zizendorf's totalitarian mind: "I swung the tuba short. I should have preferred to have some distance and be able to swing it like a golf club." Hawkes records the murder without comment—he never makes anything of it. Given the completeness of the historical nightmare, Stintz's gesture may be more absurd than heroic, for he tries to halt the repetition of history. We may lament his death as another sign of horror, but Hawkes makes it clear that one man's concern for justice and honesty is meaningless when caught up in the sweep of history.

The Mayor, on the other hand, is tortured by his participation in the elevation of state over spirit because he is obsessed with his part in the execution of Pastor Miller, a fellow townsman. Suffering from terrible guilt pangs which threaten his sanity, he tries to excuse himself by insisting that the American colonel's eagle insignia had hypnotized him into the betrayal of Miller. His guilt takes the form of nightmare, and he now fears his dreams as much as his waking hours when he is fully conscious of what he has done:

> Dream after dream the voices and horses were the same, though they wore many figures, the Priest mixed up with the Officer, his own dead wife firing the rifle, a peculiar child pronouncing verdict as the Judge, the onlooking crowd all dressed as the condemned man. But the voices were distinct, and waking he would forget that they had calmly passed sentence, enemies and friends—guilty in the eyes of his own State.   (p. 131)

Zizendorf murders the Mayor, too, burning him in his own house as part of the revolution. As he dies the Mayor thinks, in his madness, that he is playing host to Miller at lunch, an act of atonement. But release from guilt is impossible, for he has willingly participated in the nightmare. Zizendorf denies him relief: "The Mayor did not cry out, but died, I was very glad, without recompense or absolution" (p. 190).

Hawkes' conscious use of distortion and dislocation to show his characters caught in the chaos of history results in a novel which Guerard correctly describes as "radically out of focus." [10] *The Cannibal* was the first published of his full-length novels, and it is the most *avant-garde*, a deliberate effort to break with conventional fiction. The terrors of the fictional landscape most often shock unwary readers who find their standard reactions inadequate in the face of Hawkes' militantly grotesque visions. But while the sheer visual power is indeed masterful, the novel's success depends upon the ways by which Hawkes controls the distorted images and dislocated scenes. Very often *The Cannibal*'s structure poses as many problems as its visual sense for the reader who is used to a conventionally developed fictional pattern with its beginning, middle, and end. Before examining the recurring structural patterns in *The Cannibal*, we should recall Hawkes' comment upon his method:

> My novels are not highly plotted, but certainly they're elaborately structured. I began to write fiction on the assumption

10. Guerard, "Introduction," p. xi.

that the true enemies of the novel were plot, character, setting, and theme, and having once abandoned these familiar ways of thinking about fiction, totality of vision or structure was really all that remained. And structure—verbal and psychological coherence—is still my largest concern as a writer. Related or corresponding event, recurring image and recurring action, these constitute the essential substance or meaningful density of my writing.[11]

The Cannibal is particularly suited to Hawkes' definition of structure because its investigation of history's repetitions or cycles reflects structural designs which are made up of recurring images and verbal patterns. Theme and form complement each other while chronological time and logical progression are avoided. Instead Hawkes sets up these recurring patterns, visual and verbal, which are referred to throughout the novel so that narrative coherence is maintained.

The cycle of history which begins in 1914 and ends in 1945 before renewing itself with the revolution is represented throughout by *das Grab*, a fitting metaphor for the desolation of *Spitzen-on-the-Dein*. Musing on the destruction wrought by World War II, Stella feels "the vastness of community that was like burial, spreading over all borders and from family to family" (p. 17). At times the town itself is called *das Grab*, and death flows through it in a "dangerous stream." The novel opens with a description of the end of one cycle—the town is in a moment of stasis before the historical process uses Zizendorf to gain new momentum. But Stella, as the symbol of Germany, is also present at the beginning of the cycle in 1914, and the image of *das Grab* is just as meaningful then. Returning from her honeymoon following the outbreak of World War I, she and Ernst reenter the city, "into *das Grab*," while surrounded by hordes of people and dogs. At Ernst's death, these dogs howl "around the station at the port of entry to the grave" (p. 122). The point is that by 1914 the German spirit, represented by Stella's ancient father, is so feeble that it needs a nationwide effort to renew itself. Yet renewal based solely on militant

11. "John Hawkes: An Interview," *Wisconsin Studies in Contemporary Literature*, 6 (Summer 1965), 149.

nationalism quickens the country's journey to the grave. Thus, when Stella, Cromwell, and Ernst pass down *die Heldenstrasse*, acknowledging the shrines to past military glory, Mephistopheles selects a date for the new explosion of war which will not end until the entire nation degenerates to *das Grab* in 1945 (p. 47).

Germany's chance for sanity in 1914 seems to lie in Ernst, who at least has some feeling for the German spirit as opposed to the fanaticism which celebrates only land. Like Stella, he too has links with the distant past, for when he walks, he seems to "tread upon the whole world of Germany . . . back near the aurora of tabled clans, disciplined faces" (p. 44). But despite his duelling, Ernst is no soldier. Rather he is an unstable esthete, indulging his urge to collect grotesque crucifixes which soon turns into an obsession. By marrying Ernst to Stella, the Teutonic earth mother, Hawkes suggests the sacrifice of the spirit to the cannibalism of nationalism. Succumbing to Stella, Ernst loses "the thread . . . that keeps a man anchored to his nation, instrumental in its politics, radiant in its victory, and dead in its defeat" (p. 93).

In 1914 Stella welcomes Ernst with the invitation, "Come in, you poor creature." We hear it again in 1945 when she whispers the same words to the insane Balamir, thus establishing a link between the two eras. Hawkes treats the connection ironically, for the rich heritage which Ernst represents has collapsed to the mutterings of Balamir's insanity. Like Ernst, Balamir is a carrier of the German spirit, but as the spirit deteriorates, so does its representative. Balamir reflects Nazism and the new nation which Zizendorf hopes to lead, and the descriptions of him leave no doubt that his rise to prominence brings disease and death:

> All Germany revolved around Balamir. His feet were in the boots of an Emperor's son, he felt the silver sword of time and tide and strength against his hip. Growing weak and cold, he was the result of commands coming down out of the years. . . . How he sought to be that image, how the Kaiser's ghost needed him, how he would be Honor in the land he had become. But how well he knew it was a reign of terror. . . . He was the true and unknown Prince of Spitzen-on-the-Dein, followed by the castrated and the disillusioned, guided by an unknown hand

around the signs of the skull and cross-bones planted above the mines.   (p. 18)

In this description Hawkes indirectly outlines the threat he fears when historical recurrences merge with a nation like Germany. Individualism is lost as the country revolves around the leader. The leader's strength may be sapped by long centuries of repetition without the necessary periods of renewal, but the people bow down anyway. Their actions become mechanical, automatic reflexes conditioned by a heritage of obedience, so that "castrated and disillusioned," they nevertheless follow along from one crisis to another.

Balamir's warped spiritual force survives, unlike that of Ernst, because it joins Stella's nationalism and Zizendorf's love of land, and because the general populace is too conditioned not to react against what they have been trained to believe is their historical destiny. In the chaos following World War II, the union of Nazism and land is momentarily shattered, and the inmates, including Balamir, are set free to wander. Their presence in *Spitzen-on-the-Dein* goes unnoticed—the population "does not grow"—but the significance is obvious. For by the time of Zizendorf's coup, the crack in the unity of insane spirit and devotion to the state has been healed. The insane asylum, Germany, reopens its doors to the long lines of the "castrated and disillusioned," and the advent of another historical cycle—World War III—is set in motion. The terrifying extended metaphor suggests that insanity is Germany's normal state.

Hawkes has set up these repetitions of historical moments so that they are reflected in the recurring structural patterns. Balamir recalls Ernst, Zizendorf's proclamation looks back to the old general's cry of "victory," and so on. But the novel's design is best seen in the recurring references to animals, for it uses animal imagery, especially dogs and horses, as metaphors for the overall atmosphere of cyclical degradation and decay. The asylum, for example, is an "empty scorpion" in which "strange unpursued animals make lairs in the corners." The university has "dust filled caves crawling with larvae"; the market sells blue meat which flies hang over; and the town itself is "as shriveled in structure and as decomposed as an ox tongue black with ants." Cromwell is called a "wolfhound"; the Merchant dies with a cocoon in his mouth; and Ernst's mutilated hand is a talon and claw. The mysterious mobile but frozen monkeys at the asylum riot point to the widespread irrationality. Hawkes fills the novel with these metaphorical references to animals and insects to suggest the especially repulsive, terrifying atmosphere of his fictional locale. Many are mentioned only once. But with dogs and horses he extends the imagery into a pattern which provides a running commentary on the novel's development. He never specifies the meanings precisely, preferring to allow the ambiguity to heighten the nightmarish atmosphere, but the highly developed, conscious use of dogs and horses is an especially rich illustration of his definition of structure.

Professor Guerard notes that the dogs recall childhood fears or vague "symbols of defeat and death." [12] They also suggest undefined violence, the bestial side of a people stripped of humanity by their participation in a historical process which devours their spirit and implicates the rest of the world. Left vague and undefined, the dogs' shadowy presence underscores the unnamed darkness which threatens us. It is as if the shadow in the child's bedroom suddenly becomes a snarling hound with lashing fangs. The dogs' restlessness is first apparent when Stella and Ernst return from their honeymoon, and they do not stop their prowling until Zizendorf murders Leevey. In this sense the dogs suggest the restlessness of the German people. Turned bestial by nationalism and frustrated by successive defeats in two global wars, they cease to howl in protest only when Zizendorf promises to unleash them again to pursue the blood of war.

Hawkes often personifies the dogs, thus making an already terrifying vision all the more grotesque. In a scene particularly full of unspecified fear and nightmarish imagery, the dogs follow the train carrying Ernst and Stella. Yet while the description conveys terror, note how Hawkes maintains the comic tone by exaggerat-

12. Guerard, "Introduction," p. xiv.

ing the grotesqueness. The dogs all but promise not to soil the rug or chew the magazines if only the conductor will give them a ride:

> Those were certainly dogs that howled. His face pressed against the glass, Ernst heard the cantering of their feet, the yelps and panting that came between the howls. For unlike the monumental dogs found in the land of the tumbleweed, glorified for their private melancholy and lazy high song, always seen resting on their haunches, resting and baying, these dogs ran with the train, nipped at the tie rods, snapped at the lantern from the caboose, and carrying on conversation with the running wheels, begged to be let into the common parlor. They would lap a platter of milk or a bone that appeared dry and scraped to the human eye without soiling the well-worn corridors of the rug, and under the green light they would not chew the periodicals or claw the conductor's heels. As paying passengers, they would eat and doze and leap finally back from the unguarded open platforms between cars into the night and the pack.   (pp.95–96)

This especially fearful vision remains typical of the dog imagery— it is as if Hawkes has caught a nightmare on paper, complete with irrational sequences such as the comparison to the "monumental" dogs in the land of the tumbleweed. The dogs haunt Ernst until he dies, howling at his death. Gerta and Cromwell are pointedly associated with dogs, but Balamir literally longs to become "a gangling black dog racing at the herd over green slopes" (p. 11). Following Leevey's murder, Balamir thinks that his wish has been granted, and he wonders "would he whine if a thief were at the window" (p. 180). Again Hawkes mixes comedy and terror. But as clues to man's darker side, to his unconscious longing for power and violence, the dogs' bestiality is best suggested when they take precedence over men. Not only do they assume human characteristics or become "paying passengers," they also force the ambulance trains to stop. This is a particularly unnerving idea, for it points to man's degradation beyond human sympathy. Hawkes places the dogs at nearly every disaster so that they howl when the Duke finally runs down Jutta's boy or paw the leaves while Zizendorf waits for Leevey to ride into the ambush. Significantly, their restless prowling ends only when the people line up to enter a new period of insanity. We feel that these dogs reflect death, but Hawkes never supplies a reason for either the dogs or our feelings about them. They are not conceived to be discussed rationally though they do mean evil to us.

The meaning of the dogs remains purposely vague, calculated to elicit a response of undefined fear. With the horse, the most sustained recurring animal image, Hawkes is more definite. As a symbol of the state and of the historical process itself, the horse image spans the cyclical action from 1914 to 1945, and the horse's rise and fall signals the corresponding fortunes of Germany. Before the outbreak of World War I, for example, Stella loves the white prancing horses and the young men "dressed in black who could ride a horse up to the point of death on a winter's day and leave him to freeze" (p. 12). At this point in the novel the horse is white because the state has yet to be swept up in war, but Stella's admiration of the young men clearly suggests the nation's fate. By the assassination at Sarajevo, the prancing horse is "stumbling and nodding," and, significantly, it turns black when war is declared. Stella's role as carrier of the Teutonic heritage naturally urges her to try to keep the old horse alive, to offer sugar to its now "flabby lips" and "dumb groping nose," but the horse is too old. Carefully establishing this recurring pattern, Hawkes makes sure that we connect the various references to the horse into a structural design: "The black horse thrived better in the lower world. He was the same horse the students rode, shivering with the cold, tied alone to suffer the night" (p. 86). This tottering horse indicates Germany's position as the war drags on. Hawkes does not need to describe the fall to defeat—a child's cry that "the old horse is dead" is descriptive enough (p. 94).

The rise and fall of German militarism causes these symbolic changes in the horse. When Herr Snow longs in the aftermath of the war for a new horse, we could hope that the rest of the nation joins his desire for a new era. But there is no new life for Germany because the nation learns nothing from its history. Succeeding generations are swept into the cyclical motion, and the subsequent cannibalism of the children assures us that there can be no new horse. The possibility of a spiritual renaissance gives way before the recurring worship of the old horse and all it represents. The Mayor, for example, has lost his memory of history because of his guilt. He is "too blind to tend the chronicles of history," and he goes "hungry like the rest with memory obliterated from his doorstep." Unsure of himself in 1945, he has forgotten the "powerful horses of bony Belgian stock, dull-eyed monsters of old force." His fear of the one grey horse which remains in *Spitzen-on-the-Dein* is not matched by the children who ride the old grey while wearing "pasteboard Teutonic helmets" (pp. 8–9).

By 1945 the worship of the symbolic horse from 1914 materializes in a statue which stands at the center of the town. Zizendorf is fully aware of its importance, for he admits that the "eternal old horse . . . bereaved and unquiet in the night," reveals to him the secret that life and death are unimportant compared to the struggle to build the nation (p. 130). Hawkes' use of this recurring image tells us that in 1945, with Zizendorf's veneration of the horse statue, the end of one cycle and the beginning of another coincide. When Zizendorf plans the resistance, we learn that the statue is headless, a fitting description, for with it Hawkes suggests that the state is both directionless and leaderless. If Zizendorf has any knowledge that the horse was once white, he does not reveal it. All that interests him is the physical unity of the statue itself, the state or the land minus renewed purpose and spirit. Thus, it is significant that following the successful murder of Leevey, his first plan is to restore the statue. Note the ironic juxtaposition of love and militarism: "Of course I'd put the old horse statue back on its feet. Young couples would make love beneath it on summer nights. It might be better to mount it on blocks of stone, so that visitors drawing near the city could say, 'Look, there's the statue of Germany, given by the new Leader to his country' " (p. 183). All that can save the state from the resurgence of the past is youthful love, but Zizendorf effectively cancels this potentially positive force by placing the lovers beneath the statue. Youth and love are once again destined to lie under the yoke of the same old system, just as Stella and Ernst did. The physical power of the state nullifies the spiritual resources which might have both checked the rebirth of the historical cycle and provided, at the same time, something new to replace it. These patterns which are based upon the development of recurring image and action support Hawkes's statement that his novels are not highly plotted. The long series of horse images does not add anything to the plotline—indeed the plot of *The Cannibal* is relatively simple. But because he endows the horse image with increasing emotional and visual power, the pattern made up by the entire series forwards the novel's development. The emotional and visionary impact means much more than the plot of Zizendorf's plan to kill Leevey. This is why we feel that we have suffered a nightmare rather than finished just another novel when we experience the fictional world of *The Cannibal*.

Throughout the unraveling of the horror, Hawkes maintains his comic tone. As usual the humor is terrifying, often offending those readers who feel that comedy should be a harmless tickle. In most cases the humor is that of the inappropriate response, a shocking kind of humor because it relies upon the unexpected, underplayed reaction to a particularly horrible event. Some of the comedy is in the form of one-line jokes, as for example, when Stella mourns Ernst's fatal illness with the comforting thought, "At least . . . dear Ernst is not the only one." But with his sure feeling for the macabre, Hawkes reserves the most developed comic scene for the novel's most horrifying incident—the Duke's massacre of Jutta's boy. There is no way to give an adequate example of the comedy of this event because the scene is too long to quote. But it should be pointed out how delicately Hawkes maintains the balance between our outraged laughter and our horrified response. The laughter may be defensive, our only sane reaction to a horribly irrational event. The Duke's cannibalism is an hallucinated version of what happens as a result of war—something we would just as soon not face. But comedy forces the issue. While we laugh at the conscious exaggeration, we acknowledge, at the same time, the possibility that the horrifying event can have parallels in the real world which might one day victimize us. In his insanity the Duke decides that the boy is a fox. When he tries to skin and dissect the "fox" for cooking, he is especially miffed because his sword makes the task awkward. He hacks away, but misses joints; he makes incisions, but the point of the sword insists on striking buttons. When the "fox" kicks back, the Duke is horrified and curses his own clumsiness. He loses pieces in the mud, and he makes such a mess that it takes "all his ingenuity" to find the ears he hopes to keep as a trophy. He does not know which parts are edible and which should be thrown away: "The very fact that it was not a deer or a possum made the thing hard to skin, the fact that it was not a rabbit made it hard to dissect" (p. 181). Hating its "infernal humanness," the Duke begins to wish he were better prepared. And as he muses on the best method to slice up a child, Hawkes intensifies the comedy. We find ourselves laughing when the Duke contrasts the ideal way to cannibalize with his clumsy efforts. His response is out of touch with the seriousness of the action: "He would have preferred to have a light and a glass-topped table, to follow the whole thing on a chart, knowing which muscles to cut and which to tie" (p. 180). He longs for a rubber apron, some shorter, sharper blades, and his glasses. He is outraged because the dissection will not go by plan—he has always been an orderly man. Cursing himself for not having a thermos or wine bottle for the blood, "he set something aside in a clump of grass and went back to work. . . . The task was interminable and not for a layman" (p. 182). Upset with his lack of knowledge, he hurls all of the pieces together: "It lost all semblance to meat or fowl, the paw seemed like the foot, the glove the same as the shoe, hock and wrist alike, bone or jelly, muscle or fat, cartilage or tongue, what could he do?" (p. 181).

We ask the same question—should we laugh or scream? Probably both, for one reaction intensifies the other. This kind of humor is far from gratuitous as is often charged against Hawkes and other "black" humorists. In addition to revealing the characters' insanity, this comedy of the inappropriate response also suggests the lack of control which frustrates the inhabitants of Hawkes' world. Unlike the settings of conventional comedy, reality in the Hawkes vision is no longer an orderly process. It is absurd, out of joint, and what Guerard calls, when referring to history, "inconsecutive," and it lacks the standard norm of behavior which indicates the possibility of a rational, sane world. Humor which presupposes this kind of reality is bound to be unconventional. Hawkes' world in *The Cannibal* is so foreign to what we expect, so outrageous in its humor, and so innovatively rendered that we cannot possibly identify with it or its characters. Rather than reader identification, we are forced by the structural difficulties to join, as it were, the creative process, to participate in the unfolding of the historical cycle. In this way we feel the terror nearly as deeply as Hawkes, for we find ourselves active participants in the narrative process rather than the usual passive recipients of whatever the author puts before us. The difficulties of John Hawkes make reading an active experience. Using our minds, we join Hawkes' own keen objectivity and thus temper the kind of sympathetic character identification which the traditional novel invites. We remain just as detached during the Duke's attack as Hawkes is. Commenting on reader sympathy, Hawkes writes that his aim is "an attitude that rejects sympathy for the ruined members of our lot, revealing thus the deepest sympathy of all." [13] This depersonalized response governs our reaction to *The Cannibal*, even though we are also implicated in the historical cycle which might eventually cannibalize us.

13. John Hawkes, "Notes on Violence," *Audience*, 7 (Spring 1960), 60.

4

Nightmarish Western:
The Beetle Leg

PUBLISHED in 1951 as Hawkes' second full length work, *The Beetle Leg* is the most difficult of his novels and the most ignored. There are few specific critical studies of it, and the articles concerned with Hawkes' fiction generally overlook *The Beetle Leg*, giving it cursory analysis in favor of more detailed examinations of *The Cannibal* and *The Lime Twig*. Most contemporary reviewers either rejected the novel outright as incomprehensible or admired only isolated scenes and descriptions. Surprisingly few discussed the novel's coherence or suggested what Hawkes tried to do, but all commented on its originality. Even today general reactions to *The Beetle Leg* seem to be shock and surprise, as if the readers are caught off balance by Hawkes' effective parody of a peculiarly American genre, the Western.

W. M. Frohock has described the initial introduction to Hawkes' fiction as the experience of watching an old, sixteen-frame slapstick comedy that suddenly goes haywire. The pace of Hawkes' novels is the same: events spin by us at accelerated speeds, and we are rushed wildly along from one potential catastrophe to another. "But this time there is no split-second escape: the cars do collide; the thug does split the straight-man's skull; the hero dangling from the clockhand does lose his grip and plumment twenty stories to the pavement." [1] Professor Frohock's discussion of Hawkes focuses on the other full length fictions, skipping *The Beetle Leg*, but his comment is particularly appropriate to that novel because its pace is more frantic, more broken up, and more likely to explode reader expectations. This is not to suggest that *The Beetle Leg* is pure surrealism, for nothing happens that could not take place in waking life. An old tin star sheriff *could* conceive his duty to be the discovery and prevention of sexual encounters. A young man well known in the area *could* be buried alive during the construction of a dirt dam, forever haunting the lives of his neighbors. The dead man's brother *could* conceivably hook a drowned baby while fishing in the lake formed by the dam which holds his brother. And the dam operators *could* use a seismograph to track the dam's progress as it slithers forward, threatening to collapse, while the dead man's body inches along inside of it. All of these incidents could occur, yet reading *The Beetle Leg* we get the effect of nightmare because Hawkes gathers so many of these hallucinated scenes into one setting. Series after series of strange events pass before us so that we soon sense the atmosphere of dream instead of daylight reality. Hawkes develops the macabre scenes until we are forced to accept the truth that such things can and do happen—that they cannot be dismissed as purely surrealistic creations and thus as no more than imaginative quirks designed solely to shock.

Yet *The Beetle Leg* is often considered a weak spot in the Hawkes canon. Peter Brooks, for example, groups the novel with *The Goose on the Grave* and *The Owl* as novels which render a sense of disappointment following Hawkes' success with *The Cannibal*, arguing that of the three, only *The Owl* gives reward for

1. W. M. Frohock, "John Hawkes's Vision of Violence," *Southwest Review*, 50 (Winter 1965), 69.

its difficulties.[2] David Littlejohn agrees, describing *The Beetle Leg* as an "unfortunate decline" from *The Cannibal*. But he does note part of the problem when he comments that we tend to ignore radically different works like *The Beetle Leg* when we cannot discuss them with precision.[3] *The New Yorker* book section celebrates the novel's prose and many of its individual scenes, calling them "extraordinary," but the unnamed reviewer laments the "faintly realized" story and the unrelated images.[4] This criticism is the same tired observation which seems to greet any militantly new novel when it breaks with conventional forms, for the reviewer desires the security of the "well made" novel with its tendency to impose obvious relationships among the keenly developed images he admires.

The willful experimentation provides the dividing line between detractors and admirers of *The Beetle Leg*. Those who approve celebrate Hawkes' graphic imagination for its ability to create incongruous effects and apparent confusions which have a coherence all their own. Earl Rovit, for instance, groups this novel with *The Cannibal* as two novels which "present material of expansive scope and potential grandeur: the one, the successful revolt of occupied Germany; the other, a vast irrigation project in the arid American West, designed to transform deserts into gardens. Both novels could be handled in the serious 'large' manner befitting their possible importance; neither are." [5] Instead the distortions take shape in comic patterns, and the potential expansiveness is checked. Rather than blow-up his material, Hawkes reduces the world to a crossroads desert town, and he whittles down the prospective heroes of his "Western" until they are overshadowed by the incidents which mold their lives. There can be no hero in *The Beetle Leg* because the characters do no more than react to what goes on about them, especially to the construction of the dam. Its presence

2. Peter Brooks, "John Hawkes," *Encounter*, 26 (June 1966), 69.

3. David Littlejohn, "The Anti-Realists," *Daedalus*, 92 (Spring 1963), 256.

4. *The New Yorker*, 12 January 1952, p. 82.

5. Earl Rovit, "The Fiction of John Hawkes: An Introductory View," *Modern Fiction Studies*, 11 (Summer 1964), 161.

has become the most important point of reference in the area, not because it might change their lives with life-sustaining water but because it is the unmarked grave of Mulge Lampson.

In Hawkes' topsy-turvy world, the dam becomes a monument to death, thus breaking with our expectations as to what it should do to this arid land. This is one reason why *The Beetle Leg* illustrates Hawkes' "absolute need to create from the imagination a totally new and necessary fictional landscape or visionary world" and to avoid "the dangers of familiarity." [6] But despite his creation of the totally new, he uses the ingredients of the Western which, while providing him with a means to cross our expectations, nevertheless establishes a familiar frame of reference. When reading a Western, we expect certain characters like the sheriff and certain events like a shoot-out at the end. To be sure, the now classic patterns of, say, *The Virginian* or of *High Noon* are joyously abandoned, but the fictional landscape is at least accessible because we are moving through remembered territory when we enter the world of *The Beetle Leg*.

Hawkes' parody of the Western, however, is more than just an end in itself. While examining the novel in this chapter, we should see the Western in the context of the whole American experience. For part of America's peculiar expression of its own innocence is the Western which reshapes the violence, duplicity, and bloodshed used to settle the western territories into a myth of Good Guys against Bad. In the standard Western the very real ambiguities of our western expansion are simplified until we accept America's growth as innocent progress sanctioned by fate. The phrase "manifest destiny," coined to rationalize the western movement, expresses America's sense of its own innocence, and the traditional Western is a demonstration of this American dream. By parodying the Western, Hawkes expresses our distortion of that dream of innocence. He uses descriptions of sterility and images of noxious growth to suggest the reality which punctures the myth of

6. "John Hawkes: An Interview," *Wisconsin Studies in Contemporary Literature*, 6 (Summer 1965), 141.

westward expansion—in reality the American dream turns out to be a nightmare.

Admittedly this fictional world is odd and distorted, essentially a parody of the genre which exposes an emptiness in keeping with its arid desert setting. The novel is a primary example of anti-realism, for it fractures common experience, what we would call "real," in order to delineate subconscious or dreamlike experience. Distortion of this sort makes *The Beetle Leg* tough reading because we have been trained to look for the traditional development of the classic Western, our own homegrown product. Hawkes manipulates the expected patterns so that opening the book we find ourselves encountering strange events in familiar surroundings. Once again, as with his other fiction, this novel's richness is found in its language and humor, not in plot or character development. Hawkes does not narrate action so much as he investigates states of being, in this case the effect of Mulge Lampson's death upon a small desert community. This is not to say that the novel lacks action. Things do happen—births, weddings, medical operations—but they are made to seem motiveless, lacking the normal relationships of cause and effect. And character reaction to these events is often either unexpected or nonexistent.

Note, for example, the reactions of Camper and his wife Lou to the discovery that their young son has been bitten by a rattlesnake. They have stopped their flashy car in the middle of the desert, lost while trying to find the damsite and the town. Luke Lampson stumbles upon them, but Camper's first reaction is to explain why he is there rather than to show concern for the boy. He appears inhumanly calm about the whole ordeal: "You see, I had to stop. There weren't any roadstands or hotels, not a light anywhere. So I just pulled off the road and stepped out of the light and then the kid has to come too. For two hundred miles I wouldn't stop, not with warning signs posted every fifty feet. It's a hell of a thing when you can't take a leak without kicking up a pack of rattlers." [7] Camper's incongruous remark about "taking a leak" is

7. John Hawkes, *The Beetle Leg* (New York: New Directions, 1951), p. 26. All further references will be in parentheses.

typical of the unexpected comedy, but Hawkes is not through. While Luke readies the snakebite kit to save the boy, Lou decides to remain in the car. Ordinarily we would accept her decision as precautionary, a reaction based on fear of rattlesnakes. But her response is inappropriate, for she merely wants to listen to the car radio. And when Camper hears nothing except the raising and lowering of the aerial, the movement of station buttons, and the "squall of electricity on iron ore," he turns from the child to yell, "Try another station, Lou" (p. 27). All during the scene Luke plays his role of laconic cowboy. He is quiet, efficient, and strong, but his understated responses make him a comic character, too. While Luke works on the fang marks, Camper chatters away, explaining how he "practically built that dam alone." Unaware that the dam is also the grave of Luke's brother, Camper continues, "And the Slide—I suppose you know about it—was like a whole corner of the world fell in." Luke replies, "I recollect it." These unexpected responses challenge our own reactions to the scene, and our expectations are upset. Normally we anticipate parental concern and fear for the boy's health. We also look for some sign from Luke that his brother's death means more to him than just an incident to recollect. But such standard reactions remain part of the normal world, out of place in *The Beetle Leg*.

The scene appears to be motiveless—the boy's snakebite is not part of any continuing action. But it is not gratuitous. Hawkes' interest is not only in the fact of the bite or the comic reactions to it but also in the establishment of snakes as a sign of potential violence hovering in the background. In this sense the snakes recall the dogpacks in *The Cannibal*. For as those dogs gang up on the train carrying Ernst and Stella, so the snakes later attack Camper's car. Hawkes' description is particularly unnerving because he gives the attacking snake intelligence—it seems to know what it is doing as it lunges and thrusts:

> And at that moment they were attacked for the second time during the night by snakes. They ran over it. Flat and elongated, driven upon in sleep, it wheeled, rattling from fangs to tail, chased them, caught up with the car, slithered beneath it, raced

ahead into the light and reared. The snake tottered, seemed to bounce when it became blind, and, as Camper touched the brake, lunged so that it appeared to have shoulders, smashed its flat pear skull against the solid, curved glass of one headlamp, piercing, thrusting to put out the light.   (pp. 50–51)

This scene, however, does not compare in horror to the one in which Luke fishes up a baby's body lost in the flood. Rather than an inappropriate response, this time there is none. Except to close his eyes momentarily, Luke's reactions are nonexistent. He is fishing near Mulge's grave, so we expect some connection between what he is doing and the dead brother. But the hooked baby is a startling, unlooked for effect: "The eyes slept on either side of the fish line and a point of the barb protruded near the nose stopped with silt. It turned slowly around and around on the end of the wet string that cut in half its forehead. It had been tumbled under exposed roots and with creatures too dumb to swim, long days through the swell, neither sunk nor floating. The white stomach hung full with all it had swallowed" (p. 132). The description continues for two more paragraphs, but this brief part is enough to suggest the grotesqueness. There is some sympathy—the body is described as "God's naked child"—but for the most part Hawkes remains completely detached. It is significant that Luke does not react to the horror. He places the body back into the water where it can maintain its spiritual kinship with Mulge. Perhaps an experience such as this is beyond reaction, but we nevertheless expect some response if only because we are revolted. Of all the terrors in Hawkes' fiction, this one strikes me as the most horrifying. We do not know how to handle it because Hawkes' detachment leaves us free to go our own way. If anything our disgust works in favor of these damned characters. For as repulsive as they are, leading appallingly sterile lives, we find ourselves sympathizing with them when we read this scene. They are not at fault. Hawkes summons us to identify, to enter the circumstances of those who revolt us. This is what he means when he insists that "the product of extreme fictive detachment is extreme fictive sympathy."

This scene differs completely from the snakebite episode and

from the one it recalls in *The Cannibal*, the Duke's massacre of
Jutta's boy, for at least two reasons. First, there is no humor—the
mixture of comedy and terror is avoided in order to point up the
sheer horror. The dam which ordinarily should regenerate life
becomes instead a carrier of death. Not even the hope for water
can ease the pain and sterility of this wasteland. Second, the shock
of this particular incident comes from the scene itself, not from
inappropriate responses to it. Unlike the Duke's dissection of the
boy or Dolce's chastisement of the old woman in *The Goose on the
Grave*, to name two examples which are shockingly comic because
of the incongruous relationship between the event and the response, Luke's fishing experience is terrifying in itself. When the
Duke butchers the boy, we are outraged primarily because of his
improper reaction. As members of the "normal" world, we naturally expect a normal response. The slaughter, of course, is horrifying, but the Duke's reaction is worse. The fishing scene, however,
carries the full effect by itself. Hawkes describes it with complete
detachment, allowing neither the omniscient narrator nor Luke to
respond. The traditional innocence of infancy is cruelly violated
in *The Beetle Leg*, suggesting the impossibility of rebirth to counter the sterility. The effect is one of radical distortion, of systematic
reduction of the world to this desert town so that strangeness becomes the norm. And what makes it all so painful is the detachment—nothing Hawkes says colors the presentation of the events.

The spiritual aridity of the characters is reflected in the descriptions of the fictional landscape. Despite the dam's water, barrenness abides. We get the feeling of great distances, of the romantic
phrase "wide open spaces" being used ironically to underscore the
isolation of the town and its people: "Phosphorescent clumps of
weed and sage rolled airily in sight, but lone animals moved in-
visibly though a hoof click on stone carried for miles through the
warm evening" (p. 19). Mosquitoes beat against windows, horses
hang their heads, and snakes wait in the darkness. Luke's house
uses two potato sacks filled with sand for steps, and the deep skillet,
"as big around as a butter tub," is never off the stove. The flame
is continuously on, and the fat is rarely changed, boiling and snap-

ping from one month to the next as it piles up accumulations of drippings and layers of encrusted food. If one looks out across the horizon in hopes of seeing "a herd against the night sky or a lone rider nodding over the pommel," he will be disappointed. Nothing breaks the monotony and isolation, and the only event of note which seems to have sparked some interest is Mulge's death. In one remarkable description, Hawkes summarizes the desert world of *The Beetle Leg*:

> Beyond them bloomed the desert that had starved to silence the call of loveless dogs, buried under successive sand waves the hoof prints of single fading riders or the footprints of man and woman running with clothes bundled quickly beneath their arms. Any nomad tribes that had once burned raiding fires at night were gone, human drops sprinkled and spent in the sand, as bodies slipped from the edge of the horse blanket, had been settled upon and obscured by wingless insects or fried, like the heads of small but ruddy desert flowers, in the sun of one afternoon.   (p. 45)

Note the emphasis on "starved" and "loveless" and "buried." All signs of human effort to make a mark upon the land are lost to the sand. Even nomads, the people of the desert, are beaten by the emptiness. And death itself loses all importance, becoming, in the face of such barrenness, nothing more than sprinklings in the sand or bodies being "obscured" by insects. Beginning with the novel's title, insect imagery is used throughout to suggest sterility. It is as if swarms of locusts and blister beetles have literally devoured the living. The title, which calls to mind the slow but inevitable movement of insects destroying a field, is a key to the novel's imagery. For like the dam which slithers a beetle leg at a time toward oblivion, the characters, the countryside, and, by extension, the contemporary world are also being "obscured."

Over all of this hovers the threat of violence. Except for the shoot-out at the end, nothing violent happens to compare with *The Cannibal*'s cannibalism or rebellion in the asylum, but the potential is everywhere, likely to explode at any moment. This promise of violence makes the novel more fearful because no one action relieves the tension. Dogs in *The Cannibal*, Mongers in

The Owl—in this novel the Red Devils are the omnipresent carriers of potential violence. They are personifications of our under-
lives, of those amoral and indifferent impulses which haunt our
subconscious. They roam the countryside carelessly and freely, exciting our envy because of their abandon but also our sympathy
because of their damnation. Silent, grotesque demons, they seem
to be waiting for Luke when he begins his trek to town that will
take him to Camper's car. Note in the following description how
eerie Hawkes makes the Red Devils with his emphasis on their
silence and military precision:

> Each strap in place, not a buckle rattled. The Red Devils sat
> their machines quietly and their gloved hands waited over
> switches, ready to twist the handle grips for speed. They sat
> straight, tilted slightly forward, faces hidden by drawn goggles
> and fastened helmets, the front wheels in an even row all lean-
> ing to the left as tight polished boots raised, rested lightly on the
> starting pedals . . . there was never a murmur. Not a foot slipped
> nor did the saddle springs creak. . . . The black, deep-grooved
> tires were clean and hard. It was as if they had made no flying
> circuits that evening nor left rubber burns and cuts in the sand
> where few humans gather, in the gullies of rattlesnakes or be-
> fore the coils of braided whips.   (pp. 23–24)

Their affinity with the snakes makes them particularly fearful, and
this fear is compounded when we learn that unlike the snakes the
motorcyclists are everywhere. We encounter them in the sheriff's
jail, in the street ripping dogs, at the dance, at the hotel staring
in at Lou, and at the damsite. Hawkes variously describes them as
both human and beast. Inhabiting the no-man's land between humanity and bestiality, they have snouts and claws. Once, in the
scene with Lou at the hotel window, Hawkes calls the peering Red
Devil "it," a creature made of leather, straps, buckles, and breathing hose as if it were "constructed as a baseball, bound about a
small core of rubber" (p. 53). They represent the pit, the blackness
of reality which we do not want to face. And in many ways they
are our shadows, dogging our footsteps, haunting our waking hours
until they are inseparable from us. The most revealing reaction to
them occurs at the dance. Taking their role from the classic West-

ern as the band of drunken cowboys invading the peaceful town social, the Red Devils roar into town with a violent twist of accelerators, churning up the dust, braking and then exploding their engines. They make several revolutions around the gymnasium which is doubling as the dance hall, and then in a flashing column they disappear into the night. Amazed by the proceedings, a small boy says, "They had jewels all over them." Luke replies, "We don't want to hear about it" (p. 63). The point is that the townspeople hope to avoid this potential violence by ignoring it. The fictional characters may close their ears, but Hawkes does not let us off the hook so easily. One of the purposes of his fiction is to force a confrontation with the impulses and desires which we fear, for they can be dealt with only when they are faced. Luke's reply to the boy's wonder is a clue to the way Hawkes defines our position in a fractured world—we don't want to hear about it either.

One of the accomplishments of *The Beetle Leg* is Hawkes' ability to take such worn stereotypes as bad guys like the Red Devils and make them timeless and universal. Albert J. Guerard has this in mind when he celebrates Hawkes' skill in applying "his irony to familiar banalities," in this case the Western.[8] The sheriff, the frontier wife, the tight-lipped cowboy, the Indian squaw, and the showdown are all recognizable props of the American myth in the cowboy movie. But the most eerie character of all is the town doctor Cap Leech. He and Mulge Lampson, one alive, the other dead, dominate the scene. An outcast, wandering medicine man, standard character in most cowboy movies, Cap Leech appears to have direct contact with the underworld. A spirit "half stimulant, half sleep" keeps him alive as he bounces around the desert in a wagon which doubles as his house and hospital. Despite the protection of disinfectant lotions and rubber gloves, Cap's hands remain covered with warts. Hawkes describes him as a "midnight vivisectionist in a cat hospital" (p. 146). The doctor is surely one

---

8. Albert J. Guerard, "Some Recent American Novels," *Perspectives USA*, 1 (Fall 1952), 170. See also "Surrealist Western," *Newsweek*, 31 December 1951, p. 58, which calls *The Beetle Leg* "likely the most unusual western ever written."

of Hawkes' most imaginative grotesques, a man whose healing arts seem somehow strangely connected with death and decay rather than with life. This paradox is, of course, in keeping with the ironic reversals which define *The Beetle Leg*; Leech is as fearful as the Red Devils because of the power he holds over life and death. Hawkes' most extended description of him is significant, for it appropriately identifies the doctor with bloodied organs and with the general deformities of the town:

> He was a medical tinker and no longer wore his half face in the fishbowl light of an ampitheater.... If there was one last operation to perform, he thought, what would it be, since he had spread anatomy across a table like a net and crumpled with disgust a pair of deflated lungs into a ball.... If a single body could bear all marks of his blade and if it carried only the organs of his dissection, his life work would seesaw across the floor under tresses of arms and ventricles hung from the shoulders, would turn the other emasculated cheek.... He had reduced all medicine to a ringed wash basin and kept, for its good or harm, the tinkling world in a bundle under his rocking bed. In the stove he burned powders to kill disease; he lived in useless fumigation. He bled strangers in a room they could not stand in or laid them in his own iodoform dampened quilt.   (pp. 144–45)

Without making the connection explicit, Hawkes uses these descriptions to convince us of Cap Leech's secret knowledge of witchcraft or vodoo. He reduces his healing power to superstition, pain, and mysterious potions so that his appeal is to death. Yet, ironically, Cap Leech is the primary father figure. Late in the novel we learn that he is the father of the Lampson boys, a discovery which is particularly unnerving when we remember how Cap and Mulge command the countryside. Mulge's memory has become mythical, for the townspeople think of him as the restless soul in search of the peace of a marked grave. Their concern is not with the fact of his death but with the mystery of his body's whereabouts. The reaction to Mulge is awe and uncertainty, but the people plainly fear Cap. "He had the power to put them all to sleep, to look at their women if he wished, to mark their children" (p. 129). Sleep in this case clearly refers to death, and his advantage over women and children points to his negative effect upon the process of regeneration which the people of *The Beetle Leg* so desperately need. His spiritual fatherhood of Harry Bohn illustrates his position as a straddler of life and death. Summoned to attend Bohn's birth, Cap arrives "according to the law too late"—the mother has just died. But by an unexpected operation that is more "abortive than life saving," Leech saves the child. Ordinarily we would be thankful, for the death of one human is balanced by the birth of another. Hawkes, however, undercuts the possibility of rebirth. Note the word "fished": "The son, fished none too soon from the dark hollow, swayed coldly to and fro between his fingers. Leech left his scapel stuck midway down the unbleeding thigh, buried the wailing forceps in his shiny bag, stepped outdoors with the infant and disappeared, thereafter, through all his career, barred from the most fruitful of emergencies" (p. 121). His miracle is ironic. Not only does the operation cost Leech his standing as a legitimate doctor, it also produces Harry Bohn as one of the novel's comic grotesques, a man with a swollen body, a weathered mask, and an "old man's tumorous girth" who is "drawn to the expressionless genitals of animals" (p. 108). Hawkes' use of the word "fished" to describe the birth adds to a pattern of recurring scenes which includes Luke's experience with the baby and the various attempts to "fish" for Mulge's body. There are other examples: Camper has driven into the desert obsessed with his plan to fish the dam waters by night despite Luke's warning, and Thegna, the town cook, fishes for eels. Obviously Hawkes cancels the positive connotations of fishing to suggest haphazard action which results in unexpected horrors. Luke and Cap Leech literally become "fishers of men," but their efforts contribute to the sense of damnation rather than to the promise of salvation we normally associate with that Biblical phrase. The good old "doc" of the standard Western, one of the familiar banalities which Hawkes joyfully turns inside out, becomes the chief instrument of disease and negation. Births turn out to be living abortions, and we begin to suspect that in Hawkes' version of the Western there will be no final triumph of good guys over bad—the characters whose evilness or sterility comes naturally will not be punished in the end. It is simply the way things are. Movieland morals have no place in the nightmare part of reality.

Two other props of the conventional Western which Hawkes parodies in his vision of the modern wasteland are the poker game and the sheriff. The card game is ridiculous if only because the players are four women, including the mystified tourist Lou Camper who fills the role of the dude, the consistent loser. Instead of the slinky saloon girl with the lowcut dresses and fancy garters, Hawkes gives us fat Thegna. The finery and rough sophistication which we normally expect in the frontier card game are missing: "There were no watch chains on embroidered waistcoats, no weapons concealed in the finery, the feathered fronts of silken shirts. Black cigars, gold teeth, long wallets next to hot and scented breasts, these were buried under the young willow limbs of wing dams on the river" (p. 75). This scene is a good example of what Hawkes' negative critics consider to be a problem in his fiction—brilliant individual events which are essentially isolated. But this criticism reveals expectations of the conventional well-made novel, a traditional form foreign to Hawkes' intent. For while the poker game may be a momentary shot, having no direct bearing on the primary action, it is highly significant in the developing nightmare. In the midst of the game Lou suddenly hears the bells of a sternwheeler, the epitome of the plush gambling establishment. The hallucination takes shape in crystal, chandeliers, and tumblers of brandy, yet Hawkes drops hints of impending disaster with descriptions of black eyes and water, harsh silences, and "an enormous liquid dead land far from shore." Although Lou is not literally on the sternwheeler, the final description of the scene places her within the hallucination. "Feet splashed, shoulders scraped warm peeling wood and suddenly, from the deck below, against the constant lull of gamblers, a voice called up clearly between cupped hands, laughing through low fog and unaware of danger. 'Oh, Lou, Lou, where's he at now?' " (p. 76). Clearly we are to expect danger, some potential violence which is about to surface and which is all the more frightening because it is undefined. The voice is as unaware of danger as Luke Lampson is when he dismisses the Red Devils with "We don't want to hear about it." Nightmares and unexpected pain are too unsettling to face squarely. But if the characters can shut out the fearful and the unpleasing, we cannot. In the act of reading *The Beetle Leg* we confront the probability that we, too, are unaware, unwilling to hear about it.

The sheriff is not unwilling to contemplate his situation, but he puts his faith in a zodiac which promises only barrenness and famine. Hawkes calls him "rather foolish and sadistic," an apt description for this cross between country philosopher and frontier reformer. For in his fourteen years of patrolling what he calls "a lawless country," nothing much has happened. Only Mulge's death has broken the incredible apathy, so the sheriff spends his time in a one man campaign against sex. He is sadistic because of his power to warp natural urges, and he is foolish because of his comic persistency. He is highly conscious of his image, of handcuffs on the hip, rolled up sleeves, and the cartridge belt around the waist. Suspicious and tenacious, he pursues sexual encounters with such fervor that we begin to suspect him of compulsive voyeurism:

> It was the men or women who didn't have no place to hide that gave me trouble. Them people too easy found doing things a man can't talk about, things that happened or not depending on whether you arrived five minutes early or five late. They broke the law all right, directly they couldn't quiet down and talk when I was near enough to see. It almost depended on how much white showed from the side of the road before my torch was even lit. I took them in. I've got no time to waste with men like that. (p. 8)

We realize that his lack of time results from the way he spends it. But the sheriff is particularly twisted because he recruits children to spy for him and to sound the alarm. Caught between the sheriff and Cap Leech, innocence in the guise of children does not stand a chance.

Hawkes gives us one extended comic scene to illustrate. Summoned by a young girl in a bathing suit, the sheriff hurries to the river. He knows children should not play near the river, but since they run loose like their parents, he will utilize them. "And you can't tell what children see or what they find. They're skinned up and bandaged from climbing around where people big enough to do wrong have done it, or tried to, since sometimes me and my boys can stop them before they're through. Right in the middle of the desert where there is hardly sign of bird or animal you are liable to find some scrap or garment that once belonged personally to a woman. That's evidence" (p. 10). In this case the child leads the sheriff to the riverbank where they see Mulge Lampson squatting in the sun. The sheriff tries to size up Lampson, to determine what his hands are doing, whether they are "small and kind of pink with short tapering fingers." The possibility of sexual irregularity is suggested when we learn that Mulge has his pants off—yet he continues to wear his bright yellow suspenders. The sheriff sees that he is not ready for trouble, but the fact that he is alone and half dressed raises suspicions. Hawkes leaves purposely unclear what Mulge is doing—fishing, masturbating, swimming? The sheriff muses that maybe he enjoys squatting in the desert while looking at his own reflection in the river. The point is that the sheriff's pride in his prowess and astuteness is frustrated by his unfulfilled speculations, and he becomes another one of Hawkes' comic characters. He figures that if he stands up, the man will too. But Mulge continues to squat. He then decides that if he walks away, the man will swim across. But Mulge stays. Never learning what is going on, the sheriff convinces himself that this is a missed opportunity— he should have looked for trouble in the sand dunes and hollows. " 'He ain't hurt,' I said. 'He ain't drunk. I don't think he's got a gun. That's enough.' But he was something to stare at for an hour or two" (p. 14).

This comic episode makes up the novel's prologue, and it comes to nothing. Curiosity and expectations are raised which are never fulfilled, and we, like the sheriff with whom we are loathe to identify, never discover what Mulge is doing. But completion of the puzzle is impossible in the splintered world which Hawkes sees, fears, and portrays. What counts is the total absence of motive, the inexplicable events, the suggestions of perversion, the atmosphere of sterility, the union of humor with the macabre. While parodying the Western, this prologue establishes the comically grotesque world which is presided over by the death of Mulge Lampson. It all seems unreal, but Hawkes would have us accept it as the reality of nightmare.

Mulge's death will be remembered as long as the Great Slide is referred to, for it has assumed mythic importance. Desiring wild west excitement, the sheriff complains that Mulge is the only man to die during his fourteen years in office. Luke, while seeding, thinks of Mulge as a worm "crawling around in there right now, winding his way up toward the side I've sown" (p. 24). Mulge's widow Ma uses a divining rod to try to locate the body. Camper brags that he was one of the few to see part of the accident. The point is that these characters revolve around death. Although they never truly consider Mulge dead and gone, the mystery of his whereabouts governs their imaginations. They think of him as alive; they wonder what he is doing "in there," and generally they are obsessed with discovering where the body is. The irony, of course, is that Mulge gains his fame only after the Great Slide. No one remembers much about him when alive. Immediately following the Slide, for example, despite his disappearance, the search is for the "incalculable loss of small tools." Bohn's comment is comically appropriate: "It doesn't do much good to say he's buried in there . . . why, it's just like saying, 'I've got a brother buried in the Rocky Mountains'" (p. 70). But that is exactly what they do—they talk about the accident until it develops into a tourist attraction. Establishing a collection of Mulge's belongings, they set up a museum which charges admission. Stories are told and retold, and memories expand until Mulge's razor and shaving mug become sacred relics. They bestow sainthood on Mulge—Western style. And it is all done for a profit. As the barber says, "There's more ways to skin a cat . . . than bury him." For fifty cents the mementos can be touched, but none of them are for sale—they are too sacred. But the tourist can buy postcards of them if he wishes. And this is what Mulge's widow Ma does in order to preserve his memory. Hawkes tells us without comment: "It was the best she could do."

The beauty of this grim humor is that it makes us aware of the unbelievable boredom of these people, of the sheer uselessness of their lives. Cut off from larger concerns, they reduce the world to a dirt mound in the middle of the desert so that the center of their reality becomes an unmarked grave. Their awe of the mound may be an attempt to manufacture order. Dimly aware of their meaninglessness, they magnify this trivial event to the status of cosmic importance. But stability in the flux is impossible, for Mulge's grave will not sit still. Its gradual movement suggests time's erosion of their own lives, and of ours:

> It moved. The needles, cylinder and ink lines blurring on the heat smeared graph in the slight shade of evening, tended by the old watchman in the power house, detected a creeping, downstream motion in the dam. Leaned against by the weight of water, it was pushing southward on a calendar of branding, brushfires and centuries to come, toward the gulf. Visitors hung their mouths and would not believe, and yet the hill eased down the rotting shale a beetle's leg each several anniversaries, the pride of the men of Gov City who would have to move fast to keep up with it. But if this same machine, teletyping the journey into town, was turned upon the fields, the dry range, the badlands themselves, the same trembling and worry would perhaps be seen in the point of the hapless needle, the same discouraging pulse encountered, the flux, the same activity.   (pp. 67–68)

It is not only the dam that moves; the entire region is inching toward oblivion, unconcerned with attempts to stabilize the flux with museum exhibits.

Mulge does not deserve his fame. Promising to marry Thegna, he marries Ma instead in "wedding suit and cut lip, hatless and with socks hanging below his ankles . . . " (p. 73). The reference to the socks is typical of Hawkes' ability to create the grotesque effect. It minimizes Mulge in our eyes, undercuts his status as hero, and marks him as a potential comic character. Which is what he is, for we immediately learn that once married to Ma he returns to honeymoon with Thegna. The description of him as "faithless, black and cold" is understated; he somehow seems worse than that. Luke's recollections of Mulge are also negative: "I never seen him much myself"; "He wasn't good for much around the house"; "And as far as going into a field or on the prairie, not him" (p. 100). Yet as the "blindly swimming man inside," Mulge is now a scientific discovery, worthy of seismographic tracking and of a brisk tourist trade. Never quite accepting Mulge as dead, the townspeople grimly predict a riot if he "come back" because they have mourned so much. As one boy says seriously, "Not every town would have made as much of him as us." A ghostly return from the grave would not bother them as much as the disturbance which Mulge's appearance would cause to the order they have manufactured around his death. This comic discussion is topped off by the Mexican's observation that Mulge would be "a sorry sight if he showed up." Given Hawkes' fictional worlds, Mulge just might show up one day. And we have Luke's fished-up baby to tell us what he would look like—indeed a sorry sight.

The effect of Mulge's marriage proposal to Ma is the novel's best sustained piece of writing. It is a wonderfully bizarre picture of the absence of both fertility and the promise of rebirth. Mulge never enters the scene, but he acts as a magnet for Ma as she joins a group of grim frontier women for a twenty-mile trek across the desert to where the wedding is to occur. Hawkes masterfully describes the sterility of these old desert virgins. They have weak legs, "empty breasts and nameless horses," and they are as dry as the desert. The wedding promises to be a vicarious deflowering for these hags, for Ma is as old as they are. "They backtracked, chewed the sand and made their way over weary, salty miles to see one woman their own age brought to bed. Every one of them made the trip. There was not a woman in the desert who had not left the animal pens, truck garden patch and particular gully of the home to sit all day in the sun, to breathe the air of ancient lying in and love" (p. 82). Luke is horrified by it all. He longs to see a young woman, a female whose face has "not been formed and set long

ago to the sudden bloody impression of a coffin bone." But sterility
rules the day, and the absence of youth and beauty recalls the violation of children.

As always in this novel the threat of violence hangs heavy.
Mulge's mother Hattie does not want to make the trip, but Ma has
her way. Hawkes tells us that Hattie's kerchief dangles danger-
ously close to the spoke wheels of the wagon. Had she fallen, "she
would have hung before her feet once more touched the settling,
noisy track." But nothing happens this time. Reader expectations
are again crossed, and we turn from the unfulfilled promise of
terror to the comedy of Hattie's tirade against Ma. Solidly against
the marriage, Hattie criticizes Ma for being too old. She predicts,
"You ain't going to live long enough with my boy to get the yellow
off his teeth." When one of the desert women interrupts the argument to defend Ma as a girl pure as snow, Hattie ludicrously
misses the point. "I don't know anything about snow," she replies,
"I ain't ever seen none" (p. 89). Hattie, of course, is correct, though
only because Mulge dies before his teeth are cleaned and because
purity is a foreign concept in *The Beetle Leg*. We never learn why
Mulge marries Ma, and as far as we know they never live together.
But Ma remains faithful to his memory. As a parody of the griev-
ing widow, she sanctifies his unmarked grave and then tries to find
his body with a divining rod. Had he died a natural death, she
might have seen spared this ridiculous search for his remains. But
deprived of this privilege, she reasons that she deserves to find "the
slow and unbreathing, blackly preserved, whole and substantial
being of the dead man." Thus, she becomes a desecrator of graves,
literally opening many graves "to find one full." She never finds
him, of course, but she becomes, ironically, a mythic example of
perseverance, the grotesque archetype of the widow: "Ma opened
up the grave—each widow has her mile of road, the dark ridge of
her adopted name—and she revealed signs of her striking loss in
the furls of the earth" (p. 117). Her faithfulness is matched by
Hattie's. When Hattie dies, the townspeople bury her in the dam,
somewhere above her son, so that she can forever look down at
him. Note the humorous effect which Hawkes gets from the oppo-

sition of Hattie's body face down with Mulge's body feet up: "Face down, eyes in dirt, she peered through the sandy side toward her son below, where he too lay, more awkward than she, feet up and head in the center of the earth" (p. 115).

This kind of humor is not for everyone. Its mockery of motherhood, faithfulness, marriage, and death itself infuriates some readers and astounds others. Even those who laugh feel the shock of it. This is irreverent comedy at its best, designed not to amuse nor to provide a moment of quiet pleasure but to outrage, to startle us out of complacency and into a recognition of attitudes and emotions which have stultified into predictable stereotypes. Our easy acceptance of motherhood or wifely devotion mocks these qualities more than Hawkes' parody of them. Unquestioning approval reduces them to empty forms, observed out of habit and expectation. This is not to say that Ma and Hattie do not love Mulge, insofar as love is possible in the novel. But their love transforms them into full-fledged grotesques, completing a process which began as soon as they set foot in this desert community. This may be one reason why Hawkes chooses the frame of the Western. It supplies a form readily recognizable to most readers and, thus, is susceptible to ridicule. We need only think of the burial scene in a Western like, say, *Shane*, and then read the following description of Hattie's funeral to see why it is open to parody: "Perhaps a slight wind should have hummed across the miles of black land, bearing the faint lowing of faraway cattle or the sound of wheels grinding on Luke's wagon" (p. 113). Perhaps. We expect the gentle wind, the soothing sound of contented cows, the solemn arrival of the surviving son, and that expectation is the point. For such comfortable forms encourage the illusion of order and security in the face of sterility and death. Hawkes hopes to counter such complacency—the fractured twentieth-century world must be faced; the nightmare must be accepted as a legitimate part of reality.

The novel ends with the gunfight, traditional in the Western, between the Red Devils and the sheriff, Bohn, and Luke. The motorcyclists circle the sheriff's truck, playing the role of attacking Indians, while Luke and the sheriff fire their shotguns. Only

by this time in the novel we can no longer distinguish between
good guys and bad. Both sides are full of savagery and death, and
the potential violence which has pulsed as an undercurrent all
through the novel finally surfaces. Although Hawkes is ambiguous,
he implies that either Luke shoots himself or his shotgun explodes
in his face. And above the sounds of battle, "shrill and buoyant,"
there comes "that cool baying of the rising head, the call to kill,
louder and sing-song, faintly human after the flight of Devils, the
nasal elated sounds of the cowboy's western bark. Yip, yip, yip"
(p. 158). Cap Leech has the final word, a short first-person mono-
logue in which he tells us he will journey on, still in search of his
lost son Mulge. We know, of course, that Cap's decision is not parental devotion but a final expression of his obsession with death.

The beetle leg movement is the slow, inevitable settling toward
final stasis. Mulge is dead, but as far as the town is concerned, he
is only buried alive. His slowly rotting body, "dry now, untouched,
except for the soothing pressure of some tons of earth," and stuck
forever in the dam which is supposed to transform the desert into
a garden spot, suggests the slow movement of the characters, and
of ourselves, to ruin and decay. They experience death in life just
as they think of Mulge as alive in death. And Hawkes conceives it
all in the name of serious comedy. Claire Rosenfield has noted
that this kind of humor must always meet with disfavor:

> On the most obvious level, it makes obscene those vague ab-
> stractions we are taught to revere—in this instance, human dig-
> nity, religious burial, motherhood. If we admit the truth we
> discover that black humor exploits those aggressive and erotic
> impulses we also prefer to repress. And another compulsive
> concern for which we, if we are conventional readers, cannot
> forgive Hawkes is his genuine verbal facility which reduces so
> much to the merely physical. Even a cerebral process may be
> described as biology alone. Cap Leech's recognition of his son
> is undramatic: "Within the brainless cord of spinal fluid there
> was a murky solid, a floating clot of cheerless recognition." [9]

The vague abstractions which Miss Rosenfield mentions often be-

9. Claire Rosenfield, "John Hawkes: Nightmares of the Real," *The
Minnesota Review*, 2 (Winter 1962), 251.

come crutches, forms of behavior and expressions of emotion lacking the vital meaning they once had. Confronted with such irreverence, the conventional reader is appalled. Not only have the sacred cows been struck down; without the props he finds himself unsure how to react. Aggressions and impulses have been repressed for so long in the name of convention that he has come to believe them unreal. But Hawkes insists upon their reality, even at the expense of negating soothing myths.

In *The Beetle Leg* Hawkes reverses the myth of love and fertility. The novel ends with Leech searching for his lost son, but in this fictional landscape discovery of the body will do him no good. Hawkes accepts no standard myth as an ordering device for his world. The ancient fertility myth, as reflected in both love and water, is rejected, for Hawkes paints reality as a desert incapable of the traditional rejuvenation suggested by the birth of children or the discovery of water. In *Second Skin* he uses fertility rites and the celebration of "love at last" as means to defeat a world that is out to get Skipper, but to do so he must permit Skipper to abandon the world for a wandering island. No such escape is possible in *The Beetle Leg.* The Red Devils scamper away at the end, and the baby continues to haunt the lake. The best the characters can do is to insist that they don't want to hear about it. The memory of Mulge, however, grows until it becomes a substitute for myths now useless, but it centers on death. As Guerard notes, the consciousness of each character returns again and again to that moment in space and time when the Great Slide buried Mulge. It is as if something is unappeased. Time seems immobilized since Mulge's death, and the ensuing stasis promises a future of stagnation. The manmade lake waters the bodies of Mulge and the anonymous baby instead of the good earth. Thus while Luke continues to sow his daily seed in the shadow of the dam, he walks on barren ground. Hawkes' parody of the Western acts primarily as a frame which allows him to upset accepted convention and to undermine the confidence we have when we are in familiar surroundings. With the props kicked out from under us, we are more likely to note the challenge to such traditional mythic pillars as marriage, father-son relationships, childhood innocence, and the sanctity of burial. Hovering in the background of this modern desert is not the potential for life-sustaining rain but snakes and the omnipresent Red Devils. *The Beetle Leg* offers no new myth to heal the sickness of the age.

F. Cudworth Flint writes, "I suspect that beneath the somewhere-near Wyoming sagebrush of Mr. Hawkes' scenery lie the skeletons of ancient motifs—possibly most easily identified in a Greek costume—such as the anthropologist and folklorist track down through the centuries." [10] The point would be "skeletons," for Hawkes has indeed buried traditional myths in the Great Slide. Yet it would seem that Mr. Flint suggests the novel's meaning can be unearthed once we play the role of the anthropologist digging in the dam, discovering ancient mythic patterns. This is not the case, for in this novel the time-honored motifs have lost their power. Hawkes forces us to face the age without the customary protective barriers, such as fertility myths or American notions of innocence, which we rely on to insulate us from the pain of recognition. Reading *The Beetle Leg* we meet head-on the potential for violence in our daily lives. The novel makes little effort to say how things are. What it attempts to do is dismiss the forms which were once life-sustaining in order to project a situation in which we stand isolated in reality, stripped of all protections, and thus made to recognize new possibilities, be they good or bad. Myth normally assumes coherence and the hope for stability, but Hawkes denies both assumptions. The aim of his ruthless comedy is to startle us into an awareness of this reality and to expose the possibilities for the ugliness which we hesitate to accept as an everyday affair. Traditional myths have no place in a world so completely absurd.

Hawkes' impatience with complacency, with those, for example, who support the Western while unconscious of the violence behind it, is reflected in his concern with experimentation, for he is just as disturbed at those who would limit the novel to a comfortably recognizable form. His experiments in *The Beetle Leg* with

10. F. Cudworth Flint, "Fiction Chronicle," *The Sewanee Review*, 60 (Autumn 1952), 713.

distortion and nightmare are matched by his stylistic concerns. He pushes the reader to the limit, seeking to realize what Peter Brooks names "the full range of the reader's potential reactions." Not only does Hawkes make the novel shocking to experience, he also makes the reading process itself difficult. For example the following description of Bohn has been praised by Professor Guerard for the twisting syntax and "the inappropriate gnomic saws." [11]

> He had an old man's kidney. He had an old man's tumorous girth and thickly dying wind, a hardening on the surface of his armpits. Chest and shoulders were solidified against youth, bulged in what he assumed to be the paunch of middle age; he was strapping, suffered a neuralgia in winter, a painful un-limbering in the spring. A few fingers were broken, snubbed since an old man labors from stone to knife to saw to possible tractor accident and back to the single burning of a match flame short in argument. He could laugh, sparsely, at the exploits of men over fifty who enacted, he believed, all they claimed; his own prowess, he told them, had been struck off, like a head of hair, by maturity.   (p. 55)

This is an especially appropriate description of a man who is Cap Leech's spiritual son, and it is all the more ridiculous when we learn that Bohn is only thirty years old. Note the pious comment on the labors of old men and on the efforts of the body to repudiate youth. The casual acceptance of a "few" broken fingers understates the pain. The parallel of lost prowess and a balding head—prowess struck off like a "head of hair"—is unexpected.

This description is an example of Hawkes' momentary shots, artificial, carefully controlled, and what Guerard calls "bemused by its own absurd inventiveness." Clearly the author is having as much fun as we are. The early novels, especially, abound with these descriptions which seem complete in themselves, causing the complaint of brilliant but isolated scenes and images. Self-conscious and full of unexpected turns, these set-pieces account for much of the humor. But the effect is not merely stylistic, for from such absurd descriptions we also sense a vision taking shape as the

11. Albert J. Guerard, "The Prose Style of John Hawkes," *Critique*, 6 (Fall 1963), 21.

scene progresses. The inventiveness multiplies as we read, jumping from the unusual to the absurd. In Guerard's words, "The
creative necessity is to magnify and vivify everything, to leave no
part of one's fictional world neutral and inert." [12] Note, for example, a scene which most readers praise—Luke taking a shower
with his hat on and a cigarette still in his mouth. It begins with
the common enough description of Luke soaping himself and feeling the "slippery wooden slats" under his feet. He has, at least, removed his boots. The comic distortion takes shape when we learn
that the boards of the shower stall have been used in the past for
railroad trestles and the ribs of barges. Surviving a long process
from "sea craft to bridge, to tool shed, scrapped and saved," the
boards were, Hawkes tells us with a straight face, never burned.
As the description continues, we realize that the shower stall has a
history which makes it as important as the people who bathe in it.
Naturally the water is piped from the dam, but unlike Mulge, the
boards have survived the Great Slide. When the description suddenly shifts from the stall to the river, the magnifiying process is
complete. The boards "survived the Slide, floated and were towed
landward to dry. At one time the river was filled with the lattice
of new lumber, white sawdust fell on the muddy current and the
prairie ranchers . . . saw wood come into the sand country and not
only cut, but cut to special sizes" (p. 61). Obviously this new wood
cannot be the rough beams and ribs of trestles and barges which
now make up the shower stall. We have left Luke with his soap
while Hawkes creates a history of scrap lumber. This may be inventiveness in the extreme, but it is justified by Hawkes' need
to parody the Western in which, traditionally, everything looms
larger than life. Hawkes exposes this absurdity by magnifying
trivialties. The shower nearly becomes a ritual for Luke. And the
descriptions of it make us realize how out of proportion things
are in the dreary towns of Clare and Misletoe. Calling to mind the
Continental Railroad and its contribution to our westward expansion, these planks, once used for railroad trestles, have come to an
unspectacular end. They rot in the shower stall, an apt description

12. Ibid., p. 22.

of what has happened to our myth of innocence. Each common occurrence seems to assume a greater significance than it deserves, as if it were all a kind of self-entertainment by the characters. A backroom poker game suddenly finds itself aboard a glittering steamboat, and a shower leads to commentary upon a river carrying new lumber. Hawkes denies nothing; anything is possible in his world. The passages which seem obscure are saved, finally, by the sheer joy of the style, by a verbal inventiveness reminiscent of William Faulkner.

When these stylistic experiments join broken narrative patterns, plot in the conventional sense is destroyed. The reader finds himself with the responsibility of piecing it all together. What exactly does happen to Mulge? Why does he marry Ma in the first place? What are the Red Devils doing out there in the desert? Each of us can ask other questions. *The Beetle Leg* has the coherence of verbal patterns and recurring motifs instead of the structure of plot, theme, and character development. This is not to say that the novel lacks form or unity. The events themselves are unified by the fact that they all take place during one night. But, the more significant levels of form and unity are to be found in verbal and psychological coherence—the recurring patterns of sterility, death and disease, grotesqueness, the threat of violence, stunted growth. The point is that the mysterious events reflect a novel free from traditional structure which, in turn, illustrates unordered reality. Whether it applies to the fictional landscape or to the real world, order is not innate. Hawkes suggests that it must be sought out and redefined page by page or moment by moment. Lack of conventional structure in *The Beetle Leg* is an analogy for the absence of convenient order in reality.

In his review of the novel, Heinz Politzer comments that so many young novelists experiment with structural problems to hide their movements in unfamiliar territory, "in areas they do not know from their own experience." [13] But he approves of *The Beetle Leg* because he feels that Hawkes is striving for his artistic integrity within the *avant-garde* tradition. Instead of incoherence,

13. Heinz Politzer, "Five Novels," *Commentary*, 13 (May 1952), 510.

Politzer finds a "fresh air" and a "savage beauty." The territory of this novel is indeed unfamiliar, a strangely hallucinated setting that strikes a balance between the terrors which happen within it and the stylistic beauties used to describe it. But Hawkes suggests that the unfamiliarity is due in large part to our traditional unwillingness to accept the nightmare as a legitimate part of reality. We are taught from childhood that the bad dream is unreal, that the thing which goes bump in the night will not hurt us. Such is not the case in *The Beetle Leg* in which the inexplicable and the bizarre rest side by side with the "normal" and the mundane. The result is a novel which parodies the familiar in order to convince us of the reality of many things we do not want to accept.[14]

14. Some time after this study was in proof, two evaluations of *The Beetle Leg* were published. See Lucy Frost, "The Drowning of American Adam: Hawkes' *The Beetle Leg*," *Critique*, 14 (Summer 1973) , 63–74; and Frederick Busch, *Hawkes: A Guide to His Fictions* (Syracuse: Syracuse University Press, 1973) , pp. 39–60.

5

Small, Yet
Beyond Elimination:
The Lime Twig

JUST as *The Beetle Leg* parodies the trappings of a familiar genre, the Western, to expose America's myth of the West, so *The Lime Twig* (1961) burlesques the detective thriller. All of the violence, sadism, and general sordidness which we associate with the world of detective fiction are used and mocked, but again Hawkes has more in mind than parody. Manipulating the conventions of the genre, he suggests that while outwardly repelled, we subconsciously long for the thrills of violence and possible death which we normally experience only vicariously while reading a detective novel.

The Lime Twig represents a new direction in Hawkes' fiction. Despite its intricacies this novel is more accessible than his previous work. One reason for this change seems to be Hawkes' decision to forgo both the use of fantastic images in such liberal quantity and the near-surrealistic style of his earlier novels. This is not to say that *The Lime Twig* is fare for the average reader, for the initial reading will likely prove to be extremely difficult. But in this novel Hawkes shows us that manipulation of conventional reality can invoke the same intense degree of terror and comedy which

125

one expects to find in his more militantly experimental work. The banalities of conventional life frame the nightmare in *The Lime Twig*: boarding houses, kidney pie dinners, life with mother, newspaper sports columns, baffled police. Use of these conventions provides us with points of reference recognizable from our own lives, thus permitting a relative lucidity which the earlier fiction takes pains to avoid. This does not mean that *The Lime Twig* is "better" than his other novels because its evocation of nightmare is more easily read. But what it does suggest is that Professor Guerard's prediction, made over twenty years ago, that Hawkes would "move still further toward realism" was indeed prophetic.[1]

Hawkes himself has admitted this drift which has resulted in a shift of emphasis. The visual power of the earlier fiction has been limited while a more sharply focused narrative element has emerged. In a succinct summation of what this change means in part, Earl Rovit writes, "The emotional accretions of image and mood which inform *The Cannibal* are partially lost in *The Lime Twig*, although they are compensated by the proportionate increase in suspense and dramatic power which *The Lime Twig* possesses in its main story-line."[2] The point is that *The Lime Twig*, for all of its difficulty and fragmentation, has a more coherent dramatic focus, a stronger sense of developing plot. Still this novel is "realistic" not according to the traditional definition but only in its use of the conventional to create a sense of dull life as one cause for the need to indulge in fantasy and dream.

This shift of emphasis has been brought about, in part, by what Hawkes calls his need to parody the novel form. In the *Wisconsin Studies* interview, he tells us that he began *The Lime Twig* when he "read a newspaper account of legalized gambling in England."[3] Taking four years to revise, the novel moved much closer

1. Albert J. Guerard, "Introduction," in John Hawkes, *The Cannibal* (New York: New Directions, 1962), p. x.
2. Earl Rovit, "The Fiction of John Hawkes: An Introductory View," *Modern Fiction Studies*, 11 (Summer 1964), 154.
3. "John Hawkes: An Interview," *Wisconsin Studies in Contemporary Literature*, 6 (Summer 1965), see pp. 148–149.

to conventional fiction insofar as recognizable setting and developed characters were concerned. But while moving toward the traditional, he also made fun of it because of his desire to parody. For example, the voice of Sidney Slyter can be read as a parody of both the novelist's role and the commenting chorus, while the novel itself burlesques the cheap thriller.

The urge to parody remains, however, a secondary aim, for in *The Lime Twig*, as in his other fiction, Hawkes continues to violate anticipated reality so that the vision is all his own. We are drawn into what turns out to be a literal dream, pulled away from our preconceived ideas of sanity and abnormality. Not only freeing Hawkes from the limits of realism, this distortion of probability helps him investigate the deeper psychological truths which flourish beneath surface reality and beyond the dictates of rationality. What he comes up with is a novel full of fear, in some ways more terrifying than *The Cannibal*'s nightmare of history because the lives of Michael and Margaret Banks seem so close to our own. Their terrors could very well be ours. Comparing *The Cannibal* and *The Lime Twig*, W. M. Frohock writes, "Where *The Cannibal* moves in a vapor of insanity, this one is like an extremely bad half-waking dream. It is, once more, like a nightmare but not a nightmare from which one wants to wake up; one is afraid to wake up *for fear of discovering that one has not been dreaming*." [4] Knowing that man longs to break free from the limits of rational consciousness, Hawkes explores in *The Lime Twig* the question of what happens if a man's unconscious desires and "disruptive needs" were to materialize—what if.his most deeply repressed dream were to come true. The result is a mixture of longing and fear, of attraction toward and repulsion from the fantasy which limes the dreamer, ensnaring him as easily as if he were a bird. And Hawkes so deeply involves us in the dreams of Michael Banks that we, too, experience the tension of a mixed reaction, that of

4. W. M. Frohock, "John Hawkes's Vision of Violence," *Southwest Review*, 50 (Winter 1965), 75.

sympathy and repulsion for the trapped characters. How can they be so helpless, we ask, and, yet, as Sidney Slyter tells us, they could be any one of us.

Most of us rationalize our dreams, laugh them away, rely on the light of morning to assure us that the terrors of the night before were imaginary, "only" a dream. But for Hawkes the dream is the truer experience, the more meaningful reality. In the words of S. K. Oberbeck, "His aim is to make the dream a reality on paper without sacrificing its unconscious aspect of terror and indistinctness."[5] *The Lime Twig* offers a radical distortion of experience, for Michael Banks' dreams replace his everyday reality. His escapades with Larry and the gang of hoods are a manifestation of his subconscious longings, only in his case the dream becomes frighteningly real. The result is a new order of reality for Banks, one totally foreign to the little life he has been living with Margaret and one which is suddenly beyond his control. Longing for the power and thrills which an uninhibited sexual life promises, he tries to mask his frustrations with Margaret by dreaming of owning a race horse. As long as the horse remains within his dream, he is repressed but safe. This tranquility, however, is interrupted when William Hencher enters the Bankses' lives. Supplying Michael with a real horse, Hencher unknowingly unleashes all of the fury which has been trapped in Michael's dreams and which is symbolized by the angrily pawing stallion. Once released to find objectification in the race horse, Banks' fantasies take over his life—he literally experiences the dream. His unconscious desires find fulfillment in his new dream-defined reality, but entrance to his dream world costs him his life. Usually one dreams the nightmare and then awakens, brought slowly back to reality through that dimension between sleeping and waking. But Hawkes allows Banks to live his nightmare, and in so doing he reassures us of the reality of terror. Thus, this novel defines the out-of-focus world, showing us not logically motivated action but a movement from reality to dream to nightmare and death. As in *The Beetle Leg*, Hawkes destroys order, negates our comfortable concepts of a rational universe in order to show us, in Leslie Fiedler's words, "reason's last desperate attempt to know what unreason is." [6]

Fiction created from such an experimental vision is likely to be controversial, and *The Lime Twig* is no exception. David Littlejohn, for example, particularly admires the "power and intensity" of *The Cannibal* and *The Lime Twig*, and he insists that Hawkes "has no equal for the communication of revolting, inescapable terror." [7] But Littlejohn believes that too many of Hawkes' horrors are gratuitous, literary thrills used in vain unless the reader enjoys new experiences for the sake of the experience. Thus while he admires *The Lime Twig*, he feels that it is particularly "compounded of grotesquely unpleasant experiences, with little of Beckett's redeeming philosophic vision." Singling out Thick's beating of Margaret for illustration, Littlejohn says that Hawkes goes too far when he drags Margaret into a tragicomic hell of "unexplainable" terror: "Once again, I feel, he goes too far; but up to the point where an excess of sadism detaches our sympathies with a jolt, Margaret's case is made poignant and painfully clear." Finally, Littlejohn questions if the general reader can stomach Hawkes, and he wonders if the mastery of antirealistic technique does not limit his appeal to other novelists and students of fiction: "I can think of no better case-book in the re-creation of vivid and effective nightmare. Hawkes seems to know precisely what overlay of disease and sexuality, what strange dislocations of structure, what vague omissions, what tiny twists in the otherwise real, what imagery, what language, what tone can most effectively engage the root terror of the deeper unconscious."

Mr. Littlejohn's mixed opinion about Hawkes' fiction reflects a general attitude, but it is not likely that Hawkes creates terror for its own sake. Forcing us to confront terrors which we do not want

6. Leslie A. Fiedler, "The Pleasures of John Hawkes," in John Hawkes, *The Lime Twig* (New York: New Directions, 1961), pp. x, xiv.
7. David Littlejohn, "The Anti-Realists," *Daedalus*, 92 (Spring 1963), see pp. 256–258.

to hear about, Hawkes illustrates that part of experience which we would repress or ignore. It seems to me, to cite the scene which bothers Littlejohn, that the extremity of Margaret's beating is "explainable" as a manifestation of her dreams, the violence of which she never expects even though she has always been vaguely aware of the possible terror within her fantasies. Her visions of trains crushing children and of strange men feeling her legs all foreshadow and "explain," insofar as her subconscious can be explained, the physical violation which occurs when her most feared dream comes true. Critical opinion about this characteristic of Hawkes' fiction is truly divided, and it is just as easy to find supporters as it is those who believe that he goes too far. Earl Rovit, for example, describes Hawkes' novels in terms exactly opposite from Littlejohn's, arguing that they are "controlled assaults" upon readers who avoid the darkness within the self. Rather than point out possible excesses, Professor Rovit celebrates Hawkes' restraint: "The art lies in Hawkes's control, in the *restraint* of his assaults." [8] Similarly, Professor Guerard believes that the underground life is more truly conveyed in Hawkes' novels than in typical psychological fiction. Instead of appealing only to readers with an interest in fictional technique, as Littlejohn charges, Hawkes brings us much closer to reality than most of us will admit: "But *The Cannibal* does indeed convey one Germany as few realistic novels have, and *The Lime Twig*'s sordid, damp England is as authentic as Graham Greene's." [9]

One of the most authentic voices in *The Lime Twig* is Sidney Slyter's. Although we never see him, his sports column precedes each chapter and illustrates the gulf between surface reality and the depths of the Bankses' dream. Slyter is always on the edge of the mystery; he smells a rat, but his bumbling efforts to find it come to nothing substantial, only a clue here, a scattered fact there. Despite Slyter's importance, Hawkes tells us that he is an afterthought, the result of a suggestion by James Laughlin, the pub-

8. Rovit, "The Fiction of John Hawkes," p. 151.
9. Albert J. Guerard, "The Prose Style of John Hawkes," *Critique*, 6 (Fall 1963), 19.

lisher of New Directions, who felt that the novel might be "more accessible" if it had a gloss or guide for the reader:

> I believe that he even suggested the idea of a newspaper sports-writer as an appropriate kind of "chorus" to comment on the action of the novel. I don't know how I arrived at the sports-writer's name (I may have been trying to echo comically the common English term "blighter"), but at any rate that's how Sidney Slyter came into being, with his snake-like character embodied in the ugly sibilance of his name which was also related, of course, to Sybilline, the dark temptress in the novel.[10]

It is interesting that Slyter is an afterthought, for as Hawkes says, his "sleazy" character and gossipy column provide the best opportunity for "dramatizing the evil inherent" in the world of the novel. Hawkes summarizes the sportswriter this way: "Slyter's curiosity, his callow optimism, his lower middleclass English ego, his tasteless rhetoric, his vaguely obscene excitement in the presence of violence—all this makes him the most degrading and perversely appealing figure in the novel. I would say that in reporting the criminal actions of the novel, Slyter carries degradation to its final end." [11]

The significance of this description comes from Hawkes' insistence that Slyter, not Larry, is the most degraded character. Larry may be evil in the conventional sense—he is a gangster, a con man, and a murderer—but his evil comes naturally. To blame him for the violence and death is like blaming a snake for using its venom. Slyter, however, represents the establishment, the respectable world of honesty and fair play which abhors a fixed horse race. Yet the truth is that he blossoms on violence. He is a perverse man who seeks to have both his kicks and his safe reputation. The point is that we must be wary of Slyter's choral commentary. His columns precede each chapter and comment upon the action which is to follow, but he possesses only the bare facts. Cutting him off from the deeper truths, Hawkes makes Slyter an ironic commentator. Thus while the sports column may guide us to some

10. "John Hawkes: An Interview," p. 150.
11. Ibid., pp. 150–151.

of the facts, it does not reveal the significant meanings of those facts. It is still up to us to discern what really happens. No one, of course, can know the inner truths of the Bankses' tragedy unless he has access to their dreams. We as readers have that privilege, but to take advantage of it we must use Slyter's information carefully.

His certainty that he will give us the full story is what makes him so obnoxious. For example, he loves to predict and foreshadow. In his first column, which takes place during World War II, years before Michael and Margaret reach adulthood, he tells us that "one day there will be amusements everywhere, good fun for our mortality, and you'll whistle and flick your cigarette into an old crater's lip and with your young woman go off to a fancy flutter at the races." [12] Note that the tense is future, for it refers to the time after the war when life will be normal and when the horses will again run the Golden Bowl. One hundred pages and some fifteen years later, Slyter repeats this column: "—one day there will be amusements everywhere, good fun for our mortality. He has whistled; he has flicked his cigarette away; alone amidst women he has gone off to a fancy flutter at the races" (p. 163). The tense and the person change, for Slyter now refers specifically to Banks and his involvement with the fixed horse race. But while Slyter suspects a crime, he has no idea what lurks behind the scene, beneath the surface, which would urge a respectable man like Michael Banks to dirty his hands in such business. Unknown to Sidney Slyter, but by now obvious to us, Banks' "flutter" at the races has been anything but fancy, and his whistle and cigarette are about to be his last.

Such choral commentary is misleading, part of the demands which Hawkes places upon us. Possessing a wealth of factual information, Slyter is a parody of the newspaperman with connections. He has drinks with Sybilline and knows she is a tease; he suspects a mystery about Rock Castle; he tells us before the events that Cowles, the trainer, will be murdered and that Banks will be redeemed. But his connections, his facts, and his suspicions come

12. John Hawkes, *The Lime Twig* (New York: New Directions, 1961), p. 3. All further references will be in parentheses.

to nothing, and we laugh at him while he blusters about trying to uncover the missing pieces: "I want to know what's the matter with Mr. Banks. I want to know the truth about his horse. A case for the authorities without a doubt. And Sidney Slyter says: my prognostications are always right. . . . And somebody knew all this already, and it wasn't Mr. Banks. But who? Sidney Slyter wants to know" (pp. 80, 124).

Slyter's role is not a gratuitous red herring tossed into the novel to catch the unwary reader. The careless reader may indeed be led astray, but Hawkes makes much more of Slyter and his columns. As a voice from the real world, the sportswriter illustrates the shallowness of surface reality. He is baffled, as are some of Hawkes' readers, because he demands cause and effect, motivation, and a logical unraveling of events. He parallels the novel's policemen who poke into straw and inspect laundry labels in an attempt to uncover the "particulars" of the crime. But we know that the particulars will do them no good because the real truth resides in the dreams of Michael, Margaret, and Hencher, safely hidden from their probes. What makes Slyter so unbearable are his pious comments upon love and "life's pure anticipation" when, in fact, he knows nothing of purity. Nor can he ever measure up to Hencher's obsessive love or to the dreams of love which consume Michael. Ironically Slyter has his own dreams, but they reflect his egotism and are worthless. In a typical statement revealing his sense of self-importance, he compares the race he covers to the Olympic Games while proclaiming himself "God's silent servant." Indeed he pictures himself as a kind of Christ figure, one who shelters "God's own careless multitude." Such dreams do not need Hawkes' commentary—Slyter exposes himself.

The dreams of Hencher, Michael, and Margaret, however, are much more serious, for their power lures the dreamers away from reality. Like the role of Sidney Slyter, Hencher's first-person voice is an afterthought. Except for the opening chapter, which Hencher dominates, *The Lime Twig* is a third-person novel. Hencher's first-person voice acts as a prologue to the primary action of Michael Banks' dream, and it provides us with the information necessary to establish Banks' story in historical context. After reading Hencher's prologue, for example, we know that the rest of the novel centers around a lower middleclass, often grubby, residential area in post–World War II London. But while Hencher's first-person narrative is an afterthought, his character remains much more rounded than that of Sidney Slyter. On the one hand he participates in the dramatic action while Slyter merely observes. Secondly his entrapment in his dream and consequent violent death foreshadow the fate of Michael and Margaret, indirectly providing us with a more valuable commentary than any of Slyter's direct statements. Hawkes has said that Hencher "was a fully created voice that dramatized a character conceived in a certain depth." [13]

William Hencher's opening statements are among the most perceptive descriptions of loneliness in recent American fiction. Reading them we cannot help but sympathize with this fat old man no matter how grotesque his actions or ludicrous his comments. He has spent, perhaps wasted, most of his life with his mother, dragging their belongings from one cheap boarding house to another, the epitome of the devoted son because of his capacity for love: "Fifteen years of circling Dreary Station, she and I, of discovering footprints in the bathtub or a necktie hanging from the toilet chain, or seeing flecks of blood in the shaving glass. Fifteen years with mother, going from loft to loft in Highland Green, Pinky Road—twice in Violet Lane—" (p. 7). Never once does he complain. And when she dies, grotesquely burned while trying to save her cheap possessions from fire, he feels lonelier rather than free. His fondest memories are of their life together, but his descriptions of it tell us just how horrible and makeshift it was:

> I see her: it is just before the end; she is old; I see her through the red light of my glass of port. See the yellow hair, the eyes drying up in the corners. She laughs and jerks her head but the mouth is open, and that is what I see through the glass of port: the laughing lips drawn round a stopper of darkness and under

13. "John Hawkes: An Interview," p. 150.

the little wax chin a great silver fork with a slice of bleeding
meat that rises slowly, slowly, over the dead dimple in the wax,
past the sweat under the first lip, up to the level of her eyes so
she can take a look at it before she eats. And I wait for the
old girl to choke it down.   (p. 9)

The quotation's final sentence adds the comic touch, and we laugh
at a memory couched in such ludicrous details. But our laughter
does not ease our sense of Hencher's loneliness. For he is a lodger—
doomed to be one all his life—and his definition of himself reveals
how alone he has always been: "A lodger is a man who does not
forget the cold drafts, the snow on the window ledge, the feel of
his knees at night, the taste of a mutton chop in a room in which
he held his head all night" (p. 5).

This combination of love and loneliness, of devotion and the
need to dream, is best reflected in his memory of the boy and his
dog, for he uses that memory as an illustration of his own love.
Representing violated innocence, a consistent theme in Hawkes'
fiction, the boy has fresh whipping marks on his legs and a bruised
cheek. His shirt is ripped, and he plays in a place that is "empty
and wet and dead." Yet despite the absence of "fields, sunlight,
larks," this boy loves his puppy. And for Hencher the sight of the
boy and his dog amid the squalid setting and the obvious physical
abuse represents real love, for they seem to transcend pain and
deprivation. Hencher, in fact, models his love after the boy's when
he remembers "the boy with the poor dog in his arms and loving
his close scrutiny of the nicks in its ears. . . . Love is a long close
scrutiny like that. I loved Mother in the same way" (pp. 8–9).
There is an element of grotesque comedy here in his comparison,
for it inspires pictures of Hencher, devoted son, scrutinizing his
ancient mother's ears. But accusations of grotesqueness do not
bother Hencher, for he is, if nothing else, a lover, a man of such
obsessive devotion to those he loves that he will suffer death to
please them. His capacity for love is his one pride. To whistle a
tune the night through to his mother while waiting for "the kid-
neys on the sill to catch fire" is not a necessary duty but an act of

devotion which he is thankful to perform. As he remarks, "Heavy men are most often affectionate. And I, William Hencher, was a large man even then" (pp. 9–10).

Hencher's love, and his need to be loved, grow out of his loneliness. He speaks for all of the world's little people who endure grubby uneventful lives and who can only dream of passion and excitement. His first words in the novel are significant not only because they reveal his loneliness but also because they suggest the only choices which unimportant people like himself and Banks have. On the one hand he might be forced to rent his extra room: "Have you ever let lodgings in the winter? Was there a bed kept waiting, a corner room kept waiting for a gentleman? And have you ever hung a cardboard in the window and, just out of view yourself, watched to see which man would stop and read the hand-lettering on your sign." But on the other hand he might be the lodger: "Or perhaps you yourself were once the lonely lodger. Perhaps you crossed the bridges with the night crowds, listened to the tooting of the river boats and the sounds of shops closing on the far side" (p. 4). Not a very inspiring choice, and yet it describes the life which Michael Banks and Hencher now face—Banks as landlord of one-room flats, Hencher as his lodger. Confronted with such lives, they have no choice but to dream. For where else can they own race horses, pal around with people of means, participate in orgies? As Hencher says, "a man must take possession of a place if it is to be a home for the waiting out of dreams. So we lead our lives" (p. 27). Taking possession of Banks' flat, he, by fulfilling once again his role as the devoted son, shows Michael a way to make his dreams come true. But in both cases, landlord and lodger, terror and death result. Pursuing their dreams until fulfillment exceeds expectation, they pass beyond the point of no return.

Professor Rovit points out that we see *with* Hencher in the prologue instead of through him. We cannot use him as a vantage point because we become him and thus share his frustrated desires. This reduction of reader distance encourages sympathy. Hencher's eye for close detail and his tendency to expand the most trivial matter are the keys to his thwarted urge to have everything just so. His obsession is to live his life with the Bankses the way he did when mother was alive, to reshape the present in the outline of his past, to play again the role of loving son, to "scrutinize," as it were, in hopes of giving and receiving love. A sad, sordid character, Hencher nevertheless deserves our sympathy. Hawkes has said of him, "I thought of him as the seedbed of the [Bankses'] pathetic lives. To me Hencher is a thoroughly sympathetic character, though some readers would probably consider him (wrongly, I think) to be merely crippled, perverse, distasteful." [14]

Hencher sets his own dream in motion when he returns to Dreary Station some fifteen or twenty years after his mother's death. In truth he has never gotten away, for his memory is glued to this spot. Drawn back to that neighborhood because of his need to be again the devoted son, he goes directly to the same house, now owned by Michael Banks. Once he rents that room, once Michael lifts the sign out of the window, the dream, which will certainly bring pleasure before it kills them, begins to take shape: " 'My old girl died on these premises, Mr. Banks,' looking over his shoulder, feeling the wall, and he had to take me in. And then it was home again for William" (p. 17).

Hawkes' description of Hencher's first days with the Bankses is a masterful comic depiction of obsession. Paying in advance, Hencher claims one of the rooms as his while trying to smell the smoke of that old fire in the shabby walls. The first night he sits in bed smoking and thinking of mother. The second night he ventures as far as the hallway. On the third night, after he visits the lavatory, he decides "to do" something for Michael and Margaret. At this early point in the novel we have no idea what Hencher's plans for Michael are, and our curiosity is momentarily satisfied when he merely makes their breakfast. But while lulling us with Hencher's apparently generous act, Hawkes also encourages our suspicions about his motives. For an obsession like Hencher's will not rest satisfied with such trivial gestures as serving breakfast. His loneliness has been so acute, his need for love so great, and his urge to be a son again so relentless that we cannot help but expect

14. Ibid., pp. 151–152.

a significant reaction now that his years of frustration are about to be eased. Thus when Hencher stands outside the bedroom of Michael and Margaret, thinking of their clasped hands, and wondering what he might do for them, we are suspicious of his plans. He decides that night what he will do, but we are not told. We are, in fact, never told explicitly. But Hencher feels so indebted to the Bankses for what he thinks is their aid in helping him fulfill his dream that we soon suspect he will do the same for them. The Bankses will replace mother as his object of fanatical love, and he will help make their own dreams come true. The prologue ends ritualistically with Hencher outside their bedroom door at three in the morning trying to give the Bankses a sense of his own past while he repudiates his mother's memory:

> Or it is 3 or 4 A. M. and I turn the key, turn the knob, avoid the empty goldfish bowl that catches the glitter off the street, feel the skin of my shoes going down the hallway to their door. I stand whispering our history before that door and slowly, so slowly, I step behind the screen in my own dark room and then, on the edge of the bed and sighing, start peeling the elastic sleeves off my thighs. . . . Can I help but smile? I can get along without you, Mother.   (p. 28)

With this scene, Hencher's prologue ends, and the emphasis shifts to Michael and Margaret. But more importantly, the trap has been set, the twig has been limed, and Banks' repressed dreams are about to be freed. This paradox of entrapment and freedom is significant: Michael's life is so uneventful that he is forced to dream; yet if his dreams come true he will be as helpless as a trapped bird. He represses his dreams out of fear, yet he dreams more and more out of longing. Significantly Hencher hears "a little bird trying to sing" when he returns from his ritual outside of the bedroom door. The bird will finally sing—as will its mate— only when the Bankses' dreams are fulfilled, but at that moment the birds will be in the real world outside of the dreams. Michael and Margaret, not the birds, will be limed.

The motivation for the dreams of Hencher and the Bankses is love, and *The Lime Twig* is indeed a love story. But Hawkes suggests that when dreams complicate love, it gives way to fear, is then degraded into lust and sadism, and finally finds gratification only in death. Leslie Fiedler's comment on the mixture of love and terror in this novel is well known: "It is not so much that love succumbs to terror which obsesses Hawkes as the fact that love breeding terror is itself the final terror." [15] Disagreeing slightly, Professor Rovit suggests that love does not breed terror in Hawkes' novels as much as it encourages "the inhibiting soil of its own frustrations; and with these frustrations, the means to subvert them in ways that lead inexorably to the death of love itself." [16] The point is that in *The Lime Twig* love prompts horrible death. Hencher, Michael, and Margaret all receive what they long for. The Bankses, especially, subconsciously yearn for an erotic death, and they get it, while Larry and the gangsters plan the deaths of others and survive. In either case love as a means to brighten dingy lives is thwarted.

Hawkes has said that he borrowed the name Michael Banks from the Mary Poppins stories to suggest "England's anonymous post-war youth." "I saw post-war England itself as the spiritless, degraded landscape of the modern world, in this case dominated by the destructive fatality of the gambling syndicate." Hawkes also sees the drabness which threatens to stifle Banks as a direct result of the war. As an "innocent spawn" of World War II, Banks needs Hencher, who was mature during the war, to dramatize wartime England for him (and for the reader), thus "providing a kind of historical consciousness for characters who had none of their own." [17] Linked through Hencher to the destructive past, and caught in the sterile present which Hawkes says results from the war, the Bankses have no choice but to dream if they are to hope for anything better. In his near madness Hencher intuits that their needs reside in fantasies. For when he brings them breakfast for the first time, he pauses before waking them to comment upon their dreams. Note his compulsion to help:

15. Fiedler, "The Pleasures of John Hawkes," p. xi.
16. Rovit, "The Fiction of John Hawkes," p. 157.
17. "John Hawkes: An Interview," p. 151.

Behind each silent face was the dream that would collect slack
shadows and tissues and muscles into some first mood for the
day. Could I not blow smiles onto their nameless lips, could I
not force apart those lips with kissing? . . . For a moment the
vague restless dreams merely went faster beneath those two faces.
Then stopped suddenly, quite fixed in pain. Then both at once
they opened their eyes.   (p. 26)

Hencher suspects that the Bankses dream of love—he would
force open their lips with kisses. But Michael's dreams go deeper
than smiles and kisses. In his fantasies, he longs to have sexual
mastery over Margaret, to be a kind of phallic god to his mousy
wife. Their bed is one of "ordinary" down and ticking, but it has
"the course of dreams mapped on the coverlet." He is so frustrated
that he embraces two of Margaret's "hanging and scratchy" dresses
when she leaves for her fortnightly shopping. Margaret wears a
symbolic closed safety pin beneath her skirt, and Banks can open
it only in his dream. In a startling paragraph of foreshadowing,
the significance of which is not apparent until we finish the novel,
Hawkes tells us all of the sounds Banks would like to hear. He
longs to hear "tugs and double-deckers and boys crying the news.
Perhaps the smashing of a piece of furniture. Anything" (p. 31).
More significantly the darting of a small bird makes him wish for
its sound. Incredibly enough he will hear all of these sounds once
he is trapped within his dream, only the events will be multiplied
beyond his control. One piece of furniture, for example, will not
be smashed—the thugs will obliterate his entire flat, Margaret will
be beaten to death, and Banks will be crushed by the race horse
Rock Castle. But Michael does not know this, of course. Thus his
frustration mounts when he compares the exciting sounds he longs
for with the banality of Margaret's routine: "But in the silence of
the flat's close and ordinary little bedroom he hears again all the
soft timid sounds she made before setting off to market" (p. 31).
With the words "ordinary" and "timid" Hawkes pinpoints the
frustration.

Margaret is well aware of Michael's fantasy, for their dreams
seem to mingle. The crucial difference, however, is that her worst
dream—to find Michael gone one day—is the converse of his best—

to escape into a sexual wonderland. They both know that sex, violence, the horse, and destruction are all wrapped up in their reverie. Note how Hawkes joins the phallic symbol of the stallion with the smashing that Banks longs to hear:

> Knowing how much she feared his dreams: knowing that her own worst dream was one day to find him gone, overdue minute by minute some late afternoon until the inexplicable absence of him became a certainty; knowing that his own worst dream, and best, was of a horse which was itself the flesh of all violent dreams; knowing this dream, that the horse was in their sitting room . . . in the middle of the floor, the tall upright shape of the horse draped from head to tail in an enormous sheet that falls over the eyes and hangs down stiffly from the silver jaw; knowing the horse on sight and listening while it raises one shadowed hoof on the end of a silver thread of foreleg and drives down the hoof to splinter in a single crash one plank of that empty Dreary Station floor.   (p. 33)

Michael knows the horse on sight because he has dreamed of it. Traditionally the horse has been used in a negative sense to mean "a confused fantasy." [18] The raised hoof smashing all beneath it suggests not only his illusion of absolute sexual power but also his longing that this power will give him the strength to destroy his dull life, "the empty Dreary Station floor." Michael fails to realize that his obsession to smash his loneliness and thus clear the way for escape into his dreamworld amounts to his death warrant, for without his routine reality he ceases to exist. The dull life with ordinary, timid Margaret *is* Michael Banks; take away that life and he is destroyed. His sexual fantasies cover up an unconscious death wish.

Fat, old Hencher serves as their fairy godfather, for he knows where Michael can get a race horse. During the war Hencher knew Larry and his gang as "the Captain" and his men, and it is through Larry that he conceives the plan to steal Rock Castle. Hencher could not care less about the horse, but he longs "to do something"

---

18. The definition is Plato's. I am grateful to Jerrie Ashmore Stewart, a former student, who gave me this information. See Harold Bayley, *The Lost Language of Symbolism* (New York: Barnes and Noble, 1968), 2:37.

for the Bankses. So in the name of love he brings Michael in on the deal, never suspecting the resulting violence, but knowing that Michael's fantasies are somehow wrapped up in owning a horse. Choosing Margaret's shopping day as the moment to pursue his dream, Michael sets off with Hencher to meet the horse. On board the *Artemis*, a small tourist boat, Banks tries to keep his fantasies under control. His "safe" dream includes laughter, Banks and Hencher as stowaways, "an excursion life," no luggage, no destination, and a smoke with some girl. But Michael longs for more excitement, and his safe dream soon gives way to the thought that "there was better than this in wait for him, something much better than this" (p. 36).

Naming the excursion boat *Artemis* is a conscious irony on Hawkes' part. Associated with the goddess Diana, Artemis symbolizes virginity and purity, the very qualities Michael hopes to cast off. Hawkes calls attention to the "terrible" irony in the fact that the *Artemis* is carrying Banks away from chastity.[19] As the *Artemis* moves him closer to Rock Castle and to the fulfillment of his dreams of illicit love, it widens the distance between him and ordinary Margaret. He is like a little boy showing off to his girl friend, for as he meets the gang of thugs he thinks, *"She ought to see her hubby now. She ought to see me now"* (p. 47).

Hawkes develops the sense of unreality when Michael and Hencher near their destination. Using fog, haze, rats, and filth, he suggests the fuzziness of Banks' dreamworld. The landing on which they wait for the horse seems unreal because it is greasy to the touch and covered with scum. Such surroundings are foreign to Michael, especially when he moves his hands and feels rat fur. Hawkes' use of fog best illustrates this eerieness, for with it he expresses the sense of distorted reality which Banks feels when his dream arrives in the form of Rock Castle. The texture and density of the fog are so thick that his senses are confounded. Losing contact with his immediate setting, he can do no more than try to listen for the expected barge. Significantly, he suspects that his

19. "John Hawkes on His Novels: An Interview with John Graham," *Massachusetts Review*, 7 (Summer 1966), 454.

fate, undetermined though it is, will emerge from the fog. Note how he expects both to find and lose what he dreams of in the same thick haze:

> Fog of course and he should have expected it, should have carried a torch. Yet, whatever was to come his way would come, he knew, like this—slowly and out of a thick fog. Accidents, meetings unexpected, a figure emerging to put its arms about him: where to discover everything he dreamed of except in a fog. And, thinking of slippery corners, skin suddenly bruised, grappling hooks going blindly through the water: where to lose it all if not in the same white fog.   (pp. 44–45)

This quotation foreshadows much of what Banks is to suffer. Accidents and unexpected meetings will occur. Several women will emerge to embrace him, and Margaret's skin will be brutally bruised. But whereas it is all hazy and undefined in Banks' imagination, the unexpected will become clear and specific once the dream materializes and he is forced to confront it. Terror results when we realize that he can no longer cut off the dream. It is as if Michael cautiously sticks out his hand toward the fog, only to be jerked into the midst of it with no hope of escape. When the dream arrives in the form of the horse, his alienation from his dull but safe reality increases: "it was not Wednesday at all, only a time slipped off its cycle with hours and darkness never to be accounted for" (p. 49). Notations of time, distinct beginnings and endings, remain part of the real world.

One reason why Michael loses his sense of time is that the unlooked for violence upsets his bearings. He has imagined the horse smashing the floor of his flat, but never in his wildest dreams has he expected the brutality which soon follows. In the masterful scene describing the unloading of Rock Castle, Hawkes creates an atmosphere of latent violence. This scene parallels an earlier one in which Hencher watches a bomber silently crash into his London district. The airplane's descent seems gentle, as if in slow motion, and the destruction we expect never happens. A similar eeriness characterizes the unloading scene, but the suggestions of dream and violence are even stronger. The horse remains immobile, fixed in the posture of "rigorous sleep." Its silver coat gleams with "the colorless fluid of some ghostly libation" and its head smells of "a violence that was his own." And as Hencher watches Rock Castle float down to them from above, he describes his feelings in such a way that he not only ties up this moment with his memory of the bomber but also predicts the potency of the horse's strength: "Ever see them lift the bombs out of the craters? . . . something to see, men at a job like that and fishing up a live bomb big enough to blow a cathedral to the ground" (p. 51).

The arrival of the horse signals the appearance of Michael's lime twig. The practice of liming to ensnare a bird is medieval, but the image spans English literature from *Troilus and Criseyde* through Sir Thomas Wyatt's lyrics, *Twelfth Night*, *Comus*, John Donne's "Satyre II," William Wordsworth's "Merry, Merry England," and Coleridge's "This Lime-Tree Bower My Prison." As the victim of an archetype, Michael Banks is in good company, but he is not the only trapped bird. The other characters also suffer best and worst dreams. As Sidney Slyter says, any one of us could experience the same "psychic paradox" in which our best dream is the fulfillment of all of our shadowy, unadmitted desires, and our worst dream is the unexpected which would accompany the fleshing out of our fantasies.

Margaret's best dream is of a passionate love shared with Banks, but she is thwarted as much by her sense of inferiority as by his inadequacy. After she hears a child's cry and after Michael snaps off the light, she dreams "of the crostics and, in the dark, men with numbers wrapped round their fingers would feel her legs, or she would lie with an obscure member of the government on a leather couch, trying to remember and all the while begging for his name" (p. 68). But Margaret's worst dreams are of the violence and pain which come with her fantasies and which she envisions whenever she fears the loss of Michael. Her bad dreams are full of violated innocence, of particularly unnerving illusions like children being crushed by trains while toads hop off the bodies. Convinced that there is "nothing sweet for her," she has always denied her dreams.

She longs for love but is afraid to let herself go. Thus while Michael actively seeks his dream because of frustration, Margaret will be passively pulled into her fantasy because of fear. Repressing her femininity, she dodges all invitations to love though she retains the memory of each possibility. "Once the madame of a frock shop had tried to dress her in pink." But at the last moment Margaret repudiates the combination of herself and pink as outrageous. "Once an Italian barber had tried to kiss her," but she escapes in time. "Once Michael had given her an orchid preserved in a glass ball," but she has since misplaced it. "How horrible she felt in pink; how horrible the touch of the barber's lips; how heavy was the glassed orchid on her breast" (p. 65).

Hencher's unexpected death, kicked to a pulp by Rock Castle, forces Margaret into her worst dream, for with this death Michael knows he will not be returning home. Hearing mortuary bells at the moment of Hencher's death, Margaret thinks of evenings at home with Banks. With a sure comic touch, Hawkes summarizes in one of Margaret's memories the reasons for the Bankses' dreams of love: "When Banks had first kissed her, touching the arm that was only an arm, the cheek that was only a cheek, he had turned away to find a hair in his mouth" (p. 68). Plain Margaret is just that—ordinary—a girl with no other life than the one she has with Michael. No excitement for her, no laughter, no drinks at a bar. Thus when Banks telephones following Hencher's death and instructs her to meet him, she agrees for Michael's sake. Larry, of course, sets up the meeting, for he does not want her to inform the police about Michael's absence. Although Margaret is unaware that Michael is now the lure for her as Rock Castle is for him, her dream of what lies ahead foreshadows her beating by Thick. Note how brown contrasts with her fear of pink: "She was Banks' wife by the law, she was Margaret, and if the men ever did get hold of her and go at her with their truncheons or knives or knuckles, she would still be merely Margaret with a dress and a brown shoe, still be only a girl of twenty-five with a deep wave in her hair" (p. 70). She relies on her ordinariness to protect her, to help her repress the sexual suggestions of her dreams, but, significantly, when she boards the train with Larry's mistress Dora, the safety pin under her skirt is unsnapped.

Sitting in the train, her brown skirt pulled down to cover her "anonymous" knees and calves, Margaret clutches a pink ticket. She is on her way to romance but of a far different kind from that of the Italian barber. Hawkes encourages the suspense of the pulp thriller, for at this point we do not know for certain that Margaret is a prisoner. Little Dora's identity is not quite explicit, and we are not sure why Michael has instructed Margaret to take the train. The fog and haze metaphorically cover our eyes too, but not so much that we are denied a glimpse here, a hint there. But while Hawkes withholds the information for a while, he associates Margaret with enough violent images to suggest the dream of terror which she is about to enter. Visions of dead children crushed under trains are joined by her view of a dead wasp suspended on the coach window. The coach smells of darkness, and the baggage car carries coffins. Larry completely fools her, for she decides that he is gentle enough to "touch a woman's breast in public easily, with propriety, offending no one" (p. 74). But we are not fooled, for when she leaves the train guarded by Larry and Little Dora, she hears the mortuary bells again. She also envisions a "shape that might have been a murdered horse," and she imagines the oval of roses in the race course as a place in which men are murdered while torn-up stubs flutter by. What makes it all so terrifying is that these dreams will come true. And our suspicions that latent violence boils under the surface of Margaret's comic reaction to Larry's "gentleness" are confirmed when Hawkes springs on us without comment the fact that Margaret is indeed a prisoner, dressed in only a white hospital gown, watched over by Dora and Thick. As readers we are disturbed because we carry similar fantasies. Participating in their nightmares as we read, we tend to go beyond sympathy to identify with the Bankses' plight. Margaret and Michael never mention their dreams to each other, but each is aware of the other's longings. And like them we fear the potential but as yet submerged power of our deepest desires.

They are now trapped like the medieval birds: he literally tastes lime when he climbs into the horse van, and she tastes green when she first sees the race track. Hawkes insists all along upon the innocence of these impoverished souls. Caught in a banal daily routine, they have no recourse except to dream. They are the kind of innocents who are born to be destroyed by those who ruthlessly victimize innocence. But we want to remember that *The Lime Twig* is a sort of love story, and that even Larry the victimizer has his dream of love. Late in the novel, when the race is about to begin, Larry straightens his green sun glasses and says to Little Dora, "A bit of marriage, eh? And then a ship, trees with limes on the branches, niggers to pull us round the streets, the Americas—a proper cruise, plenty of time at the bar, no gunplay or nags. Perhaps a child or two, who knows?" (p. 165). The lime image, of course, tells us that he will be snared one day too, but for the moment he remains untouchable. His bulletproof vest, his reliance on sheer force, and his complete dominance of the gang establish him as the perfect character for the job of controlling nightmares. Hencher may lead a willing Michael Banks into a dream-world, but once there Larry grabs control. Like Zizendorf in *The Cannibal* and Miranda in *Second Skin*, Larry manipulates the nightmares of his victims so that in the process of fulfilling the dream he destroys the dreamer.

Yet Larry is more important as the personification of the Bankses' dreams of sexual ecstasy than as a victimizer. The phallic thrust which Michael longs for first takes shape in his fantasy of owning a stallion. But that fantasy assumes human form in Larry, and Hawkes carefully establishes the connection between the gangster and Rock Castle: "The man was big, heavy as a horse cart of stone; there was not a wrinkle in his trenchcoat over the shoulders, his chest was that of a boxer" (p. 73). This is how he first appears to Margaret, when she imaginatively grants him permission to touch her breast, but she fails to make the connection between his shape and Michael's image of the horse. Hawkes sees Larry in two ways: as a parody of the tough guy in the dime thriller, "Larry the Limousine," and as a godlike figure of destructive power, something larger than life, that part of Banks' dream which he cannot control.[20] Larry personifies Margaret's perfect lover and, more importantly, Michael's ideal conception of himself. Several times she refers to the thug as an angel, and Banks envies the man who can push around police inspectors, ignore the "killing of the kids," and warn knowingly, "There's power in this world you never dreamed of" (p. 147).

This power is indeed Michael's problem, for he generates enough in his own fantasy to kill Hencher, Cowles, Monica, Margaret, and himself. Banks himself, not Larry, is his own worst enemy. His dull lonely real life may encourage dreams which reel out of control, but he has unconsciously willed the disaster. What begins as the fulfillment of fantasy terminates in terror. Although he first tastes lime immediately before Hencher's death, he does not feel personally threatened until he realizes he is trapped. Hawkes does not pinpoint the exact moment of Michael's realization, but he does give us a superbly comic scene describing Banks' first serious attempt to escape by hiding in the filthy men's room underneath the grandstand. Crouching at the base of toilets beside the light green walls, he tries to whistle up his courage. But he is not a whistler, and the words "barrels of fun" going around in his head soon give way to memories of a humorous obituary he had once read of a man who died on a toilet—from fear. While remembering how he could never "bring himself to touch the copper ball, slime-covered, gently breathing, that lay in the bottom of a toilet tank," he hears footsteps. Naturally he is recaptured—the limed bird does not escape—and the three men who find and threaten him with pellet bombs become "the triangle of his dreams, the situation he dreaded at the sound of sirens" (p. 94). Sitting on a piece of broken toilet, his eyes half shut, he returns to the "green world."

The line of demarcation between reality and the lime-green world of the dream is often fuzzy. But while Hawkes avoids mention of an explicit jumping-off point, he takes pains to let us know when the Bankses' transition to the dream is complete. Michael

20. Ibid., p. 455.

first fears that he will not be going home again when Hencher dies. Yet through Margaret he maintains a connection with reality even though he does not know that she is also a prisoner. Following his thwarted effort to escape, however, Larry severs the final links between the dream and reality, sealing the Bankses forever in their fantasies. He orders Thick and Sparrow to the flat in Dreary Station where a scene of extraordinary destruction takes place. Bolting the door, the two thugs literally destroy everything in the apartment. They strip the houseplants, quietly break the china in towels, and cut the stuffing away from furniture before sawing the wood into "handy" lengths:

> Bare walls, bare floors, four empty rooms containing no scrap of paper, no figured piece of jewelry or elastic garment, no handwriting specimen by which the identity of the former occupants could be known: it was a good job, a real smashing; and at dusk, on a heath just twenty miles from Aldington, they stopped and dumped the contents of the van into a quagmire round which the frogs were croaking.   (p. 102)

Their real life symbolically smashed, Banks and Margaret cease to exist in the surface world. Michael's longing to personify the power of a race horse comes true when he meets his ideal self in Larry.

Now permanently ensnared, he unexpectedly spies Margaret trying to escape. Because this is the first time he has thought of his wife since instructing her to take the train, his response is comically inappropriate. "My God, what have they done to Margaret," he wonders as he watches her attempt to sneak away while disguised in an enormous hat and tassled gown so large it drags the ground. Note that his concern is not for Margaret's safety or whereabouts, but for the way she is dressed: "A dress from another age, too large, too old, Margaret clothed in an old tan garden gown and lost. 'She's not yet thirty,' he thought, shoving, using his elbow, 'where's their decency?' " (p. 106). When Margaret is suddenly pulled away into the crowd, Banks feels panic for the first time.

Michael is, however, too caught up in the promise of his dream to worry about Margaret. Rock Castle is the original lime twig which traps him. Once caught, Larry's other girl Sybilline is the lure to keep him ensnared by satisfying his wildest erotic fantasies. The life she represents contrasts totally with his dull routine. She is the lady of mysterious messages: "Sybilline's in the Pavilion"; of sexual knowhow: "Don't you know what eggs are good for, Michael?"; and of the good time: she has come to the races for "rum, a toss, a look through a fellow's binoculars." Drinking with her, he forgets that he is caught in a situation full of terror. Once again he allows his fantasies to blot out the unsatisfactory, his fear in the men's room, Hencher's death, his panic when seeing Margaret. Drinking with Syb, he thinks not of Cowles' murder nor of the depressing flat in Dreary Station but of "a love note he had written at the age of twelve when the city was on fire. . . . In his arms she was like the women he had thought of coming out of comfort rooms" (p. 121).

Sybilline personifies Michael's ideal conception of Margaret. The opposite of a dull wife who thinks pink too daring, Syb has red hair, "like the orange of an African bird" studded with pinkish pearls, and she loves pink gin drinks. Margaret smiles shyly, relying on her innocence to protect her, while in Sybilline's voice Banks detects "laughter, motor cars and lovely moonlit trees, beds and silk stockings in the middle of the floor" (p. 120). Margaret jerks her skirt over her knees, but Syb teaches him to dance. Margaret is only twenty-five, but acts the spinster, while Syb gives the illusion of first love despite her sexual experience: "that was the fine thing about Sybilline, the way she could kiss and play and let her spangles fall, keep track of all the chemistry and her good time, and yet be sighing, sighing like a young girl in love" (p. 144). Like all of Michael's erotic fantasies, this one is full of warnings, but he is too far gone to resist the lure. He ignores the fact that her soft lips are also venereal.

Sybilline makes good her promise at least three times and another woman, the widow, at least once. Michael's confidence builds to ludicrous proportions, and he begins to swagger like the stud he longs to be. Ready to take up any prospect of sex, he responds to the news that another lady wants to see him with "I should imagine so." When this lady turns out to be his next door neighbor Annie, his visions are complete—his dream girl gives herself to him. Note the use of fog, timelessness, and silver, Rock Castle's color, to suggest the dream: "She was twenty years old and timeless . . . at three o'clock in the morning she was a girl he had seen through windows in several dreams unremembered, unconfessed, the age of twenty that never passes but lingers in the silvering of the trees and rising fogs" (p. 155). He is, to quote Leslie Fiedler, "screwed silly."

But when Michael leaves Annie to join the gang downstairs, his dreams of sexual mastery come tumbling down. Sporting a fresh bruise from Larry for being too good to Michael, Sybilline clings to Larry's arm while Little Dora strips him to the waist. When they marvel at Larry's dazzling torso, Banks can do no more than look away, a defeated man. Only now does Hawkes make explicit the connection between the Bankses tangled within their dreams and birds trapped on a lime twig. As dawn approaches, Banks thinks, "Even two oven tits may be snared and separated in such a dawn. He listened, turned his head under the shadows, and reflected that the little bird was fagged. And he could feel the wet light rising round all the broken doors . . . himself fagged and tasteless as the bird on the sick bough" (p. 159). Fulfilled but unsatisfied, Michael's dream lures him to his death.

Though in another part of the house, Margaret has undergone a similar kind of violent fulfillment. She, too, is permanently cut off from reality when Thick burns her clothes and identification card. Trapped within her fantasies, she is easy prey for the uncontrollable horrors which swiftly follow. Thick's beating of Margaret is probably the novel's best known scene. Maintaining his metaphor of two oven tits snared and separated, Hawkes coordinates Margaret's beating with Michael's sexual satiation—both begin at two a.m. But whereas Michael's exploits are ironic—the would-be seducer being seduced—Margaret's experience explodes in unbearable pain. An expert at his job, Thick uses his rubber truncheon professionally and proudly, rupturing her insides without leaving marks. With each hit he draws the truncheon across her loins and abdomen before raising it to swing once more. "It made a sound like a dead bird falling to empty field." Robert Scholes defends the incredible violence of this scene against charges of morbidness and of excessive brutality by pointing out what the careful reader should readily see—that Margaret's physical pain does not interest Hawkes as much as "her situation as helpless victim." [21] This observation is certainly valid, one which those who dismiss Hawkes as no more than a purveyor of senseless violence need to consider. By stressing Margaret's isolation rather than the potentially gory details, he impresses upon us her plight as victim. No help can possibly arrive in the nick of time. After all, she is trapped within her own dream.

But what makes this scene so memorable is the successful mixture of horror and humor. Hawkes is just as interested in Margaret's inappropriate response to her beating and in the comic effect which her unexpected response produces. The violence is so far removed from her past experiences, so unbelievable, that she does not know how to handle it. Though bound by rope and hemorrhaging to death, she humorously decides that the position she is tied in is good for her figure. She expects that she is badly hurt, but she is more upset because she lacks a free hand with which to rub her injured parts. She suspects that there "is an enormous penalty" for what has been done to her, but she cannot think what it could be. Her funniest response is her most consistent: the beating is terrible mostly because "it was something they couldn't even show in films." No matter how much she accepts the terror—as if she has any choice—she knows it is "something they couldn't show in films. What a sight if they flashed this view of herself on the screen of the old Victoria Hall where she had seen a few pictures with Michael. What a view of shame. She had always dressed in more modest brown, bought the more modest cod, prayed for modesty, desired it. Now she was hurt—badly hurt, she expected" (pp. 129–130). This inappropriate response to the experience, not

21. Robert Scholes, *The Fabulators* (New York: Oxford University Press, 1967), p. 84.

the experience itself, makes the scene comic, and the humor balances the violence.

This scene perfectly illustrates the victim-victimizer theme which is apparent in so much of Hawkes' fiction. Margaret and Michael unconsciously long for their deaths as the only limitation to their fantasies. Margaret has dreamed of her violation, has even craved it, so that she turns Thick's beating into a sexual attack to satisfy her own repressed lust. When he nudges her thigh with the truncheon, she makes no effort to pull her leg away. When he moves in for the kill, she notes that he is wearing his trousers with the two top buttons open. The horror hits us when we realize that Thick is no more than a means to the end of her final gratification, an instrument to make her dreams come true. His beating encourages her erotic fantasies of intercourse with a phallic god, an illusion which literally happens when Larry rapes her. Margaret sees an angel's whiteness on Larry's face when he approaches her, and she notes how all of his gestures are considerate, calm, and careful. Even though he purposely cuts her wrists when he slashes Thick's ropes, she takes a "little" pleasure in it. Larry rapes her in retaliation for Michael's overindulgence with Sybilline. Yet with the rape, Michael and Margaret metaphorically experience the kind of sexual fulfillment with each other which they have been unable to feel in their real lives. An ideal, phallic Michael finally makes love to a captured but willing Margaret in a dream world with all of the sadism we associate with erotic fantasies. The safety pin which Margaret locks under her skirt when she goes shopping and which she feels pull free on the train is completely open following Michael's orgy. She finally approaches Michael's ideal woman, sexually loose and available. Margaret becomes Sybilline, and Michael becomes Thick and Larry. She may be a victim of their violence, but Thick and Larry are just as victimized by her longings.

The pink ticket has taken her to the lime-green room in Aldington where she can no longer be "merely Margaret with a dress and a brown shoe." She calls on her innocence to protect her, but

Hawkes draws a clear parallel between Margaret and Sybilline's child Monica. As Margaret personifies innocence in the real world, so Monica, dressed in green, is innocence in the dream. But as Margaret's innocence is violated in her fantasy world, so Monica's is shattered by nightmare at night. Monica suffers nightmares while Thick beats Margaret, and their screams mingle together:

> But at night there were horrors. At night [Monica] sweated her innocence and, bolting up in her shift, declared she'd been swimming in the petrol tank of a lorry, or watching three rubber dolls smartly burning, or sitting inside a great rubber tire and rolling down a steep cobbled hill in the darkness. And Margaret remembered these dreams. Now Margaret's sobs and Monica's screams commenced together and continued together, variants of a single sound, screaming and weeping mingled.   (p. 132)

Hawkes suggests their identification with the statement that Margaret somehow remembers Monica's dreams. Because both Margaret and Michael cling to childhood memories as a possible refuge for innocence, they remember the past as they sink deeper into their illusions. We recall that when drinking with Sybilline, Banks thinks not of the series of terrors he has encountered but of a love note he wrote at age twelve. Similarly, Margaret remembers after the beating that she had been a docile child. But there are no sanctuaries in this novel, and certainly not that of childhood. On the train to Aldington, Margaret tells Little Dora that she does not recall much of her youth. But through her identification with Monica's nightmares, she participates in a childhood which she had thought to be free from fear. Harmless memories turn out to be deadly dreams in Margaret's fantasy, and she discovers that past reality shapes her present illusions. For example, her dreams of unknown men feeling her legs and of her cousin dressed in a white hospital gown during an operation on the abdomen come true in unexpected ways. Her vision of children being crushed by trains materialize when the constable shoots Monica. When we link these suggestions to the fact that Margaret does remember Monica's dreams, we see that Monica personifies that image of childhood innocence which Margaret hopes will save her. Hawkes hints that

Monica's nightmares are Margaret's own from childhood. Thus, the child must be killed because Margaret is about to die.

Monica's murder gives Banks his first chance to try to break free from the snare. The murder, which occurs while Larry rapes Margaret and immediately after Michael finishes with Annie, is like a bucket of cold water in Michael's face. He "recognizes" the child as someone who had always been "coming over a bridge for him." Attacking the constable, he at least protests the killing and regains some of his humanity. But he is not ready to awaken fully. The constable knocks him unconscious, and he falls back into his vision of jolly evenings with Syb. Only when he repudiates Rock Castle can he free himself forever. He has no idea what has happened to Margaret, but he now knows that he has betrayed both himself and her. Whispering his wife's name as the race begins, he dashes out onto the green in an effort to strike down the horse. Intent on bringing "wreckage to horses and little crouching men," Michael is, as Hawkes pointedly characterizes him, "small, yet beyond elimination." The crowd screams, and in a wonderfully controlled account of a man meeting a violent dream with violence, Hawkes describes Michael's act of redemption:

> He was running in final stride, the greatest spread of legs, red-
> ness coming across the eyes, the pace so fast that it ceases to be
> motion, but at its peak becomes the long downhill deathless
> gliding of a dream until the arms are out, the head thrown back,
> and the runner is falling as he was falling and waving his arm
> at Rock Castle's onrushing silver shape, at Rock Castle who was
> about to run him down and fall.   (p. 171)

We know that the dream is over because Michael is once again aware of time. When he and Hencher first meet the horse arriving on the barge, time is suspended. At the race track the clock is covered with canvas. But when Banks dashes onto the track, "the green, the suspended time was gone" (p. 170).

The black ending of *The Lime Twig* is obvious. But what is not as clear is that both the comedy of the ending and the success of Michael's attempt to redeem himself encourage the sympathy we have felt all along for these damned characters. When Banks dies crushed beneath Rock Castle, the dreamworld literally collapses but in a comic way because the track is strewn with fallen horses and men. Larry's plan to marry Dora among the lime trees in the Americas is also foiled since he will not have the money for the trip. Michael atones for his betrayal by destroying the dream which, because it has becomes his reality, necessitates his own death. In doing so he shatters what Hawkes calls the "Golden Bowl of earthly pleasure." [22]

His successful act of redemption is, nevertheless, a hopeless act. For while he repudiates the evil when he jumps in front of the horse, he is still a victim of that evil in which he has so willingly participated. Hawkes denies the possibility of conventional poetic justice in this topsy-turvy world where dreams come true with such violent results. Banks' sacrifice may redeem him, but he, Margaret, Hencher, Monica, and Cowles are all dead. Larry and the gang still escape, and the police of the real world fumble about ineffectively in search for the facts of the case, unaware that those facts are buried in the dreams of Hencher, Banks, and Margaret. Yet it is a mistake to term Michael's death meaningless and to call Larry triumphant at the end as Charles Matthews does.[23] The ending may not suggest hope, for Hawkes himself admits that he is "reluctant to argue too strongly for the necessity of hope." [24] But it is still an atonement for Banks. He does not commit suicide; he redeems himself through sacrifice—certainly not a meaningless act. Nor does Larry triumph. His plan fails because he is identified with the horse. When Rock Castle goes down, Larry's scheme falls too. He may go scot free, but he is not victorious.

The only possibility of hope which Hawkes grants comes from the novel's "general pairing off of sensual and destructive experiences," from the "fictional rhythm itself." [25] He says that he is leery of the theological meaning of Banks' redemption because he is not a religious writer. But insofar as Michael makes amends for

22. "John Hawkes: An Interview," p. 154.
23. Charles Matthews, "The Destructive Vision of John Hawkes," *Critique*, 6 (Fall 1963), 51.
24. "John Hawkes: An Interview," p. 155.
25. Ibid., pp. 154–155.

his mistake, he is redeemed: "And I suppose that despite of all my interest in evil, all my belief in the terrifying existence of Satanism in the world, I guess by the end of that novel I somehow intuitively must have felt the human and artistic need to arrive at a resolution which would be somehow redemptive." Hawkes absolves Banks of his fatal error because Michael is not just a pawn of the gang. Banks follows his own dream willingly, though it destroys him. "And he had to die. And I take that to be a very sympathetic treatment of his death and an act of great power. Because to stop that great mythic race horse, Rock Castle, is really quite a feat." [26] Sidney Slyter has pondered the same things: "But what power, force, justice, slender hand or sacrifice can stop Rock Castle, halt Rock Castle's progress now? Sidney Slyter doesn't know" (p. 140). Slyter may not know, but we do. The force is sacrifice, and Michael Banks meets the test. Quoting from Djuna Barnes' masterpiece *Nightwood*, Hawkes clarifies his connection of dream and destruction: "When a long lie comes up, sometimes it is a beauty; when it drops into dissolution, into drugs and drink, into disease and death, it has a singular and terrible attraction." [27] Hencher, Michael, and Margaret are drawn to this terrible attraction, and by implication any one of us can be too.

The illusion of dream is supported in this novel by the recurrence of image. Things appear, disappear, and reappear with no apparent explanation, just as they do in dreams, and often in distorted or oddly shaped form. The casual reports of nonhuman death, for example, crop up here and there, carefully placed by Hawkes to enhance the nightmarish effect. Immediately after Hencher's death, Hawkes mentions, without developing the image, a hive of bees stinging to death a sparrow. A few pages later, Margaret stares at the train window and spots a dead wasp. Swarming bees begin and end the scene in which Cowles has his throat cut. And bees are mentioned before the description of Margaret's beating for no reason other than the fact that the accumulative effect

---

26. "John Hawkes on His Novels," p. 457.
27. John Hawkes, "Notes on the Wild Goose Chase," *Massachusetts Review*, 3 (Summer 1962), 787.

of this image now suggests horrible death. We could also trace the pattern of the mortuary bells which Margaret hears following Hencher's death and which are still ringing when the bumbling police arrive to uncover the particulars of the crime. Or we could follow through the more complex image pattern of lime, green, and birds which is associated with the bee-wasp imagery when the police take note of a dead wasp on a green splinter.

The point is that we are presented with a total experience which happens to be a dream. Most of the recurring images help to provide coherence, but they are also important as a means to suggest the disjointedness and irrational quality of dreams. Although we can "explain" why the Bankses are snared by the lime twig, we need not look for a determining cause and effect to elucidate all of the various visual effects within the dreams. To do so is to become Sidney Slyter or the police, characters in search of the facts, of the clues which will lead them, they hope, to the bottom of the case. But such characters belong to the standard detective thriller in which all the pieces fall neatly into place at the end. In *The Lime Twig*, a parody of the thriller in which the certainties of ratiocination are exchanged for the irrationalities of dreams, motive and logically determined cause and effect are absent, nonexistent, and irrelevant. Slyter and the police remain caught up in the problems of surface reality, exactly where the reader is who demands readily discernible answers to explain the fragmented pieces.

Such a fictional world is bound to be absurd but not only because the novel jumbles cause and effect. As Professor Rovit points out, much of the absurd effect comes from Hawkes' dismissal of such godly notions as mercy, justice, and order. This kind of comic novel contradicts George Meredith's theory of comedy, discussed in chapter one, which insists that the true comic wit "springs to vindicate reason, common sense, rightness, and justice." A world void of these once stable notions is bound to be both terrifying and absurd. The genius of *The Lime Twig* is that Hawkes fashions the terror in comic form.

6

Love at Last:
Second Skin

WITH *Second Skin* (1964) Hawkes moves even further in the direction of the conventional novel. But suggestions of conventionality, first noted in *The Lime Twig*, must be approached cautiously, for these last two novels appear more nearly conventional only when compared to the radical experiments of *The Cannibal* and *The Beetle Leg*. The earlier novels abound in highly controlled set-pieces full of self-conscious inventions and amusing twists, whereas the later fictions keep a tighter rein on language and imaginative vision. Visionary power has been toned down in exchange for a greater emphasis upon lyrical description, intricate interlocking image patterns, and even a bow to traditional plot conventions. This exchange does not mean, however, that *Second Skin* is for every reader—the novel remains a highly experimental fiction.

Hawkes' statements about the development of *Second Skin* reveal how conscious he is of this drift in his fiction, but he cautions that *Second Skin* only "appears" to resemble the traditional novel. Thus, we should hesitate to use a word like "clarity" for fear of misrepresenting the novel's intricacies. We should, rather, call attention to the emphasis upon narrative coherence in a novel which is as violent and as experimental with time and chronology as the rest of his work. One of the reasons for *Second Skin*'s supposed clarity is the presence of a consistent point of view. This technique has been noted by every commentator, for it seems to be the basis for value judgments concerning the relationship of *Second Skin* to the other novels. Peter Brooks, for example, likes *The Cannibal* and parts of the earlier fiction, but he feels that they tend toward the brilliance of the isolated image instead of toward overall coherence. Hawkes' radical unconventionality makes the reader, according to Brooks, long for an "orientation provided by a strong point of view." [1] This orientation is supplied in *Second Skin*, but the novel remains difficult because Skipper's point of view may be unreliable.

Hawkes admits that he wanted to make parts of *Second Skin*, at least the comic tone, more accessible. Obviously upset at the persistent misreadings of his work as fiction saturated with an obscene delight in violence, he began *Second Skin* with a conscious effort to write a funny book: "Comic vision always suggests futurity, I think, always suggests a certain hope in the limitless energies of life itself. In *Second Skin* I tried consciously to write a novel that couldn't be mistaken for anything but a comic novel. I wanted to expose clearly what I thought was central to my fictional efforts but had been generally overlooked in *The Cannibal, The Lime Twig, The Beetle Leg.*" [2] His other conscious goal was to experiment with the first-person narrator. Thus, while he was making the novel's comedy more obvious, he was also continuing his manipulation of traditional fictional methods. He tells us that Hencher's first-person prologue in *The Lime Twig* led directly to *Second Skin*, his first full length novel written entirely in first person.[3]

The creation of fifty-nine year old Skipper, ex–naval officer and

1. Peter Brooks, "John Hawkes," *Encounter*, 26 (June 1966), 70.
2. "John Hawkes: An Interview," *Wisconsin Studies in Contemporary Literature*, 6 (Summer 1965), 146.
3. Ibid., p. 150.

accomplice to numerous suicides, represents a new element in Hawkes' fiction. Skipper's sustained first-person voice provides us with a necessary touchstone in this involved novel, and thus it seems to ease our efforts to piece together the chronologically jumbled events. Yet *Second Skin* remains complicated because Skipper is more than simply a commentator. In addition to our suspicions that his account may not be totally reliable, we soon realize that Skipper is the main character in a novel who comments directly to us about the novel he is writing in which he is the main character. The introduction of other characters, time sequences, and general chronology depends not upon the claims of rational exposition or logical sequence but upon Skipper's demands as a storyteller. As author of his own tale, in his words his "naked history," Skipper reserves the right to interrupt any chapter in progress when he feels the need to elucidate some other aspect from his violent past. He has total control of his narrative, and he tells his story with a purpose. All of his efforts are directed toward convincing us of his undaunted affirmation, of the triumph of his survival, and of his faith in the belief that "virtue always wins." But Skipper is such a blunderer, so naive and unprotected, that we are tempted to challenge his faith in love and virtue. The questions to be pursued in this chapter are why does Skipper survive and why does this extraordinarily violent novel seem so much more affirmative than Hawkes' earlier work? A related question concerns whether or not Skipper is a hero despite his numerous setbacks at the hands of malevolent forces and designing friends.

Hawkes himself has called Skipper ineffectual, a man who somehow survives against the odds: "The novel is about a bumbler, an absurd man, sometimes reprehensible, sometimes causing the difficulties, the dilemmas, he gets in—but ending with some kind of inner strength that allows him to live. And he lives, of course, with the memory of his daughter." [4] This is a significant quotation, for it hints at our mixed reaction toward Skipper. We despise his ineffectiveness, his incredible innocence in the presence

---

4. "John Hawkes on His Novels: An Interview with John Graham," *Massachusetts Review*, 7 (Summer 1966), 460.

of clearly defined evil, and his absurd efforts to save his daughter Cassandra from suicide, which succeed only in hastening her death. We want to scorn him, to rouse him to action when he blinks at the malignancy surrounding him. And yet we sympathize with his predicament. Despite his culpability, Skipper seems caught up in a world of pernicious designs which are not of his making and beyond his control. For all of our dismay at his bungling, we do applaud what Hawkes calls that "kind of inner strength that allows him to live." And the fact that he does live while those around him embrace death is indeed a major point.

But why is Skipper successful? Does he confront an absurd world, challenge it and lose, but finally accept its absurdity and transcend its chaos? Or does he survive because he retreats from it when he realizes that he cannot win? The questions remain debatable, but the second suggestion seems to be the most likely answer. No matter what we may think of Skipper during the revelation of various episodes from his past, our total evaluation of him is colored by the fact that he continues to live and love while others die. Our tendency to despise him for his individual failures is balanced by our need to celebrate him for his unlikely survival. And as Hawkes points out, Skipper's durability is one of the key reasons for *Second Skin*'s affirmative tone:

> [Skipper] himself undergoes all kinds of tribulations and violations and by the end of the novel, I think we do have, in effect, a survivor. This is the first time, I think, in my fiction that there is something affirmative. In other words, even I got very much involved in the life-force versus death. The life and death in the novel go on as a kind of equal contest, until the very end, when a newborn baby, perhaps the narrator's, is taken to a cemetery on a tropical island, on an imaginary island, really, taken to a cemetery on All Saints' Eve with candles lighted on the graves and so on. And out of this, I think, does come a sort of continuing life.[5]

What makes the evaluation of Skipper's survival difficult is the technique of the first-person narrator. We have only his word

5. Ibid., pp. 459–460.

for what has happened. The possibility remains for a contradiction between the way we see him and the way he defines himself and his past. He wastes no time in beginning the process of self-definition which, he hopes, will convince us of his goodness. The novel's first words read, "I will tell you in a few words who I am. . . ." [6] And the first thing he tells us is that he is a lover of many things: hummingbirds, the bright needlepoint of "humorous old ladies," a small naval boat, and "poor dear black Sonny, my mess boy." But what Skipper loves most of all is his "harmless and sanguine self." In addition to describing his love, the first page also tells us that Skipper is a victim and "a man of courage as well." The rest of the novel is an explanation of his victimization and a justification of his claim to love and courage. No other character is in a position to question his self-assessment. That challenge, if it is to be made, must come from us.

Skipper believes that he is fated to endure the agonies heaped upon him by friends and family. Note the pat on the back he gives himself: "A few of us, a few good men with soft reproachful eyes, a few honor-bright men of imagination, a few poor devils, are destined to live out our fantasies, to live out even the sadistic fantasies of friends, children and possessive lovers" (p. 18). In this statement Skipper points to his ability to "live out" the sadism of others, but he also mentions his own imagination and fantasies. As he tells us his story, he may very well be using his fertile imagination to remake his painful past into something he can handle. Hawkes suggests that Skipper's myth-making tendencies may be an important factor in his survival, just as they may point out the possibility of unreliable narration. Thus, when he recalls his courage during the horrifying scene in which Cassandra forces him to have the name of her homosexual husband, Fernandez, tattooed on his chest, we are not sure if he is trying to convince us or himself: "There were tiny fat glistening tears in the corners of my eyes. But they never fell. Never from the eyes of this heavy bald-headed once-handsome man. Victim. Courageous victim" (p. 19).

6. John Hawkes, *Second Skin* (New York: New Directions, 1964), p. 1. All further references will be in parentheses.

Only when the novel unfolds is it clear that Skipper can call himself courageous not because he refuses to cry out but because he holds on to the courage to live. His juxtaposition of courage and victim in this definition of himself is indeed important, for we soon realize that Skipper is as much a willing victim as he is ready prey for victimization by others. Obviously proud of this willingness, he brags about his role as an absorber of pain when he comments on those "persons whose love I have lost or whose poison I happily spent my life neutralizing with my unblemished flesh, my regal carriage, my impractical but all the more devoted being" (p. 5).

The most striking examples of his role as willing victim occur on the ironically named "gentle island" of the widow Miranda and Captain Red. On this island the natural process is from life to death. Skipper is bound to lose, but to him the dire predicaments only provide additional opportunities for him to neutralize pain with his flesh. He longs, for example, to gather the family burial mounds of the island's fishermen and give them his life. During an early morning walk his first day on the island, he watches all the mystery and hints of pain begin to emerge: an "inhuman" sky, a "condemned" lighthouse, "a crafty makeshift" world. But rather than heed the warnings, he excuses himself as too proud and trusting to retreat from the signs of evil. Even if the hints were made obvious, he still would not have turned back:

> But how could I know that Captain Red's boat, the *Peter Poor*, lay invisible and waiting only fifty yards from shore in its dark anchorage? How could I know that we, Cassandra and I, would sail away for our sickening afternoon on that very boat, the *Peter Poor*, how know about the violence of that sea or about the old man's naked passion? But if I had known, if I had seen it all in my glimpse of Jomo's pumps and Bub's useless bicycle and the old man's smoke, would I have faltered, turned back, fled in some other direction? No. I think not. Surely I would have been too proud, too innocent, too trusting to turn back in another direction.   (pp. 56–57)

There is a note of pride in this statement, a boasting tone about his willingness to be victimized despite the consequences. He parades this pride, innocence, and trust during his sojourn on the gentle island. We wait for something to move him, some event so unexpected that it finally shocks him into action, but his reactions are always ineffective. Inappropriate responses to highly serious situations turn Skipper into a comic blunderer. Jumping this way and that, he exerts every effort to dodge the implications of evil while directing all the pain onto his own shoulders. The truth which he will not admit is that the world is full of malevolent people all waiting for a chance to bring down an innocent like himself. He would rather ignore Miranda's slaughter of the baby bottles—broken glass, spilled milk, slashed nipples—and comment on his "self-sacrifice" while cleaning up the mess. He would prefer to avoid the "noxious odor of grief, death and widowhood" which permeates his house on the gentle island. Note his reaction when Miranda forecasts his bloody future by pinning his naval uniform to a dressmaker's dummy: "—oh, it was a jaunty sight she had prepared for me. But of course I ignored it as best I could, tried to overlook the fresh dark gouts of ketchup she had flung down the front of that defiled figure, and merely shut my door, at least spared my poor daughter from having to grapple with that hapless effigy of my disfigured self" (p. 67). The phrase "of course" summarizes his attitude. What Skipper does not know or will not admit is that his "poor daughter" Cassandra enjoys torturing him as much as Miranda does. She spurns his smothering protection, but "of course" he prefers not to see it.

But willingness to victimize himself is not the only reason for our ambiguous attitude toward Skipper. Too often we suspect that he is an unwitting accomplice to the very actions he hopes to thwart. Not much could be done to prevent the ruined baby bottles or the disfigured naval uniform. Although we wish that he would protest, perhaps confront Miranda with her handiwork, we do not blame him. None of it is his fault. But we cannot excuse him so easily when, for example, he suspects Cassandra's willing seduction by Captain Red and his sons Jomo and Bub following the high school dance. The consequences of this scene are tragic, for Cassandra will eventually commit suicide. But the scene in iso-

lation is comic because of Skipper's frantic efforts to counter all
suggestions of evil. Leaving the dance as the newly crowned cham-
pion of the belly bumping contest, he finds himself stranded in the
snow. The others have left without him so that they can enjoy
Cassandra's charms without fear of his interference. Skipper, naturally, will not admit that Cassandra wants an evening of sexual
sport, so he hurries through the snowdrifts "for Cassandra's sake."
Finally reaching home, he finds Miranda waiting for him on the
porch. And it is here that our frustrations develop. For although
he suspects what is going on in the darkened house, he follows
Miranda, the decoy set by Captain Red, to her car, all the while
protesting that it is against his will, against his better judgment.
Skipper is caught between his urge to "save" Cassandra and his
fear of discovering exactly what is happening. He does not know
what to do. But considering that all of his efforts are aimed at
preventing Cassandra's suicide, we cannot watch sympathetically
while he trudges through the snow to Miranda's car. Quickly
stripping, she pulls him into the car to prevent him from barging
in on the orgy. What frustrates, even angers, us is not so much his
hesitation but his refusal to see that he is being made a fool. Note
the series of comic questions he asks to avoid the obvious:

> Drunk? Out of her mind with passion? Or spiteful? Who could
> tell? But in the rusty disreputable interior of that frozen junk
> heap she had mocked me with the beauty of her naked stern,
> had challenged, aroused, offended me with the blank wall of
> nudity, and I perceived a cruel motive somewhere. So I clawed
> at the scarf, tore loose the scarf, and supporting myself palm-
> down on her icy haunch for one insufferably glorious instant I
> gathered my weight . . . kicked my way out of the car and fled.
> Burning. Blinded. But applauding myself for the escape.
>
> (p. 96)

How are we to respond to such ridiculousness? He brags about his
escape, but we know that he should not have been trapped in the
first place. And Miranda is certainly not drunk or out of her mind
with passion—she knows exactly what she is doing. His reactions
are comic, but while we laugh at his attempts to excuse himself,
our frustrations at such bungling increase. His willing victimiza-

tion can be admirable at times, but too often his self-sacrifices cause him to turn away from possible evil and, thus, indirectly complete the event he hoped to prevent. Because he recognizes this weakness, he adds "accomplice" to the definition of himself as lover and victim.

This kind of self-awareness maintains reader sympathy, but it does not check the incredible series of violent acts which bombard Skipper. In terms of sheer numbers, *Second Skin* is Hawkes' most violent novel, a work saturated with suicides, murder, and pain. But the violence is not gratuitous, and it is not designed to assault the reader. In his study of the uses of violence in art, John Fraser suggests that the most meaningful creation of violence is not aimed at the reader's decent impulses but at encouraging his empathy with others.[7] We experience this kind of empathetic awareness of Skipper's plight when we follow his tortured road to survival. As Hawkes insists, malice is useless unless it fosters reader sympathy. One way to generate sympathy is for the author to remain detached: "But mere malice is nothing in itself, of course, and the product of extreme fictive detachment is extreme fictive sympathy. The writer who maintains most successfully a consistent cold detachment toward physical violence . . . is likely to generate the deepest novelistic sympathy of all, a sympathy which is a humbling before the terrible and a quickening in the presence of degradation."[8] In other words, reader sympathy can often be nurtured in direct proportion to author detachment, and Hawkes is always detached. Never once does he comment on Skipper's trials. But empathy with the victim can also be encouraged by the reader's familiarity with him. Significantly, Skipper, unlike Zizendorf, Cap Leech, or Il Gufo, is normal, recognizable to us all, and an acceptable object of our sympathy. The more he suffers violence, the more we sympathize, despite his bumbling, because we know him to be a good man. For this reason we continue to be shocked, rather than dulled, when the novel's savage events pile up. In a

7. John Fraser, "An Art of Violence," *Partisan Review*, 36, No. 3 (1969), 366–367.
8. John Hawkes, "Notes on the Wild Goose Chase," *Massachusetts Review*, 3 (Summer 1962), 787.

lesser work of art we might be satiated by the quick succession of numerous disasters. The result would be a lack of reader involvement with the violent scenes because satiation finally produces dullness. But in an artistic novel like *Second Skin* the distance between us, violence, and Skipper is narrowed. Fraser comments: "And it is characteristic—and one of the greatest strengths—of the rare works or episodes in which violence is truly shocking that they close the gap between us and violences so that there is no longer on the one hand a normal and natural world that we ourselves inhabit and in which we are safe, and on the other a variety of worlds or activities in which violences happen merely to other people." [9]

Skipper's general life experiences may seem strange and otherwordly, but this is because he relates to us only the highpoints of his battle with the "seeds of death." By sifting out irrelevant details and episodes, he leaves the impression that everything which happens to him is exotic. But the violences he endures are not part of that other world in which violence happens only to other people. In general the violent acts are recognizable events, not bizarre at all: suicides, murder, snowball fights, tattoos. Only the iguana scene and, perhaps, the belly bumping contest seem unusual. Yet despite this relative normality we are left with the *feeling* that the violences which threaten Skipper are indeed abnormal. The reasons, I suspect, are twofold. First, the heightened language which Skipper uses to relate his naked history provides a sense of the unusual. His poetically charged descriptions place everything in a new perspective. Second, the violences taken individually may be familiar, but they appear extraordinary when they all happen to one person. Hawkes successfully creates tension between the credibility of violence in *Second Skin* and the aura of strangeness. This tension is often made possible by references to normal, everyday objects as evidence that the nonviolent world continues. For example, the belly bumping contest seems unreal, perhaps beyond the reach of normal affairs, but Hawkes surrounds

9. Fraser, "An Art of Violence," p. 376.

it with a recognizable scene: a high school dance, a slightly off-key danceband, chocolate cake, teenagers dressed in their Sunday best. As Fraser points out, speaking generally of violence, "What shocks profoundly . . . is not just that someone is assaulted or tortured or killed but that someone else is undisturbedly willing to do these things and to ignore the conventional safeguards of innocence or ignorance or helplessness." [10]

This observation has particular relevance for *Second Skin* because in spite of Skipper's naive helplessness, Cassandra, Tremlow, Miranda, and a host of others, even his wife and parents, stand ready to attack his innocence. What finally shocks us the most about Skipper's predicament is not the particular malignant events he endures but the presence of so many people who are out to get him. And as usual in a Hawkes novel, the malevolence remains motiveless, unexplained, and irrational. Hawkes is not about to tell us, for example, why Skipper's wife Gertrude must sleep with members of Skipper's naval crew, or why Tremlow holds a grudge against him. To do so would upset the tension between credibility and strangeness. But Hawkes, too, is obviously shocked. As Fraser notes, "Good art doesn't shock only the bourgeoisie, it shocks *everyone*." [11] Although Hawkes maintains detachment and refuses to comment on the violence, he does not look on comfortably while we remain outraged at Skipper's trials. We feel that he, too, is shocked by the hot bite of that tattoo needle, by the pain of the snowball fight. Skipper's violators have passed beyond accidental violence, have exposed the nightmare at the souls of their beings, and consequently, because we do believe that all this could happen to Skipper, have revealed to us and to Hawkes life's very real potential for extreme, truly shocking violence. This urge to expose violence is often balanced by a corresponding need to show what Hawkes calls "graceful action." He has commented on his "need to maintain the truth of the fractured picture, to expose, ridicule, attack, but always to create and

10. Ibid., p. 379.
11. Ibid., p. 387.

to throw into new light our potential for violence and absurdity as well as for graceful action." [12] Significantly, even while Skipper unfolds his naked history with its countless violent events, he also insists upon the ability for graceful action which he has successfully protected:

> Even today I take these same slow-paced, deliberate, impervious footsteps, using the balls of my feet in proud and sensual fashion, driving a constant rhythm and lightheartedness and a certain confidence into my stride through the uninhibited and, I might say, powerful swinging of my hips. Of course there are those who laugh. But others, like Sonny, recognize my need, my purpose, my strength and grace. Always my strength and grace.
>
> (p. 3)

Second Skin seems more violent than Hawkes' earlier novels because it is set primarily in a more easily verifiable locale, instead of in a surrealistic nightmare, and because it uses the first-person narration of a fully developed character, a technique which invites reader sympathy. The violence of, say, *The Beetle Leg* seems to rest at some distance from us because of the nightmarish atmosphere and freakish characters. Cap Leech and Luke surely do not encourage our sympathy as much as Skipper does—they are so strange. But we recognize Skipper at once. And because we can identify with him, the violence he experiences seems somehow worse, much closer to home. W. M. Frohock notes that Hawkes' preoccupation with violence is "authentically" American, for violence is a staple in our fiction. Yet Hawkes maintains his own vision, creating something entirely his own. The peculiar grotesqueness of his episodes suggests how original his depiction of violence is. The fictional characters of the twenties and thirties "accepted violence with stoic resignation as a part of life." [13] But Hawkes' heroes often react to violence. Like Skipper they throw up, or like Michael Banks they finally strike out even if it guarantees their

12. "John Hawkes: An Interview," p. 144.
13. W. M. Frohock, "John Hawkes's Vision of Violence," *Southwest Review*, 50 (Winter 1965), 78–79.

own death. Violence revolts Hawkes, and his treatment of it is unusual. Professor Frohock writes: "On the whole, the older novel of violence passed for a true report; it was supposed to show us the actual content of life in given circumstances and was a kind of document. What Hawkes gives us documents nothing at all. He retains all of the characteristics of American preoccupations with the violence of life, but . . . what he offers is essentially a vision of life's not always lovely potentialities." Rather than record a violent reality, Hawkes fractures reality to create a vision of it which suggests in heretofore unimagined forms not only our potential for violence but, sadly enough, our obvious need for it.

As a sympathetic victim of violence, Skipper is a kind of hero. Fraser argues that heroism and victimization by violence often coexist, if only momentarily, when the feeling generated by the work of art underlines the reader's kinship instead of his differences with the victim. One of the triumphs of *Second Skin* is that Hawkes so successfully lures us into Skipper's absurd world that our own relative values no longer seem to hold. We adjust our angle of vision to Skipper's, reevaluating, as best we can, what happens to him in the light of his own sense of things. A particularly effective result of this reevaluation is the importance given to various acts of violence which involve Skipper. A snowball fight and a belly bumping contest would not ordinarily seem as vicious and cruel as the claws of a thirty-pound iguana dug into a lover's back or the discovery of a murdered and mutilated son-in-law in a waterfront flophouse. But because Skipper's values are determined not by our real world but by his own absurd situation, such is the case. The snowball fight and the belly bumping contest involve Skipper personally and therefore they pose serious threats to his shaky status as modern hero. From our perspective these two events appear to be minor, perhaps no more than additional examples of Skipper as bumbling buffoon. But from his point of view—the one we must accept if we are to understand the significance of his survival—these events are hostile traps. True, his inappropriate responses make the scenes hilarious, and we laugh at his initial refusal to accept himself as a target for deliberately aimed iced snowballs. Only an innocent would try to convince himself that the snowballs are invisible birds:

> But I stopped. Listened. Because the air seemed to be filled with low-flying invisible birds. Large or small I could not tell, but fast, fast and out of their senses. . . . One dove into the snow at my feet—nothing but a sudden hole in the snow—and I stepped back from it, raised my hands against the unpredictable approach, the irregular sound of motion, the blind but somehow deliberate line of attack. Escaped homing pigeons? A covey of tiny ducks driven beserk in the cold? Eaglets? I found myself beating the air, attempting to shield my eyes and ears, thought I saw a little drop of blood on the snow. And I was relieved with the first hit.   (pp. 86–87)

When he can no longer deny that these are snowballs smashing his face and drawing blood, he shifts the focus of his rationalization. He stops trying to call the snowballs birds. But comically enough, he feels relieved because he now knows that he has "nothing to fear from any unnatural vengefulness of wild birds." This scene is one of the funniest in the novel, but the fact remains that Skipper suffers badly from the packed snowballs. In his world the snowball fight in the cemetery turns out to be a real massacre during which he recalls his degradation by Tremlow. And the belly bumping contest is elevated in Skipper's point of view beyond a silly annual show to a perverse obscene tournament which causes the "death of modesty." Although we laugh when "the fat begins to fly," we nevertheless realize his acute embarrassment and suffering.

Conversely, violent acts which we would insist on as horrifying in our world are no more serious than the bumping contest in Skipper's perspective. The iguana's claws dig into Kate's back, not Skipper's, and the narrative emphasis skips over her feelings to concentrate on his futile attempts to defeat the dragon which threatens his lady. Similarly, Fernandez's murder, though surely horrible with the amputated fingers, seems no more painful a massacre than the snowball fight. The point is not that Catalina Kate and Fernandez do not suffer but that we never feel their pain. More important to Skipper, and thus to us, is the agony he undergoes because of these experiences. He is convinced, for example, that he must protect Cassandra from the knowledge of Fernandez's death. Later he decides that his decision was wrong—that he should have told her immediately. He had hoped that she might spare herself if she were ignorant of the exact circumstances of her husband's disappearance. His decision to tell her is based on the same motive. Thus, when she jumps from the lighthouse, he suffers all the more guilt because he does not know which decision was correct. The pain associated with Fernandez's murder is a felt presence only as it affects Skipper. The result is that the relative impact of violent acts has been readjusted. Experiences which we would not normally assume to be dire turn out to be pain-inflicting and degrading, on a par with iguana's claws and murder. What finally matters is not *our* evaluation of what is horrific but Skipper's. We must adjust to his world, rejecting the standard impulse to evaluate his trials according to what we consider normal.

Skipper's survival of these violent experiences encourages our feelings about his heroism. None of Hawkes' earlier novels have heroic characters with whom we would like to identify. In *Second Skin* he creates a good man who survives, and it may well be that in the perspective of the novel Skipper is indeed heroic. And yet we still tend to withhold total approval of him for a while. Despite the first-person narration which usually narrows the distance between narrator and reader, we hesitate to identify with a hero who shows such a marked propensity for naiveté and bumbling. From our point of view Skipper is too good-natured, too innocent, too loving, too willing to be maimed for the sake of those he loves—in short, too much the sacrificing fool. Yet the fact remains that he is heroic in the absurd world of *Second Skin*, and we finally applaud his victory. If men like Skipper can survive, then hope lives for us. His chaotic world is no more absurd than ours—its events are simply more compressed so that what seems like an unusually abundant number of violent experiences falls upon him.

Hawkes has endowed Skipper with standard heroic characteristics which should enable him to meet his enemies. He is a large, heavy man, for example, yet proud of his graceful movements. He has various names which, though comic, call attention to his uniqueness: Papa Cue Ball (he is bald), the A.I. (artificial inseminator), even the name "Skipper" itself. From our perspective his victory in the belly bumping contest, made possible by his sheer size, or his position as leader of the fertility rite in which he is the A. I., may seem preposterous—how can we identify with a "hero" whose feats of strength and skill are so absurd? But our perspective does not matter to Skipper. Only his own assessment of his trials finally counts. And in the world of *Second Skin* belly bumping victories over the "King of the fat" and fertility rites with cows count for significant deeds worthy of heroic stature.

Skipper's heroism is untraditional, for he is a modern hero who searches for ways to neutralize his suspicions. A good example, and one of the most important violent experiences from his past, is Tremlow's mutiny. Tremlow, whom Skipper calls "a perfect Triton," clobbers Skipper, takes over the naval vessel after dancing a hula while dressed in a grass skirt, and rows away in the lifeboat. There are suggestions that Tremlow assaults him homosexually, but we cannot be sure. Through it all, Skipper desperately dodges unmistakable hints of insubordination and mutiny. Hearing machine gun fire, he dismisses it as no more than gunnery practice. When Tremlow grins at one of Skipper's orders, he turns away, bragging because "at least I had been too quick for Tremlow, once again had managed to avoid his deliberate signs of insubordination" (p. 138). When he sees bodies go over the side, he comments to Sonny about how amusing Tremlow's hula must have been. Compare Skipper's reaction when Tremlow beats him to his response to the snowballs, and note his inability to accept evil or deal with it. Once again his inappropriate response provides the humor:

> He knocked down my guard with a tap of his bright fist, and vaguely I thought it wasn't fair, that he was supposed to respect my age, respect my rank, that he was supposed to be down in the shack communicating with the rest of the fleet. Knocked down my guard and socked me in the mouth, and I should have ducked at least because the line of that blow was clear as hate

in the steady eyes, though I still missed the idea, the plan, which was surely riding far forward by then in Tremlow's eye. . . . But he hit me in the mouth again. Same fist, same mouth, more bloody mud, more pain. Why not the nose, I thought, or the naked eye, or the stomach, why this furious interest in my loose and soft-spoken mouth?"   (p. 146)

This scene is hilarious, but Skipper's inability to act in the presence of evil nevertheless causes him great pain. His stature as hero rests not on his power to defeat evil but on his strength to survive it.

The iguana scene makes clear his ironic relationship to classical standards of heroism. Summoned by Sister Josie to the aid of Catalina Kate, Skipper becomes the modern hero who fails to save his lady from the dragon. The heightened language and heroic allusions testify to the significance of this episode. He calls Kate "my brown Joan of Arc" and the iguana "Succubus." He describes himself as a colossus meeting the monster: "So I straddled her—colossus over the reptile, colossus above the shores of woman—and hearing the lap and shifting of the sea, and wiping my palms on my thighs and leaning forward, I prepared to grapple with the monster" (p. 106). But the iguana's claws are dug in too deep. All he can do is apologize to Kate and wait for the monster to withdraw: "So the round goes to the dragon, Kate. I'm sorry." Skipper is no St. George. Again we laugh at his bumbling efforts to play the knight in shining armor, to slay the forces of evil. But this episode is different because it takes place on the magical wandering island, not on the mainland or on Miranda's gentle island—the locales of his most grievous defeats. His bout with the iguana can be seen as a kind of victory, for on the wandering island he learns to outwait the monster, though he must acquire his patience from Sister Josie and from Kate, the suffering damsel herself. So although his efforts are thwarted, he nevertheless achieves a victory of sorts. For once he does not plunge blindly into the enemy's lair. With time now on his side in this place of "no time," he simply outlasts the horror.

The significant point of *Second Skin* is not Skipper's failure to save Catalina Kate from pain or Cassandra from suicide but rather his ability to save himself. The very fact that Skipper survives with his need to love still intact while Father, Mother, Gertrude, Fernandez and Cassandra all die testifies to his heroism. And we commend his will to live and love. By the novel's end our reluctance to identify with this far from ideal hero has diminished somewhat, for we realize that his apparently insignificant victories, like finally smashing Bub's face or sweeping the little lizards off the gravestone even though he cannot dislodge an iguana, are for him immensely important feats which reveal his new found ability to take action, however weak. Hitting Bub's nose and removing the lizards may not measure up to the mythic hero's defeat of the giant or the dragon, but in the chaos of Skipper's world such action is meaningful. Sheer survival, his ability to redeem the others' preoccupation with death, finally qualifies him as a modern hero.

What happens to Skipper during his journey to the wandering island is cruel and sadistic, but the sadism is a perversity of the malevolent characters, not a quality of the author. Skipper's principal antagonists may deal in death and negation, but Hawkes' overall vision in *Second Skin* is affirmative. Behind the individual violent acts we feel the joy in the life forces and the celebration of love which both frustrate Skipper's many devils and counter accusations of the author's gratuitous horror. Hawkes has argued that he has no desire to be sadistic or cruel: "Of course, I myself actually, in real life terms or in art terms, I would tend to reject this sick joke, if it is merely a kind of dissolving into mindless and heartless obscenity or sadism. Cruelty." He wants fiction to live "out of a concern for humanity," and he insists that comedy has a "saving" attitude. Shocking humor often encourages the recognition of what Hawkes calls "the lasting values, the one or two really deep permanent human values. I think any writer of worth is concerned with these things." [14] *Second Skin* nicely illustrates this argument, for its grotesque humor is a means to reaffirm the lasting values of love and the will to live. The extreme violence of this novel finally has a positive meaning. *Second Skin* leaves no

14. "John Hawkes on His Novels," p. 461.

doubt that the life force can equal death even though both are part of the same cycle. When Skipper celebrates Kate's baby's birth in the cemetery, he shows his awareness of this truth.

Hawkes has always been very much caught up in the interplay between the life and death forces, but only in the later fiction has he tended to emphasize life's power to balance death. The earlier novels are much bleaker, much more concerned with detailing man's potential for and submission to violence beyond his control. The strength of life's "lasting" values is weak to the point of nonexistence in *The Cannibal* and *The Owl,* and, consequently, the violent events assume even darker perspective. All of the horrors and violence of the earlier novels are present in *Second Skin,* but Hawkes' emphasis has changed. By reaffirming the life forces, he calls attention to our ability to "live out even the sadistic fantasies of friends, children and possessive lovers." One of Hawkes' comments in his review of Edwin Honig's poetry is especially appropriate here, for it points to birth and death as "deplorable and astounding processes." "A highly moral poetry, true enough: but very nearly all of these poems construct a kind of ghostly and biting double exposure, or hold in some mercurial suspension, suasion, the two deplorable and astounding processes—that of dying and that of birthing. Hence the felt morality, the moral judgment, the extreme moral prescience, is most often lodged in soft anxiety-provoking antithesis or jocular paradox." [15] The point for us is that the antithesis of life and death can carry the felt morality. Faced with these "astounding" processes, Skipper experiences both the anxiety and the joy Hawkes describes. The novel's morality emerges from the tension between these two primal forces. In his essay on Flannery O'Connor, he argues that "in the most vigorously moral of writers the actual creation of fiction seems often to depend on immoral impulses." [16] The apparently immoral impulses of *Second Skin,* and of all Hawkes' fiction, would appear to result in the lavish descriptions of torture and death and the

15. John Hawkes, "The Voice of Edwin Honig," *Voices: A Journal of Poetry,* No. 174 (January–April 1961), 40–41.
16. John Hawkes, "Flannery O'Connor's Devil," *Sewanee Review,* 70 (Summer 1962), 398.

seeming commitment to soulless people who glory in pain. But his fiction never celebrates these characters. Rather it violates anticipated probability to expose the very real presence of evil. In *Second Skin* we have his clearest statement of his faith in the life force when faced with that evil. In other words, Hawkes' intense awareness of evil helps him create his most affirmative revelation of the life-death paradox.

Having survived a series of violent deaths, Skipper is now aware of this paradox as he muses on his past. From the very beginning of his naked history he calls attention to his lifelong involvement with death. Claiming that he was never afraid, he tells Cassandra, "I grew up very familiar with the seeds of death; I had a special taste for them always" (p. 12). His familiarity, in fact, nearly convinces him that he is a carrier of death. Realizing that the recipients of his love always die, he wonders, "But if my own poor father was Death himself, as I think he was, then certainly I was right to tell Cassandra how familiar I was with the seeds of death. Wasn't I myself, as a matter of fact, simply that? Simply one of those little black seeds of death?" (p. 161). Until he reaches the wandering island, Skipper has every right to believe himself a harbinger of death. He feels, for example, that he was a "child-accomplice" to his father's suicide. The great comedy of this scene—fat boyish Skipper frantically playing Brahms on his cello outside the bathroom door while his father shoots himself on the toilet seat—carries over to his description of Gertrude's suicide when he misses his own wife's funeral. But comedy gives way to horror in most of his memories of his involvement with death. His discovery of Fernandez's mutilation causes him to vomit: "Stabbed, beaten, poked and prodded, but he was finally choked to death with the guitar string. And the fingers. Yes, all five fingers of the left hand. All five. The clasp knife, the wine-dark pool, the fingers themselves, it was clear, too clear, what they had done and that the severed fingers were responsible for the spidery red lines scattered over everything" (p. 156). There is no humor here, and the heightened language which Skipper uses to describe this murder reveals how revolted he is.

Cassandra's suicide, of course, tortures him the most. Until she jumps from the lighthouse she represents his most painful association with the death force, for it is her death he fights against the hardest. Easily recognizing her cooperation with death and pain, he variously describes her as "lifeless," as having a death-mask face, and as showing a "sadistic calm" during the tattoo ordeal. But he also tries to erase these definite suggestions of death by emphasizing her childish looks and by equating her with the "BVM" (Blessed Virgin Mary). These descriptions appear early in the novel, and they point to his confused attitude toward Cassandra. He suspects that she wants to kill herself, but he cannot discover her motive. Is it because suicide seems to be hereditary in his family? Is it because of Fernandez's disappearance? Or would her death be the easiest way to hurt him? He is never sure, but he mistakenly believes that by retreating with her to the gentle island he can devote all of his energies to the prevention of her suicide. But the gentle island turns out to be death's citadel. During that early morning walk right after their arrival, he has a vision of Cassandra's death. He thinks he sees a naked woman lying between himself and the high rocks of the beach: "Vision from the widow's photography magazine. Woman who might have leapt from the lighthouse or rolled up only moments before on the tide. She was there, out there, triangulated by the hard cold points of the day, and it was she, not I, who was drawing down the eye of the bird and even while the thought came to me—princess, poor princess and her tower" (p. 58). Skipper's innocence will not allow him to think about the meaning of this vision, and he promptly forgets it. Yet the scene foreshadows Cassandra's suicide exactly, and during the remainder of their stay on the gentle island, she pursues, almost leisurely, her death.

We sympathize with Skipper's apparent defeat by death's forces on this island, but at the same time we are angry at his innocence. His refusal to act in the presence of imminent danger is the primary reason why we agree with his designation of himself as "accomplice." He was a child when his parents died and, thus, not responsible. We do not know the details surrounding the deaths of Gertrude and Fernandez, so we do not blame him. But he does tell us the full story of Cassandra's death, and we realize that his naiveté aids her pursuit of death. Their excursion on Captain Red's fishing boat, the *Peter Poor*, is a good example. Admitting that there was "no chance really for Cassandra after that," he now tries to discover why he permitted the trip in the first place. The dawn comes up red, a sailor's warning, yet he goes. He tells us that he swore off sailing after Tremlow's mutiny, yet he climbs aboard the *Peter Poor* knowing that Red plans to seduce the willing Cassandra. He reminds Cassandra that her full skirt is inappropriate for a sailing trip, yet he lets her wear it. When he protests, "I should have known," or "I wanted to stop her," we agree, and our frustration at his inaction turns to anger when he proudly tells us, "But I, at least, made an effort to see the landmarks he thought worthy of our attention" (p. 181). Despite the "dawn curse," the black water, the "malevolent unpromising scene," and the smell of dead fish, Skipper decides that the only thing he can do is turn the excursion into a sightseeing voyage. He fools only himself when he insists, after Bub hits him with a tire iron, that he should have taken over the ship: "Had it not been for Crooked Finger Rock I might have done something, might have reached around somehow and caught Bub by the throat and snatched away the tire iron and flung it at Red. Somehow I might have knocked Red down and taken over the *Peter Poor* and sailed us back to safety before the squall could threaten us from another quarter" (p. 185). But we know better. As long as Skipper remains on the gentle island he is powerless to take effective action against the death force. Later when he hits Bub following his desperate drag race to catch Cassandra, we cheer his belated move to strike back, but even here he remains the comic bumbler. Bub has fooled him, and Miranda drives off in his car, leaving him to run up the beach, all the way to the lighthouse. Once there he allows Cassandra her final torture. He climbs the stairs on his hands and knees, even though he knows that she has jumped, because he is expected to do so:

> Even as I approached the black doorless opening in the base of the tower I was quite certain that she had planned it all, had

> intended it all, knowing that I would come and call to her and force myself to climb that tower, climb every one of those iron steps on my hands and knees, and for nothing, all for nothing. Even as I thrust one foot into the darkness of Dog's Head light I knew that I could not possibly be in time. (p. 197)

Only now does he remember his vision of the dead girl on the rocks. His final act on the gentle island takes place appropriately in a cemetery when he places Cassandra's fetus, a "present" from Miranda, on her grave.

His determination to maintain his innocence and his inability to act in the presence of evil make him partly responsible for Cassandra's death. In the long run he may not have been able to prevent it, but the fact remains that he has facilitated her suicide. Because he has an intimate acquaintance with the death force, all of the major events of his life take place in cemeteries. The contrast between his placing the fetus on Cassandra's grave and his celebration of Kate's baby on a timeless gravestone is clear enough. His defeats and victories take place amid the dead. Only when he reaches the wandering island does he realize the unity between the life and death forces. Since childhood he has tried to counter death, to use his own flesh to neutralize its sting. His chosen role as willing victim is often admirable, but it renders him impotent. Obsessed with trying to hold off the death force, he makes no effort to create life. Early in the novel Sonny tells Skipper, "No more cemetery business, Skipper? I trust there's no more of that cemetery stuff in the cards. That stuff's the devil!" (p. 21). We later learn that Sonny fears gravestones. But "that cemetery stuff" is one of the novel's key points. For all of his ignorance, Skipper is at least aware that cemeteries should not be avoided. He even defines his adventures as "our journey between two distant cemeteries" (p. 31). But he makes the grievous mistake of seeing the cemetery as his "battleground," as the place where he must take his stand against death. On the wandering island he finally learns that birth and death are two "astounding" processes, each inextricably involved with the other, each a necessary force in its own right. Completely changing his perspective, he sheds his role as a failed preventer of death and assumes his new status as the primary provider of life.

An unmistakable symbol of Skipper's new ability to integrate life and death is the presence of the blackbird on the wandering island. The crow or blackbird seems to hold special meaning for Hawkes, pointing to his fascination with the life-death process. Commenting on Edwin Honig's use of it in the poem "Island Storm," he writes, "the darting of the crow, that bird of death, indicates that this world's end will come again and again, without cessation." [17] The blackbirds on the wandering island also promise the full swing of the life-death cycle. They are not malevolent, for they cheer at the impregnation of Sweet Phyllis the cow. But their presence at the rites of artificial insemination and at the graveyard ritual which celebrates the baby's birth tells us that Skipper has not erased death. His victory is not over death but over his earlier attempts to negate it. He learns to accept the "jocular paradox" involved in the mixture of the tomb and the spawning role, of grief and the cycle of genesis, and he attains the "essential" solace of a man who has found love at last.

His survival is an act of defiance in a chaotic world. For many modern literary heroes, the choice of living in an absurd reality is irrational; hence suicide is the only sane decision. Skipper's will to live with absurdity in spite of the indignities piled upon him is something different, what T. A. Hanzo calls a rejection of fashionable antiheroism, but his reason for living, love, is not new at all.[18] To the bafflement of those who would hurt him, Skipper's love enables him to survive their negation. Their refusal of his love is an offshoot of their repudiation of life, for only by deliberately rejecting Skipper can they plunge headlong into their various deaths. Even in the very act of suicide they try to hurt him. Attempting to stretch the power of hate beyond the grave, they fashion their suicides in ways which they hope will chip away at Skipper's desire

17. Hawkes, "The Voice of Edwin Honig," p. 44.
18. T. A. Hanzo, "The Two Faces of Matt Donelson," *Sewanee Review*, 73 (Winter 1965), 111.

to live. But all of them, especially Gertrude and Cassandra, underestimate the power of his love. Replying to Gertrude's declaration "You are going to hate me, Edward," he insists, "But she was wrong. Because the further she went downhill the more I cared. And Gertrude was no match for my increasing tolerance" (p. 131).

Yet Skipper's survival is more than a stoic stance, and his naked history does more than record the bleak events which have made up the hideous joke of his past life. Rejecting the premise that life is dominated by fear, a condition to be tolerated only by negating it through death, he moves beyond mere endurance of his trials to insist upon his affirmation of joy. He is as much an apostle of life as Tremlow is a disciple of the devil. The durability of his joyful innocence testifies to the novel's moral vision. Note his serene confidence in the novel's final statement: "Because now I am fifty-nine years old and I knew I would be, and now there is the sun in the evening, the moon at dawn, the still voice. That's it. The sun in the evening. The moon at dawn. The still voice" (p. 210). Not only is he confident of survival, he also accepts the world's absurdities. The emphasis in the last sentence is reversed—sun in evening, moon at dawn, a still voice—to suggest life's fragmentation. Skipper survives on a wandering island which is beyond time. As a modern hero of love and life, he now transcends time. These last sentences show how far he has come, show his awareness of his present timeless state which overcomes his past fragmented life.

Skipper's situation may be abnormal in the sense that we do not want to believe that so many dire events happen to one man, but his narration of his naked history is so sane that we end up believing him. His method of narration is indeed a key to *Second Skin*. We have no choice but to accept the heightened language and the rhetorical flourishes which give what may seem to be undue importance to certain events. Despite his reluctance to discover the full account of why a particular calamity has befallen him, he remains our only access to the story he wants to tell. His tone is alternatively banal, apologetic, bragging, and fearful, but never once is he insane like Zizendorf or preoccupied with private fetishes like the sheriff, Il Gufo, or Hencher. Though *Second Skin* undergoes these shifts in tone, Skipper's point of view stays constant. We need only realize that his history unfolds not by plot or character development but by his particular narrative requirements at specific points in his story.

Many times he steps to center stage to address us or to speak directly to his characters:

> And so I have already stepped once more from behind the scenes of my naked history and having come this far I expect that I will never really be able to conceal myself completely in all those scenes which are even now on the tip of my tongue and crowding my eye. The fact of the matter is that Miranda will have to wait while I turn to a still more distant past, turn back to a few of my long days at sea and to several other high lights of my more distant past.   (p. 99)

This is the statement of a man who is highly conscious that he is writing a novel with a particular point of view to stress. He even addresses the ghosts of his tormentors and warns them that he is about to tell their tale: "So hold your horses, Miranda! Father and Gertrude and Fernandez, sleep! Now take warning, Tremlow!" (p. 110). But is he about to tell their tale? Without testimony from someone else, we cannot be sure. Their side is never revealed, of course, and Skipper apparently does not want to know their motives for hurting him. Just as important as his manipulation of past events is his control of our reactions. He takes pains to see that we will read his novel sympathetically and accept the spirit with which it is told. Again and again he underscores the affirmation, dismissing as dead wrong any effort on our part to read defeat into it: "High lights of helplessness? Mere trivial record of collapse? Say, rather, that it is the chronicle of recovery, the history of courage, the dead reckoning of my romance, the act of memory, the dance of shadows. And all the earmarks of pageantry, if you will, the glow of Skipper's serpentine tale" (p. 162).

At first glance he seems to be apologizing for his bumbling, attempting to convince us that despite his defeats he is neverthe-

less a man of love, grace, and courage. His narrative voice sounds
like a confession of his involvement with the life-death cycle. He
himself may not be sure what to make of it. Only by putting the
story on paper can he come to terms with a past which once seemed
dominated by the seeds of death. His story is an explanation and
an apology to both himself and us. From the first page we realize
that his love is too indiscriminate, too blind to the machinations
of those who inflict pain. He calls attention to his love so much
that we suspect it of being an excuse for defeat, perhaps a mask.
But reading on, we discover that Skipper's confessions are not a
revelation of incompetence but an exposé of a nightmare world
in which brutal acts consistently thwart good intentions. His frustration increases with each act of violence because he never knows
why it happens. We are frustrated too because we want him to
fight back. But once we realize the horror which surrounds him,
once we understand that his confessional mode is an acceptable
reaction to a life inundated with death, then we can see that his
love, indiscriminate though it may be, is neither a pose nor an
excuse, but rather the only response possible if he hopes to survive. If he is not to commit suicide himself, he must constantly
reassert his love in an effort to balance the life-death cycle. Following his failures on the gentle island, he gives up his efforts to
rationalize the violence. But he never abandons his need to love
and to affirm life. Hawkes' decision to make Skipper an artificial
inseminator is significant. For if Skipper has been impotent when
dealing with death, he can at least become fertile when affirming
life. Be it with a herd of cows or with Kate, he resolves to create, a
god of modern fertility rites. His eagerness to celebrate the baby's
birth while sitting amid the gravestones shows us how far he has
come. Incompetence no longer matters when he finds love at last.

The style which Hawkes uses to tell Skipper's story is every bit
as important as the narrative voice. Highly lyrical and sensuous,
it approaches poetry. Emphasis is often on pure description, and
Hawkes uses alliteration and assonance to full effect—for example:
"Wet hands on the flaking white sill. Sudden shock in nose, chin,

cheeks, sensation of the cold glass against the whole of my inquisitive face" (p. 73). Some readers find these stylistic effects excessive. T. A. Hanzo, for instance, writes:

> Skipper's hypersensitivity is allowed to be the vehicle of a nearly delirious registering of sensation, often stimulated by experiences which scarcely seem worth the telling. . . . Hawkes's novel suffers in its stylistic excesses from the consequences of a serious choice. Having perceived the necessity for a radical statement (the return, in *Second Skin*, to the earth and to her priestly service), he was also urged by the universal implications of his theme to a radical reassessment of the emotional content of his language.[19]

Instead of calling attention to apparent stylistic excesses, I would argue that the poetic language results from Skipper's present perspective—that of the magical wandering island. Having already survived, he now looks back on his past while surrounded by all of the pastoral serenity and other-worldly life-style of a tropical paradise. The novel's language testifies to Skipper's intensity and to his hypersensitive awareness of all that has happened. As Hanzo suggests, his evocation of sensation is often stimulated by what we might call minor experiences. Yet we must remember that they are not minor to Skipper. One of his worst faults is his inability to discriminate, his failure to size up people and events. He lavishes love on everyone, deserved or not. And his descriptions of his past result from this same tendency. To him the belly bumping contest is as much an outrage as the mutilation of Fernandez's body, and thus it deserves the same level of emotional response. Skipper's heightened language is not so much the result of stylistic excesses on Hawkes' part as it is testimony to Skipper's need to feel with intensified emotion everything which affects him. The novel's language forces recognition of vivid fragments and isolated scenes lovingly described. Because Hawkes takes the time to create unusual phrases and combinations of images, we, too, linger over the lyrical passages with the result that we are drawn into a rich verbal atmosphere which seems to order Skipper's disordered past.

19. Ibid., pp. 113–114.

But as Tony Tanner notes, this conscious style also prevents total reader involvement. We are always aware that we are reading a skillfully created piece of fiction. Called upon to search out parallel or corresponding images, echoes of one event in another, and fragments of action which combine to make a pattern, we are kept back from "total absorption into the landscape." [20]

Skipper's mastery of the language which reports the events of his past far outstrips his mastery of the events themselves. As Tanner points out, he may be using his art to transmute the pain and chaos of his experiences into a benign whole. If this is so then Skipper is truly a modern hero in the sense that he forges his own world. But how truthful is his account? As we have noted, his history is in the form of an apology, a kind of rationalization for his part as accomplice to so much pain, yet it is couched in a self-congratulatory tone. Could his narrative thus be unreliable? Is he trying to impose on us his own account and justify his private version of what Tanner calls "events which might well have afforded a different reading?" [21] Since we have only Skipper's word, the question is unanswerable, but it does call attention to his freedom to create his own view of the past. His justification for his refusal to tell Cassandra of Fernandez's death is pertinent here: "Yet wasn't I deceiving her even then? Wasn't I sparing her certain details, withholding others, failing somehow to convey the true tonality of the thing? Well, I should hope to God! Because how could I or anyone else convey the true tonality of Second Avenue . . ." (p. 149). But what about the true tonality of his entire narrative—can he possibly convey it? Skipper has suffered so intensely that he uses art to ease the memories. He finds that artistic creation, rather than his willing flesh, best neutralizes the sadistic fantasies of friends and possessive lovers. The point is that now, safely away from Tremlow, the tattoo parlor, and the gentle island, he is free to construct his own myths by narrating his history in any way he chooses.

20. Tony Tanner, "Necessary Landscapes and Luminous Deteriorations: on Hawkes," *TriQuarterly*, No. 20 (Winter 1971), 164.
21. Ibid., p. 175.

One of the ways he chooses to exercise this artistic freedom is in his role as the namer in his novel. Hawkes has always delighted in stringing red herrings across the reader's trail and in upsetting mythical or classical allusions. But in *Second Skin* the use of these allusions does not seem a deliberate attempt to mislead us as much as an illustration of Skipper's need to write his own story from his private point of view. He tells us, for example, that had he been born a girl, he would not have been Clytemnestra, cause of murder and revenge, but Iphigenia, unsuspecting and trusting. Yet though he would have been more willing than she to be knifed down, he is sure that somehow he would have been spared. He also equates himself with Hamlet because of his preoccupation with death, and he sees himself as a modern Menelaus who leaves his beloved in the care of Paris while he travels to a distant island. Unlike Prince Paris, however, Skipper finds love and, thus, he pities the man who lost Helen. Some of these classical allusions are ironic, but we are never sure if Skipper is aware of the irony. He tries to see Cassandra as the BVM, and he equates her driving with that of Thor. He calls Tremlow "Triton," Miranda "Venus," and himself "Colossus." Even some of the non-classical names seem ironic. Skipper's real name, Edward, means guardian of property, a job at which he fares very poorly. But his choice of the hummingbird as his favorite bird is meaningful. This particular bird is known for its apparent ability to suspend motion in seeming violation of gravity, thus suggesting the wandering island's freedom from the limitations of time and space.

But the suggested meanings of these names are not nearly as significant as the evidence they provide of Skipper's control of his narrative. He is free to set up whatever classical allusions he likes. It does us little good to track them down. His narrative voice and lyrical flights of language enable him to translate the negation of his real past experiences into the affirmation of his mythical present paradise. What he calls "my naked history" is just that—his own unsubstantiated account of what he alone says happened. The point, however, is not that he may be manipulating the past to fit his present needs. It makes no difference that he never tells us why

Cassandra insists upon the green tattoo or why Tremlow attacks him. What does matter is his survival. Hurt so badly and so often, he feels he has the right to be ecstatic about the promise of his new situation. Clearly he is using his skills with language to pattern his past, but the translation of past facts into the stuff of his dreams is not a shortcoming. Although his story is about past events, it is also most certainly a thrust toward the future. The accuracy of his facts does not count nearly as much as the assurance we now have of his future happiness.

A good way to understand Skipper's combination of stylistic effects with truly terrifying events is to examine one of the means by which Hawkes orders Skipper's fractured past. The novel's color imagery, for example, helps to structure the narrative, but color also serves to emphasize the disorder of Skipper's life. Because each character and event is described in a color that has more than one level of meaning, Hawkes suggests the impossibility of Skipper's hope to isolate segments of life in an attempt to establish stability. No such stability is possible. Skipper survives, paradoxically, not on the hard, stable gentle island, but on a wandering island. Only when he accepts life's ambiguities can he settle down to write his naked history. And as he composes it, his control of structural patterns and his flair for language create a coherence which may have been missing from those past experiences he describes. Structure in *Second Skin*—those images, events, and verbal patterns which point to the novel's internal coherence—is based upon cross-references, parallels, and contrasts. This technique enriches the nightmarish overtones of all of Hawkes' novels and gives them their poetic quality. We recall Hawkes' statement that structure is his greatest concern: "Related or corresponding event, recurring image and recurring action, these constitute the essential structural or meaningful density of my writing." [22] He goes on to insist that this kind of structure is not "planned in advance but can only be discovered in the writing process itself." Clarifying his point, he suggests that he consciously uses materials which are liberated from his unconscious in the writing process.

22. "John Hawkes: An Interview," p. 149.

Careful, conscious writing leads to a scaffolding that is developed from unconsciously discovered details.

Second Skin is a particularly intricate example of this means of structure. Various patterns can be traced which illustrate Skipper's efforts to control his disordered life by art—color imagery is only one of them but it is an effective example. For while Hawkes dismisses conventional ordering devices, he uses color imagery thematically to provide a frame of reference for the fragmentary, often motiveless action and for the violent time shifts. The colors provide guidelines for us as well as change the novel's tone. They function as objective correlatives because they can register clashing hard notes or soft tones, thereby affecting our response. In some cases, of course, the colors suggest the literal description of an object. But most of the references to color illustrate thematic considerations to such a degree that, depending upon Skipper's geographical position at the time, the mention of a specific color helps to bring a desired response from us. Although numerous colors are mentioned in isolated instances, in general Hawkes plays with variations on two pairs: green and yellow, normally positive shades, and black and white, usually negative. Yet he does not use the colors in pairs, preferring to choose one of the four for relative prominence in different sections of the novel. Yellow is used, for example, to suggest the nature of reality as it affects Skipper at a given moment. Establishing a tonal declension from golden to yellow to urine, Hawkes modulates the color in terms of Skipper's location and predicament. It is positive or negative, depending on where he is and how he feels.

Skipper remembers only two events from his childhood, the separate deaths of his parents. He prefers to linger over the memory of his mother's death because she literally withdraws from life, leaving him with his private vision as to how she dies. He chooses to see her waiting patiently for death as if preparing for a dinner date. Death arrives with his face hidden, driving a yellow machine, and as the mother climbs aboard, "the vehicle, severe and tangled like a complicated golden insect," gains speed and carries her serenely away (p. 9). From this point in the novel, Hawkes uses yellow to suggest the painful circumstances of Skipper's situation. The odor of Gertrude's death room, for example, reminds him of lemon, and the sky on the day of her funeral emerges with a "pure lemon color." The references to Skipper's pain-filled reality continue to be described with yellow as he narrates his experiences on the West Coast and on the gentle island, but when he is personally involved, the color often degenerates to urine. In the tattoo parlor, Skipper remembers standing in the "urine-colored haze of a guilty light bulb" (p. 15). Thus, when he describes his house on the gentle island and comments upon the "fireplaces packed with the rank odor of urine," we are keyed to look for the coming disasters. The dance in the high school gym recalls the tattoo parlor, for it is lighted with an "uncertain yellow glow." And just as he undergoes the torture of the tattoo, Skipper suffers through the brutal snowball massacre in the cemetery next to the gym which is partially illuminated by a "pale lemon-colored light."

While yellow may be the normal reference for light, Hawkes consistently equates yellow with pain so that the mention of the color encourages a reader response. When Skipper and Cassandra board the *Peter Poor* and don the yellow oilskins, we expect the disaster which soon follows. Cassandra commits suicide, and Skipper's final act on the gentle island is to carry the fetus, Miranda's "present," to the cemetery which is described in yellow in such a way that all the memories of pain, suffering, and death are merged. Miranda's weapon is destructive sexuality, and she dresses to play the role. Skipper first views her in "canary yellow slacks. Soft thick canary yellow slacks tight at the ankles . . . binding the long thighs, binding and so tight on the hips—yellow smooth complicated block of flesh and bone . . . yellow from the waist down . . . lovely specimen of broad flat stomach bound and yellow and undulating . . ." (p. 59). She wears these slacks when she attempts her seduction of Skipper following the dance and when she gives him the fetus. In the face of such consistent pain, Skipper's love remains undaunted, but the suffering takes its toll. As if gathering all the horrors of his predicament for one concise symbol, Hawkes dismisses any positive meaning with yellow. Skipper notices, at the discovery of Fernandez's murder, that the golden threads of the eagle on his naval cap are turning black. This revelation hits us with full force; no amount of expanded description could carry more weight.

Although Hawkes uses black, white, and green in a similar manner, the references to these colors are complicated by the traditional equations of death with black, ambiguity with white, and life or regeneration with green. As long as Skipper recalls his childhood, the West Coast, or the gentle island, the traditional meaning of black holds true. Musing on his youth, Skipper remembers his mortician father and the weekly chore of hosing down the shabby black limousine. Similarly, he pictures the driver in the vision of his mother's death as a figure who wears a black muffler to hide his face and who summons the mother with a squeeze of the "black bulb of the horn." Black associated with death plagues Skipper until he leaves the gentle island. The tattoo artist writes innocently enough with a "black stub of pencil," but Skipper's repressed scream is brilliantly described as "a strenuous black bat struggling, wrestling in my bloated mouth" (p. 19). Hawkes uses other examples to equate black with suffering and death, notably when describing Fernandez and Tremlow, but the most developed use of the equation refers to Miranda and her island. The description of the island with black hues is common enough. What is significant, however, is that normal human relationships are lost in a dark atmosphere of sadism and pain. Skipper describes the Sunday dinners as "our black entanglement" during which they wait around "for something—the first snow? first love? the first outbreak of violence?" (p. 71). Miranda's spell over Cassandra is symbolically presented when Cassandra holds the black yarn while the widow knits. Seeing this also as a "black entanglement," Skipper laments that the yarn is a halter on Cassandra's wrists, a "black umbilicus, the endless and maddening absorption in the problems of yarn" (p. 70).

The thematic use of black reaches its greatest development with Miranda. Skipper's first confrontation with her is not with her person but with her flag—a "black brassiere that dangled as large and stark as an albatross from the tin shower curtain pole" (p. 52). Although she never wears the garment, it is present at each disaster. When Skipper boards the *Peter Poor* with Cassandra, he runs into the black brassiere swinging like a pendulum from a hook. At the dance Miranda is "dressed in black, of course—her totem was still hanging in the bathroom—and around her throat she wore a black velvet band. Her bosom was an unleashed animal" (p. 75). Skipper calls her "the black beauty," and as she dances with Red, who is also dressed in black, he sees them as another black entanglement, as "two tall black figures locked length to length."

This traditional association of black with death holds so long as the scene is the gentle island. Each reference to the color recalls an earlier one; as, for example, when Jomo's black hot rod, an indirect cause of Cassandra's death, calls to mind both the black interior of Fernandez's car and the funeral limousine. Such traditional references aid us. With white and green, however, Hawkes upsets the traditional suggestions of ambiguity with white and of life or fertility with green, thereby adding to the novel's grotesqueness. As with the first mention of yellow and black, that of white refers us to Skipper's childhood when he remembers his mother dressed in white. The personification of death which summons the mother also wears a white cap and coat, but as the yellow death car glides away, the coat turns brown, just as Skipper's gold braid later turns black. White joins black as a prevailing signal of death. As Skipper undergoes his long years of suffering, he makes numerous references to his dirty white naval uniform. It is described as "crumpled" and as a "sullied field of white." And true to the novel's structure, the uniform receives its worst treatment on the gentle island: remember Miranda's symbolic defilement of it with "fresh dark gouts of ketchup." This act units the pattern of imagery which begins with death's white coat turning brown and which ends with Skipper's gold braid turning black.

Miranda, too, is associated with white. As she slips out of the canary yellow slacks during her attempted seduction of Skipper, Hawkes indirectly informs us of the potential catastrophe, exchanging one shade of death for another: "Icebergs. Cold white monumental buttocks. . . . Desire and disaster. Pitiless. A soft breath of snow swirling in that white saddle . . ." (p. 96). Our last view of Miranda comes when she gives Skipper the "present." This moment of death recalls the earlier scene in which she symbolically shatters the maternal instinct by slashing the bottle nipples. For this final perverted act, Hawkes gathers together the three colors and describes Miranda: "Black eyes and sockets, uncombed hair, white face. And after all these months she was wearing the canary yellow slacks again" (p. 201). Ordinarily the reader could suspect that the primary color yellow has been employed to undercut the effect of the negative death-colors, black and white, but yellow is just as lethal. Because of the thematic overtones developed, this final view of her is the portrait of a demon.

White is, however, a secondary color for Miranda, used in an untraditional way to support the traditional suggestions of black. All the effects of the color as it pertains to her are summarized by the "white plastic skull" which she uses for the knob on her car's gearshift and which recalls the black bulb of the horn on death's car. Hawkes reserves the most significant use of white for Cassandra despite the relatively few references. Her face reminds Skipper of a "little death mask of Pascal," and during the bus ride her face is "dead white." Skipper insists, however, upon her youth and innocence, preferring to associate her face with that of the plastic Blessed Virgin Mary which Fernandez attaches to the dash of his car. This confusion of death mask with the face of Mary reaches its climax when Cassandra jumps from the white lighthouse. Standing on the top floor of the lighthouse, Skipper is unable to distinguish between Cassandra's "small white oval face—it was up there with me as well as below on the black rocks—and the small white plastic face of the BVM" (p. 199). But we feel no such confusion because for us the white plastic statuette recalls the white plastic skull in Miranda's car. White has been associated with but one general theme on this island—lack of innocence and death. Any less malevolent associations with the color must remain the product of Skipper's befuddled mind.

A similar use of reversed connotation is developed with the color green, normally a positive hue, for in Skipper's pain-filled world, the traditional associations of life and rebirth with green no longer hold true. The color points to the humiliation and torture of the tattoo. Cassandra demands that Fernandez's name be tattooed in green, "a nice bright green." The tattoo artist warns her (and us) that green is a "bad" color, one that will "hurt like hell," but she insists upon her sadistic game. Hawkes describes the tattoo in such a way as to suggest the full impact of the pain which Cassandra will inflict on Skipper in the course of the novel. The letters are "thick bright green, a string of inflamed emeralds, a row of unnatural dots of jade . . . the large unhealed green name . . . this green lizard that lay exposed and crawling" on Skipper's breast (p. 20). The mention of lizard sets up another series of cross-references which orders the novel. Three soldiers who kiss Cassandra are described as "three deadly lizards," and the leader has "lizard eyes." And the "dragon" in the iguana scene is described as "thirty pounds of sprawling bright green putty . . . gorgeous bright green feathery ruff running down the whole length of him" (p. 106). Rather than life and rebirth, green suggests the extreme pain associated with Skipper's torturers. Fernandez's marriage to Cassandra is ill-fated from the start, and Hawkes indirectly informs us with three key references to green. Fernandez's car, which carries them to the honeymoon hideaway, is an "old disreputable forest green sedan." Married in a white linen suit, Fernandez nevertheless wears green socks. And before retiring for the wedding night, he retrieves his green guitar from the sedan, explaining "there would be no romance without my green guitar" (p. 126). This comment is ironic, not only because romance is impossible, but also because green signals the opposite of romance. Death and green go hand in hand—we learn later that Fernandez is strangled with guitar strings.

Similarly, green dominates the references to Tremlow's mutiny. Hawkes describes the day of the mutiny as dawning pink and green. The shoal water reminds Skipper of "broken bottle-green glass," and by evening green is a symbol of fear. He notices that his

palms and hands are green and that he is soaked with green per-
spiration. These descripions in green of fear and betrayal on the
naval ship provide a cross-reference to Skipper's and Cassandra's
short cruise aboard the *Peter Poor*. At low tide the vessel lists in
green mud. And when Bub hits Skipper just prior to the orgy,
Skipper, in extreme pain, feels that he is "a fat sea dolphin suspended in the painful silence of [a] green underseas cavern" (p.
186). As he comes to his senses, the synesthetic effect of his question drives home the significance of his painful defeat: " 'Where's
the Salerno Kid,' " he asks, "and it was a thick green whispered
question" (p. 188). Most of these color references would have little
significance were it not for Hawkes' conscious reliance on them to
create motifs and order. Although the traditional meanings associated with the colors are often reversed, the symbolic impact of
each color remains consistent as long as Skipper describes those
characters who cause him pain or the surroundings in which the
pain is experienced. But this consistency does not hold true for the
entire novel. When we turn to Skipper's exploits on the wandering
island, we must readjust the symbolic suggestions for each color.
Hawkes complicates the problem further because he dismisses normal chronology in order to place chapters about the wandering
island amid those about the gentle island. We find ourselves dealing with two general sets of motifs and thematic colors and facing
an even more difficult novel than is apparent from the first few
chapters. Yet order remains because the new symbolic associations
for each particular color stand consistent as they are repeated
throughout the chapters about the wandering island. We need
only make sure not to confuse the two general uses of each color.

This first significant hint that Hawkes plans to assign symbolic
associations to his colors other than those which refer to pain and
death occurs in the first descriptions of the wandering island. Celebrating his triumph over Miranda and his escape from the gentle
island, Skipper insists:

> behind every frozen episode of that other island ... no matter
> the rocks and salt and fixed position in the cold black waters of
> the Atlantic—there lies the golden wheel of my hot sun; behind

every black rock ... behind every cruel wind-driven snowstorm a filmy sheet, a transparency, of golden fleas. No matter how stark the scene, no matter how black the gale or sinister the violence of Miranda, still the light of my triumph must shine through.   (p. 48)

This description begins the completion of the tonal declension associated with yellow, for gold acts as a positive color at the other end of the scale from urine, the most negative use of yellow. Having come full circle, the symbolic associations with the color are no longer to pain but to contentment. The story of Skipper's survival becomes an "evocation through a golden glass," and the thematic associations for each color are developed anew to support a second theme—this one of life and fertility. The equation of black with pain and death does not hold for "poor dear black Sonny ... fellow victim and confidant." Significantly, black, on the wandering island, refers to genuine romance as opposed to that of the green guitar. Skipper finds comradeship with black Sonny, spiritual love with black Sister Josie, and sexual love with black Catalina Kate, thus controverting the dazzled, self-projected "white-innocence" imagery which had befuddled him during his life with Cassandra. The birth of Kate's black baby nullifies the sterile sexuality of Miranda, a white woman consistently associated with black. Thus while black is feared on the gentle island, it is now celebrated, as when Skipper describes the blackbird: "As for a blackbird sitting on a cow's rump, there surely is the perfect union, the meeting of the fabulous herald and the life source" (p. 101). This description is a specific point of reference for us because three chapters later Skipper impregnates a cow, and a "dense tribe of blackbirds" cheers at the completion of the ritual.

As Hawkes lifts black away from its traditional connotation on the wandering island, he readjusts the descriptions in white. The white house on the second island, for example, recalls the white house of pain, but this time white suggests beneficence. Skipper and Sonny wear white as Cassandra usually does, but the color seems now to refer to their fertile sexuality with Kate. Oscar the bull, the other source of life on the wandering island, has a white head. The literal level of interpretation with these colors is clear, but Hawkes suggests various levels of meaning by his conscious use of color for cross-references and structural purposes.

Similarly, green, when found on the wandering island, loses its connotation of horror and resumes its traditional association with life and fulfillment. There is no better symbol of this reversal than the discovery that Skipper's green tattoo is covered and healed by the golden sunlight. Even the green iguana finally departs, an agent of pain but not of malicious intent. Fertility, love, and survival all merge in the color green when Skipper finishes with the impregnation of the cow. Turning to Catalina Kate, now eight months pregnant, Skipper watches as she tears off "a flower—leaf, flower, taste of green vine—and looking at me put it between her teeth, began to chew" (p. 173). We need no further explanation—Skipper has finally found love.

The concluding short chapter draws many of the motifs together for a final celebration of Skipper's victory. Carrying Kate's newborn child to the cemetery, Skipper acts out a symbolic ritual. He places stubs of candles on the stone markers and observes "the shades and graves and little yellow teeth of light." Although reminded of the cemeteries which hold his parents, Gertrude, and Cassandra, our interpretation now develops from a different angle. Skipper's life, both defeats and victories, is always with the dead, and the yellow candlelight dancing on the tombs is the triumph of his final victory. He can now afford to celebrate life beside gravestones, an act which, Hawkes suggests, must be performed if we are to survive. Death and life are one, a truth which Kate senses. For when Skipper asks whom the baby resembles, she answers, "Him look like the fella in the grave." Skipper breaks out "black blood sausage" and white wine for the ritual feast, and one of his final acts provides the last stitch in a thread which has unified the novel. Kneeling beside a "great monumental outline of old stone that had survived grief," a symbol of himself, he quickly sweeps "the little lizards off the rim of it" (p. 208). With this motion he purges his past; his naked history is complete. The intricacy with which Hawkes puts related events and recurring images together testifies to the care he takes to help us grasp the shifting narrative, the unconventional characters, and the thematic suggestions of each grotesque event. Hawkes' interest in structural coherence is reflected in Skipper's efforts to shape our opinion of his narrative. Proud of his mastery of language, Skipper may very well have used his art to point out the interpretation he desires—art may have created history.

Memoirs of a Sex-Singer:
The Blood Oranges

THE Blood Oranges (1971) is Hawkes' third consecutive novel about the varieties of love. In *The Lime Twig* repressed sexuality generates erotic dreams which lure Michael and Margaret Banks to nightmare and violent death. Cruelty and malevolence, normal by-products of love in *The Lime Twig*, are even more extreme in *Second Skin*. Saturated with suicides and grotesque events like the tattoo which make pain appear exotic, *Second Skin* would be Hawkes' most depressing fiction about the close relationship between violence and love were it not for the affirmation of love's final victory. Skipper's discovery of "love at last" on the lush wandering island testifies to his faith in the regenerative process and to his belief in the maxim that virtue always wins. *Second Skin*'s serene atmosphere and confidence in the healing power of love seem at first glance to carry over to *The Blood Oranges*. Hawkes' most extended discussion of love, *The Blood Oranges* appears to take up the theme at the point where Skipper finishes the final flourish of his naked history.

Once again, for example, Hawkes creates a first-person narrator,

Cyril, who has complete control of his tale as he relates his adventures in what he terms the "tapestry" of love. Establishing an atmosphere and tone suitable for a love story, Cyril uses a lyrical, sensuous prose which recalls Skipper's heightened language:

> Sinuous smoke, sun on the back of my hand, smile reaching out for the pain that lay behind the skin of her face, the sound of my voice already gone, frames of golden eyeglasses warm on the bridge of my nose and behind the ears, and smiling in silence, leaning forward, waiting, receiving no answer.[1]

This description could just as easily have come from *Second Skin*, and, indeed, the epigraph to *The Blood Oranges* seems a direct reference to what Skipper calls his land of spices:

> Is there then any terrestrial paradise where, amidst the whispering of the olive-leaves, people can be with whom they like and have what they like and take their ease in shadows and in coolness?   —Ford Madox Ford: *The Good Soldier*

Reading this epigraph, the reader familiar with Hawkes' fiction nods affirmatively to Dowell's question and thinks immediately of Skipper's wandering island. Surely Skipper's final retreat is an earthly paradise free from threats of designing friends and full of lovers who dreamily pursue the regenerative cycle.

Cyril would like to persuade us that he has found a similar paradise of ease and love, and for a while he sounds convincing. But repeated readings of his narrative suggest, despite his insistence to the contrary, that he will find his paradise only in an imaginative reconstruction of past events which seems at odds with the horrors of his reality. Thus the answer to Dowell's question, insofar as *The Blood Oranges* is concerned, is "no." Cyril remains in Illyria but so do the realities of Hugh's death, Catherine's illness, and Fiona's departure. Perhaps only within the texture of his visionary tapestry can he experience the earthly paradise which Dowell wonders about and which Skipper attains.

As noted in the chapter on *Second Skin*, Hawkes specifically

---

1. John Hawkes, *The Blood Oranges* (New York: New Directions, 1971), p. 8. All further references will be in parentheses.

states that Skipper developed from Hencher's role in *The Lime Twig*. The suggestion that Cyril finds his genesis in Skipper seems just as valid. In both cases a primitive life-style finds expression in fertility rites, submission to pastoral rhythms, and acknowledgment of the subconscious need for sexuality and love. Both Skipper and Cyril celebrate their strength to endure tragedy, to slough off the debilitating effects of violence, and to survive intact. Both reconstruct their stories after the fact in a prose style reminiscent of a love lyric. And most of all, both proudly call attention to their success as lovers and to their creations of timeless locales which give substance to their narratives and support to their roles. But the similarities end here, for Cyril finally exposes himself as the negative side of Skipper's innocence. It is almost as if Cyril is Skipper's dark shadow, a personification of the deceit which lingers in all of us but which Skipper successfully represses.

Skipper loves in order to help others, to neutralize with his own flesh the poison of their hate, and to reaffirm his faith in life itself while those around him pursue death. But Cyril loves in order to fulfill his own sexuality and to express his theory of sex-singing. Skipper's love is so compassionate that he grieves for the cruelty and violence in the very people who hound his life, willingly suffering extreme pain for his faith in virtue. But Cyril claims to transcend grief because he believes that love depresses pain. Finally, Skipper's love is fertile, an expression of the earth's cycle with an emphasis on beginning again, but Cyril's sex-singing is sterile, an exhibition of sexuality which consumes the passions of those about him. Some may question Skipper's protestations of heroism, but all would agree that he is an affirmative person. Cyril, on the other hand, is a hero to no one except himself. His devotion to fertility rites and his submission to pastoral serenity produce only sterility and eventual death. Cyril's Illyria is Skipper's wandering island sullied by perversion of the one force Skipper suffers for in order to keep pure—love. In *Second Skin* neither suicide nor malicious hate, nor even murder, can annihilate the love force. But in *The Blood Oranges* Cyril, the self-proclaimed priest of love, unknowingly distorts love by limiting it to sexual freedom.

His story is much less complicated than Skipper's. Establishing his subject in the first paragraph, he immediately associates himself with love's golden thread and all of its mystery: "Love weaves its own tapestry, spins its own golden thread, with its own sweet breath breathes into being its mysteries—bucolic, lusty, gentle as the eyes of daisies or thick with pain. And out of its own music creates the flesh of our lives. If the birds sing, the nudes are not far off" (p. 1). The rest of the novel is Cyril's effort to explain as much to himself as to us how his own tapestry of love came to be ragged and torn and how he plans to mend it. Like most of Hawkes' fiction, *The Blood Oranges* reveals an intricate narrative pattern full of time shifts, each with its own storyline, and interlocking cross-references rather than an involved plot. Cyril is primarily concerned with two specific times: the immediate past when he and his wife Fiona attempt to initiate another couple, Hugh and Catherine, into the mysteries of sex-singing; and the present when he convinces Catherine to help him mend the metaphorical tapestry following Hugh's suicide and the subsequent break-up of what he calls their "symmetry."

Hugh's death is a near fatal blow to Cyril's experiments with sexual freedom, though it is by no means the novel's most grotesque scene. At first Cyril and Fiona appear to have found the perfect locale for their life of love. Situated in a strange, pastoral land identified only as Illyria, they are the sole Westerners among a group of natives who speak an undecipherable language. There are vague references to past love affairs for both Cyril and his wife, but Hawkes avoids the exposition most readers expect. He supplies no details of their lives prior to the novel's time periods, and he refuses to tell how they found this remote country. They are simply there, isolated in a primitive life-style, and apparently happy. When Hugh, Catherine, and three daughters arrive from "beyond the mountains," Cyril's philosophy of sexual multiplicity begins to take shape. He easily seduces Catherine, but Hugh, a handsome one-armed man who likes to photograph nude peasant girls, rebuffs Fiona's advances. The four begin a kind of sexual picnic beneath the tropical orange sun, full of nude swimming, erotic games, and Cyril's theorizing about the pleasures of sexual freedom. Hugh is content to pair off with Fiona, but he will not consummate the affair until the pressure to do so shatters what Cyril calls his "conventionality." Stripping nude and then hanging himself, Hugh manages with his death to warp their symmetry. Fiona leaves to care for his children, Catherine suffers a traumatic shock, and Cyril finds his tapestry in tatters. But he remains undaunted. In his narrative of the novel's "present" time, he reveals his slow, intricate, and often humorous efforts to break through Catherine's depression and thus, by reclaiming her as his mistress, to reestablish his role as love's agent.

If degree of difficulty is limited only to determining what happens, *The Blood Oranges* is much "easier" than *The Cannibal, The Beetle Leg,* or even, perhaps, *Second Skin.* The negative barbs usually tossed at Hawkes' fiction, such as gratuitous opaqueness, do not apply here. Readers uneasy with experimental fiction and extremely violent humor will not be so totally shocked by *The Blood Oranges.* Yet none of Hawkes' novels, including this one, can be grasped in one reading. The published comments about and reviews of *The Blood Oranges* testify to the wildly mixed reaction Hawkes' fiction always elicits. Covering the gamut from unqualified praise to scathing dismissals of the novel, these comments show that with his eighth novel Hawkes remains just as controversial as he was in 1949 when he published *Charivari.* A discussion of these critical opinions will lead us to an examination of Cyril's theories, the elaborate symbolic references he uses to express them, and the reasons for his current predicament.

In general, reactions to *The Blood Oranges* focus on three areas: Cyril as narrator, the original setting, and the intricate symbolic allusions. Writing for the *New York Times Book Review,* Thomas McGuane expresses complete approval.[2] Suggesting that Hawkes is "feasibly our best writer," McGuane praises him as the one American novelist who can "so well arrest that perpetually terrified portion of the inner mind with unnerving images of things

2. Thomas McGuane, "*The Blood Oranges,*" *New York Times Book Review,* section 7, 19 September 1971, p. 1.

going to pieces." He reserves most of his praise for the novel's un-relenting originality. Noting that Hawkes is unapologetic about his fiction, and admitting his difficulty, McGuane nevertheless wonders why Hawkes is not better known. He decides that it is the reader, and no longer Hawkes, who is now being tested, for he sees *The Blood Oranges* as Hawkes' most accessible novel to date.

Ronald De Feo, in an article for *Saturday Review*, also approves of *The Blood Oranges*, though he seems less convinced than McGuane.[3] He celebrates Hawkes' "remarkable ability to create dream landscapes," worlds which are so mysterious that added de-tails only heighten our sense of disorientation, and settings which have a puzzling, unfamiliar logic all their own. But while he finds the novel "original and haunting," he does not think it as "com-pelling" as *Second Skin* or *The Lime Twig*. His primary com-plaints are that some of the language is overwritten and that it is not as technically adventurous as the earlier fiction.

Walter Beacham's mixed reaction to *The Blood Oranges* carries De Feo's criticism a little further.[4] Admitting that Hawkes has achieved a considerable reputation among readers who enjoy sub-tle fiction, he nevertheless finds this novel "short on plot, short on setting, short on interesting characters, and too long, apparently, on theme and symbol." Despite such sweeping charges, Beacham avoids complete condemnation. He finally cannot make up his mind about the book, a common reaction upon first reading a Hawkes novel. On the one hand he does not think it a good piece of fiction, but on the other he wonders if it might not one day be a classic: "It doesn't seem to be a very good book, especially to come from the pen of John Hawkes; yet there is something peculiarly alluring and sinister about the whole attempt, and the reader sus-pects this might be one of those novels that will become better, perhaps even a classic, as the critics explicate the subtleties for us." The nagging sense of importance which the novel encourages is for him never revealed.

3. Ronald De Feo, "*The Blood Oranges*," *Saturday Review*, 23 Octo-ber 1971, pp. 92, 94.

4. Walter Beacham, "Hawkes' New Novel Imparts Nagging Sense of Importance," *Richmond Times-Dispatch*, 5 December 1971, p. F–5.

Beacham's observations suggest the controversy surrounding Hawkes' fiction in general. But we need to look at Roger Sale's comments to complete the spectrum, for Sale unreservedly damns the book.[5] He begins his review with an attempted knock-out blow by stating unequivocally that *The Blood Oranges* fails because it is the product of a "contemptible imagination." Why is Hawkes' imagination contemptible?—because, writes Sale, he has always been "more an unadmitted voyeur of horror than its calm delineator." He finds this novel more deserving of scorn than Hawkes' previous efforts because "in this new novel the pretense that what is being described is horrifying is dropped, and we have only the nightmare vision of a narrator unable to see how awful he is." He goes on to argue that because Cyril's cruelty is unadmitted, it "is not even palliated by the relish of sadism." Sale's major complaint is that he sees the author Hawkes standing with the narrator Cyril, nodding his head in agreement with each of Cyril's pronouncements on love. Commenting on Cyril's criticism of Hugh's belief in chastity, for example, Sale argues that both author and narrator are at fault for imagining that chastity, not Cyril, should be blamed.

Sale's dislike of *The Blood Oranges* is based less on criticism of Cyril, setting, and symbolic patterns than on a quarrel with the fictional technique used to create Cyril as narrator. He seems more upset with Hawkes' method than with the novel it produces. Acknowledging possible loopholes in his observations, he tries to cover his tracks by admitting that Hawkes' many admirers will note that "I have completely missed the fact that it is a put-on." And, indeed, Gilbert Sorrentino, for one, takes up the challenge in print.[6] Terming Sale's review "silly frothings at the mouth," he insists that Cyril's self-justifications, elaborate theories about sex, and celebration of the joys of adultery are sufficiently clear shortcomings to portray him mean and hateful. But what is more significant to a discussion of *The Blood Oranges* is not this particular

5. Roger Sale, "*The Blood Oranges*," *New York Review of Books*, 21 October 1971, pp. 2–6.
6. "Letters," *New York Review of Books*, 2 December 1971, p. 36.

observation, nor the original review which prompts it, but Mr. Sale's reply to the Sorrentino letter. His rebuttal does more than defend his previously stated argument—it reveals him to be the type of reader who demands demonstrable evidence that the author, aloof from his narrator or not, is at least indicating authorial pressure on the invented storyteller. Sale apparently believes that every author is obligated to the reader to tip his hand, to establish precisely where he stands in relation to his fictional material. And he insists on all or nothing. Since Hawkes remains totally uninvolved with his narrator, *The Blood Oranges* remains, in Sale's view, contemptible.

These astonishingly varied reviews, from McGuane's high praise to Beacham's hesitancy to Sale's angry dismissal, testify to the controversial responses which Hawkes' fiction encourages. Although *The Blood Oranges* is one of his most accessible novels in terms of what happens, it promises, nevertheless, a difficult reading experience. Even the theory of fiction which informs the novel is challenged. Mr. Sale's notions of what fiction should be clearly conflict with Hawkes' previously published opinions about experimental writing. What should be recalled here are Hawkes' comments about his goal of disrupting the novel's more conventional forms and his insistence upon an "increasing need" to parody the conventions. Calling for wit, the comic treatment of violence, and extreme detachment in experimental fiction, he singles out detachment as the center of the novelist's effort.[7]

It seems to me that recognition and acceptance of the distance between Hawkes and Cyril are the keys to evaluating Cyril's narration. Sale argues that Hawkes is "dabbling in the boring and hateful," but Hawkes would contend that such malice in a novel is nothing without corresponding sympathy: "But mere malice is nothing in itself, of course, and the product of extreme fictive detachment is extreme fictive sympathy." Successful maintenance of consistent detachment toward the violence of his characters enables him to generate this very deep sympathy defined as a "hum-

7. See John Hawkes, "Notes on the Wild Goose Chase," *Massachusetts Review*, 3 (Summer 1962), 787.

bling before the terrible, and a quickening in the presence of degradation." Thus Hawkes justifies his understanding of the relationship between author and narrator—a complete lack of authorial pressure. The author remains free from any obligation to reveal where he stands. If we are to understand that Cyril is contemptible, no matter how idealistic and lyrical, then Hawkes must be allowed to create him in such a way that Cyril exposes himself and, simultaneously, arouses in us sympathy for his degradation. Insisting on total freedom from the constraints of traditional point of view, motivation, and the logical progression from cause to effect, Hawkes creates the impression that his characters are free to go their own way. His fictions may be the product of an intensely personal vision, but once he begins to write he erases his own personality. The authorial distance maintained throughout *The Blood Oranges* contributes to the blackness of the novel's humor. How are we to react, for example, when Hugh clamps the ancient chastity belt around Catherine's loins? Hugh's gesture is ridiculously funny, but one which nevertheless causes pain. Without hints and nudges from Hawkes, we are left to our own devices, forced to participate in the narrative in order to discover for ourselves where the humor leads and what it might mean. Significantly, Cyril the narrator is as detached from the horror as Hawkes the creator. The result of such total objectivity is that we are isolated with a terror that becomes more intense as the detachment is realized. Neither real author nor implied author supplies guidelines.

Recognition of the function of comedy is nearly as important to a reading of *The Blood Oranges* as acceptance of Hawkes' extreme fictive detachment. We note Mr. Sale's complaint that Cyril's cruelty is beyond sadism because it is unadmitted. Yet to criticize the novel on these grounds is to ignore comedy's role. Hawkes has never sought to minimize the cruelty or sadism in his fiction, but he insists that awareness of the humor must join recognition of the terror: "But though I'd be the first to admit to sadistic impulses in the creative process, I must say that my writing is not mere indulgence in violence or derangement, is hardly intended simply to shock. As I say, comedy, which is often closely related to poetic use of language, is what makes the difference for me." [8] The negative comments about *The Blood Oranges* make no mention of the comic impulse at work behind the obvious terror, giving shape and perspective to the violence. As Hawkes notes, comedy not only creates sympathy. It also helps to expose evil, to convince us that we, too, may be involved in malicious processes, and most of all, to suggest futurity, "a certain hope in the limitless energies of life itself."

We distort *The Blood Oranges* when we insist on Cyril's meanness without a corresponding recognition of his ridiculousness. His egotism is soon obvious despite efforts to convince us of his gentleness and purity. Admittedly the humor of his narrative is not as easily seen as the cruelty because Hawkes rejects authorial suggestions which could point to the comedy. Leaving Cyril alone to expose himself, he relies on his narrator's pompous theorizing, overconfident manipulation of others, and frantic efforts to reweave the tapestry, to reveal Cyril for what he is—a comic idealist who is a slave to a philosophy of polygamy. In *The Blood Oranges*, as in all Hawkes' fiction, comedy does not soften the cruelty, for Cyril's humorous though lyrically narrated theories do have tragic consequences. But we reduce the novel to gratuitous violence if we discuss Cyril's deceptions and ignore the comedy which finally mocks him.

The point is that Hawkes rejects the sick joke, the kind of humor that degenerates into mindless cruelty. He sees, rather, the function of comedy as a saving attitude, a means to reacquaint us with the eternal verities. Recall this key statement in his theory of fiction: "If something is pathetically humorous or grotesquely humorous, it seems to pull us back into the realm, not of mere conventional values but of the lasting values, the one or two really deep permanent human values." [9] The lasting value linked with

8. "John Hawkes: An Interview," *Wisconsin Studies in Contemporary Literature*, 6 (Summer 1965), 145–146.
9. "John Hawkes on His Novels: An Interview with John Graham," *Massachusetts Review*, 7 (Summer 1966), 461.

grotesque humor in *The Blood Oranges* is love. By fashioning Cyril's musings about love in such a ridiculous manner, Hawkes persuades us to reexamine the meaning of love. Once we realize that Cyril is utterly serious about sex-singing, we find ourselves redefining love in reaction to his distortions even while we laugh at him. Love may be warped in *The Blood Oranges*, but the distortion is not Hawkes' doing. All of the blame must rest with his narrator who, once created, takes on a life of his own. Our laughter at Cyril's efforts to defend his extraordinary sexual freedom remains meaningless unless we reconsider at the same time what love means to us.

Cyril, of course, is unaware that he is funny. Much of his humor results from incongrous remarks about or inappropriate responses to serious situations. When, for example, he tries to rekindle Catherine's love following Hugh's suicide, he whispers reverently as if he were an ordained savior, "Arise, arise, Catherine . . . climb to your feet, and let's comfort each other" (p. 13). Or note his use of medical terminology when he describes the equality which middle-age gives each of the four adults: "Too big for mere caprice, too old to waste time and yet old enough to appreciate immodesty, we were all four of us imposing in height, in weight, in blood pressure, in chest expansion" (p. 16). Cyril consistently identifies himself with the white bull or the golden ram in love's tapestry, but he does not realize how our laughter at his use of the word "menagerie" undercuts what he thinks is a serious remark: "Was it dream, change, coincidence, or was my state of mind a menagerie of desire from which real animals might spring?" (pp. 92–93). How can we accept his role as supreme lover when he interrupts his first seduction of Catherine to comment: "Her hardly audible vocal throb subsided, she did not move. I swung away and for a moment devoted precise fingers to the carefully tied laces of my tennis shoes" (p. 116)?

Yet humor does not shake his confidence, and it is complete assurance in sexual matters which makes him both misguided and ridiculous. His description, for example, of a snail hunt with Rosella, a young peasant girl who serves as his cook, turns a routine chore into a grotesquely funny seduction scene. They do not understand each other's language, but they join together to track down the "sticky silver trails" of the snails. The scene includes Cyril's accidental spilling of the snail pot, his glimpse of Rosella's thighs and buttocks, the appearance of a hunchback who gives Rosella a love offering of dead sparrows, and the preparation of snails and sparrows for dinner. Cyril admits that when he and Rosella sit down to the meal, there will be "no touching of knees," no "meeting of bare feet." But her sticky lips arouse him. He ends this wonderfully funny scene wondering if Rosella's gravy-spattered lips are not a sign that love is about to reclaim him: "Had I gone too far? Had I somehow raised false hopes? Was that whole vast tapestry beyond villa, cypresses, village, crying out for my re-entry into the pink field? Was my very skin about to be fired again in the kiln that has no flame? At least the sparrows inside me were already singing a different song, and I was listening" (p. 53). All this because of gravy-spattered lips? We are listening too, incredulous at his arrogance but amused by his anticipation. His belief that love speaks to him alone results in pain for his friends, laughter for the reader, and frustration for all. The creative spirit behind *The Blood Oranges* is comic while the fiction itself is dark, constantly recalling what Hawkes has termed the "ultimate thunderclap." Revolving around Cyril's tale are the paradoxes of love causing fear, sexuality spawning sterility, and a pastoral timelessness producing death.

Reader interest in *The Blood Oranges* does not center on the book's action but on how Cyril evaluates what happens. All of Hawkes' novels minimize plot, and *The Blood Oranges* is no exception. The plot is again a vehicle for the display of intricate language, the pleasures of grotesque comedy, and the experiments with, often parodies of, narrative technique. To be sure things happen—a bus accident, an expedition to an ancient fortress to search for a chastity belt, a suicide—but Hawkes is more interested in his narrator's reaction to the events than the action itself. If *The Blood Oranges* has a plot in the traditional sense, it is Cyril's attempt to piece together for us and, more importantly, for himself not only what happens but why. For despite Cyril's command of language and allusion, he cannot determine the reasons for what he considers to be serious interruptions of his efforts to create sexual harmony among four middle-aged adults.

There is little controversy concerning the novel's limited action, for the simple plot is part of Hawkes' general plan when writing fiction. But to say, as Mr. Beacham does, that this novel is short on setting is to invite disagreement unless he means conventional setting, for Hawkes is not interested in realistically described localities. The setting of *The Blood Oranges*, a remote Mediterranean country, is intended more as a frame suitable for Cyril's musings about the definition of love. Detailed descriptions of the pastoral landscape are not ignored, but the primary effect of this particular setting is to convey a feeling of timelessness and to gain from us agreement that such strange adventures could indeed occur there. Hawkes provides not a specific account of where Cyril pursues his theory of polygamy but rather an air of exotic lushness, pastoralism, and remoteness which passes for a modern Illyria.

Atmosphere is much more significant than detail. Kept purposely vague, nearly abstract, this novel's setting is more an illusion than a definite place. Cyril's metaphor of the tapestry is apt, for it testifies to the artifice which he can fashion in such a locale. The fictional landscape is typically Hawkes—dreamy, unusual, promising violence and pain. It is described as "primitive," and artifacts from ancient Italy are mentioned, such as "a low urn containing the ashes of a Roman lover." Prominent in the landscape are "the stinking depths of the timeless pestilential canal" which is variously described as being "historically significant," and as having a "deep intestinal tug." This strangeness is balanced by a rich pastoralism. Numerous references are made to cypress trees, arbors heavy with grapes, beaches warm enough for nude sunbathing, and shepherds watching flocks of goats. Cyril describes a typical scene as he goes to visit Catherine:

> My slow bike ride takes me from the villa where I live by choice with Rosella, through the poor coastal village with its ruined aqueduct and small houses of charred bone (that wet dark place

always fetid with the faint bulbous aroma of sewer gas still rising from the deep pits dug by ancient barbarians), then out of
the darkness and up the crusted slope of the hill. . . . The same
each week, from dead snails and sediment and the stately gloom
of the funeral cypresses to the sudden light, peace, charm of this
walled sanctuary. . . . The sanctuary is simple and mysterious too,
is antithetical to the brambles and broken tiles of the primitive
landscape above which it is set. Surely the sanctuary was conceived and built by someone who could never vocalize the harsh
unimaginative language of this terrain.   (pp. 5–6)

Later in the novel Fiona asks rhetorically where they are, and
Cyril shouts, "We're in Illyria." This reference to Shakespeare's
pastoral country in *Twelfth Night* is not a chance occurrence, for
Cyril mentions Illyria at least a half dozen times.

Such a consciously fashioned setting can easily carry the weight
of most of the elaborate symbolic references, for we know that we
are reading not an account of verisimilitide but the musings of a
narrator who seems determined to weave the bits and pieces of
real life into a stylized design expressive of his views of sex and
love. But while the fictional landscape guarantees credence for
most of the symbols, the novel may nevertheless be overcharged
with allusions and references. Mr. Beacham's criticism that *The
Blood Oranges* is "too long, apparently, on theme and symbol"
seems worth considering. Complaining that potential symbols are
never developed, Beacham suspects that even "witch hunters" will
feel uncomfortable tracking down the blatant symbolism. He may
have a point. As noted in earlier chapters, Hawkes has always
heightened his comedy by suggesting symbols and mythological
references which more often than not are secondary to his primary
purpose. Classical allusions, peculiar names, nature references, and
religious trappings are, in many cases, red herrings, designed more
to support atmosphere than to create specific meanings. This device is present in *The Blood Oranges,* and it may be extreme because the sheer quantity of the allusions nearly overwhelms the
reader. Yet the elaborate symbols do unify into patterns of cross-
references and parallels which normally point to narrative coherence in Hawkes' fiction. Recall that in *The Cannibal* the appar-

ently disjointed animal imagery provides indirect commentary upon the status of Germany as well as indicates the novel's internal coherence. Color imagery in *Second Skin* is so highly developed that it helps us grasp each thematic suggestion of Skipper's misadventures. In *The Blood Oranges* these allusions retain suggestive meanings and often develop into the expanding narrative patterns we have come to expect in Hawkes' work.

In many cases the symbolic variations are ironic, for (in the guise of Cyril's narration) Hawkes again parodies the novelist's role. The point is that the symbolism seems to get away not from Hawkes but from Cyril. No reader of the *Blood Oranges* wants to be a "witch hunter." There is always danger of overreading the symbolism in a Hawkes novel. And yet the allusions send us to Shakespeare and to books on mythology with such frequency that some discussion of them is called for. Since Cyril consciously uses mythological allusions and symbolic references to heighten his story, we should follow his lead at least part way and investigate the more important symbolism to which he alludes. If he sees himself as a mythic character in love's tapestry, we must note the references in order to understand how he defines himself. The most significant of them are to male animals, flowers and vegetation, and Illyria.

Cyril consistently associates himself with bulls and goats. On the second page he calls attention to his sexual role when he defines his place in the tapestry:

> Throughout my life I have simply appeared at Love's will. See me as small white porcelain bull lost in the lower left-hand corner of that vast tapestry, see me as great white creature horned and mounted on a trim little golden sheep in the very center of Love's most explosive field. See me as bull, or ram, as man, husband, lover, a tall and heavy stranger in white shorts on a violet tennis court.   (p. 2)

On first meeting Hugh and Catherine, he decides that Hugh has a "saintly goatish face." This should be a happy sign, for it suggests to him Hugh's readiness for sexual multiplicity. But after Hugh rebuffs Fiona's advances, Cyril calls a goat "our rigidly approaching nemesis" because he knows that sex will ruin their idyl by driving Hugh to despair. Goats appear everywhere—significantly accompanied by a girl, in the face of a lusty old man who celebrates the launching of a boat, even in Cyril's smoke rings.

In *The Golden Bough*, J. G. Frazer summarizes the mythological meaning of bulls and goats. Dionysus, the god of vegetation, was often represented in animal shape, especially a bull or goat, thus establishing links between seasonal fertility and sexual lustiness. As a goat, Dionysus can hardly be separated from the minor divinities, Pan, the Satyrs, and Silenus, all of whom are represented in the form of goats. For example, Pan was regularly portrayed with the face and legs of a goat. The Satyrs were depicted with goat ears and often with horns and short tails. And Silenus was represented clad in a goatskin.[10] The bull and goat have been well established as symbols combining the reproductive seasonal cycle with human fertility rites. But Cyril's consistent identification of himself with these animals of love is ironical, for his sexuality amounts to lechery, reproducing nothing, expressing no fertility, and causing suicide and pain. Though he insists that he is not against domesticity, he and Fiona have long since decided not to produce children. Indeed this is the key difference between the two couples, for Hugh and Catherine have three daughters. Fiona pinpoints the gulf separating Cyril's sexuality from Hugh's when she instructs Cyril on their wedding night: *"Don't bother being a husband, baby. Just be a sex-singer"* (p. 97). Cyril's scorn of Hugh's conventional sex within marriage causes him to describe Hugh as "doomed": "But I for one was conscious of bodies, hands, squinting eyes, positions in line, was well aware that Fiona stood on my left and Catherine on my right and that Hugh was doomed forever to the extreme left and could never share my privilege of standing, so to speak, between two opposite and equally desirable women" (p. 118).

But Cyril remains unaware that his sterility is at odds with his view of himself as a modern Dionysus. Rather than give nourish-

10. James George Frazer, *The Golden Bough: A Study in Magic and Religion* (New York: MacMillan, 1923), p. 464.

ment to his idyl, he destroys the sexual symmetry which he longs to make permanent. His unconscious self-destruction parallels Frazer's observation about the role of the goat deity in ancient myth. Noting that the fertility god, personified as a goat, often destroys its own subsistence by feeding upon it, Frazer writes, "The inconsistency of a god of vegetation subsisting upon the vegetation which he personifies is not one to strike the primitive mind. Such inconsistencies arise when the deity, ceasing to be immanent in the vegetation, comes to be regarded as its owner or lord; for the idea of owning the vegetation naturally leads to that of subsisting on it." [11] Destroying his own life source, the god soon experiences poverty. Cyril suffers the same fate. As a self-proclaimed god of love, he feeds on love until he exhausts it. His situation in the novel's "present" time testifies to his poverty. He muses about his past, and he explains to us his current courtship of Catherine while living in a rundown villa "with broken red tiles and fireplaces like abandoned urinals . . . where I knew my last mistress, sang my last song, last spread the legs of my wife" (p. 2). Shabby clothes, muddy shoes, rusty bicycle, and cigarette butts for smoking illustrate his present state as a victim of his own interpretation of love. Never admitting he was wrong, and at a loss to explain the sudden absence of sex-singing, Cyril wonders if love purged him when it rid itself of Hugh's conventional love. Note his bewildered tone:

> Why, after more than eighteen years, does the soft medieval fabric of my tapestry now hang in shreds—here the head of a rose, there the amputated hoof of some infant goat? Is it possible that in purging her field of Hugh's sick innocence Love (impatient Love) purged me as well? Eliminated even her own faithful sex-singer from the joyous field? It is possible.   (p. 3)

Coming as it does so early in *The Blood Oranges*, this statement suggests the rationale for Cyril's story—he needs to determine why he fell from love's favor, whether or not he was at fault, and what hope he has for restoration. He remains confident that he will soon recover his identification with bull and goat. Telling himself that

11. Ibid., p. 465.

"this abandoned man survives the period of his uselessness, that no catastrophe can destroy true elegance," he now initiates a new ritual of seduction, hoping that Catherine will once again welcome him to her bed. He clearly refuses to accept the poverty which mythological gods of fertility suffer when they devour their nourishment.

Cyril's ironic identification with the animal personifications of the gods of fertility finds a further expression in his association with flowers and vegetation. One of his most effective erotic stimulants, for example, is the "grape-tasting game." Grapes have long been linked in mythology with fertilizing powers.[12] Using the grape-tasting game to arouse desire, Cyril describes his grape arbor as "clearly the place for the bedding down of lovers" (p. 183). He suspects that Hugh's reaction will be distaste and impatience, but as love's agent, Cyril feels obligated to awaken Hugh to the joys of grape-tasting. Hands behind back and standing on tip-toe, he sticks his face in among the grape clusters: "methodically I sucked in that simple plump dangling grape and gave a tug, closed my mouth, split the skin, began to chew" (p. 185). Obviously affected, Hugh takes his turn, straining to reach the grapes. When Cyril says, "They're only grapes," Hugh replies, "Nipples, boy, that's what you mean" (p. 186). Once again Cyril's association with an ancient symbol of fertility is ironic. His successful stimulation of sexual passion in both Hugh and himself is worthless because this modern fertility rite reproduces nothing.

Similarly, the ironic relationship holds true with Cyril's affinity for lemon and orange trees. The folklore of trees traditionally associates the lemon with passion and discretion and the orange with fecundity, chastity in marriage, and eternal love.[13] References to oranges and the color orange fill the novel from the title to the orange marguerites which stand beside Cyril's bed as he makes love to Fiona and which he describes as "deeply orange" and "in-

12. See Frazer, *The Golden Bough* (London: MacMillan, 1919), 5:165; and Ernst and Johanna Lehner, *Folklore and Symbolism of Flowers, Plants and Trees* (New York: Tudor, 1960), p. 117.
13. Lehner, pp. 75, 119.

nocent." Surely he understands the traditional folklore surrounding oranges, for he uses it so consciously while narrating the story. He would like to be known as a faithful lover. But like the association with the goat deity the development of references to oranges finally exposes him. Rather than suggesting chastity and eternal love, Cyril's oranges point to pure eroticism. His most extended use of orange occurs during recollection of the sun bathing party with Fiona, Catherine, and Hugh. Cyril and Fiona are dressed daringly in sparse briefs, while the other couple is modestly covered. The setting sun, described as an "enormous smoldering sun . . . like a dissolving orange suffused with blood" clearly affects them all (p. 37). The lower the sun falls, the more their bodies glow, and the orange color lulls them to inertia and dreams. When the orange light makes them unrecognizable, Cyril quickly removes Fiona's bathing bra. She stares at the blood orange sun while its color seems to affect the size of her breasts. Although Cyril enjoys the eroticism, he is more interested in persuading Hugh to become a sex-singer. This scene nicely illustrates his longing for symmetry and harmony, for he now waits for Hugh to remove Catherine's bra. Growing impatient, he wonders if "this momentary idyl would pass before the rose and golden metallic threads could begin to spin our separate anatomies forever into the sunset scene, would come to a sudden conclusion, incomplete, unbalanced. What was the matter with Hugh? Why was he not holding up his end?" (p. 42). Fearing that Hugh may be blind to their "sex-tableau," he watches while Catherine completes the symmetry and exposes her breasts herself. Cheered and fulfilled, Cyril now foresees many sunsplashed days of sexual harmony, but he fails to recognize that this apparent bliss is bathed in the orange light of a dying sun. Hugh's refusal to succumb to the sexually stimulating orange glow is our first substantial hint that he defines love as more than sexual pleasure. In Cyril's eyes, of course, this definition is reason enough for Hugh to be purged from love's tapestry. Some readers might agree with Cyril this early in the novel. But once we realize that his consistent use of mythology and symbols is unconsciously ironic, we can see how Hawkes uses Cyril's own allusions to expose him while maintaining, at the same time, extreme authorial detachment. Cyril selects orange to suggest eternal love because in his mind love equals passion.

An equally significant symbolic pattern develops from his numerous citations of flowers. Descriptions of grape arbors, orange groves, and flower-covered fields add to the pastoral quality of the fictional landscape, but Cyril's choice of flowers again turns out to be ironic. Flowers in general have long suggested fertility and the course of true love. Frazer, for example, comments on the rite of midsummer eve when maidens would twine garlands of flowers in their hair in order to encourage dreams of future lovers.[14] In a scene remarkably similar to this ancient ritual, Cyril acts out his role as the personification of love and fashions garlands of flowers for Hugh's daughters. He takes pride in his knowledge of flowers, for he consistently uses the Latin names. The irony develops when he fails to reveal the discrepancy between his use of the scientific names and the connotations which some of the flowers carry. We must track down the information ourselves despite the danger of overreading the scene. He tells us, for instance, that the *Pisum elatius* is Fiona's favorite blossom. Yet this flower connotes happy marriage and fertility, sentiments hardly appropriate to Fiona and Cyril.[15]

The point made in the scene with Hugh's daughters is the difference between the flowers he weaves for Meredith, the oldest girl, and those he reserves for himself. Though a child, Meredith distrusts Cyril. She is a threat to his continued liaisons with Catherine because she dislikes his sunbathing excursions, and she disapproves of his dominance of her mother. Her whispered comment to him upon witnessing Catherine remove the bathing bra, suggests that she suspects his sexual involvement: "Don't think I don't know what you're up to." Aware of this mutual suspicion between Meredith and Cyril, we note with interest some of the

14. Frazer, *The Golden Bough*, 11:45–75.
15. I am indebted to Professor Jack Ashley of the University of South Carolina for much of the information concerning the symbolism of flowers. See also the Lehner study.

flowers which he directs the girl to gather. Among them are *Cyclamen persicum*, *Echium diffusum*, ghostly asphodel, and *Anemone coronaria*. According to plant folklore, these flowers traditionally mean, respectively, resignation and a bad luck gift to a woman; courage; languor, regret, and the Greek emblem of death; and refusal and abandonment. Nearly all of the connotations are dark, suggesting pain and the eventual defeat of women. Yet the flowers from which he makes his own garland convey the opposite meaning. He chooses *Laurus nobilis* (interestingly, the plant of the sun, suggestive of glory and renown) and *Genista cinerea* (ardor and humility). Considering the specific traditional associations with each of these flowers, it seems inconceivable that Cyril could be unaware of the scene's meaning. He calls himself the "flower god at play," perhaps hinting at his desire to cast a dark spell on Meredith while simultaneously praising his own efforts on behalf of love. He would like for us to read this scene on the literal level only, for it limits his game to a gentle pastoral exercise with children. What he does not count on is our pursuit of the symbolism, at least to the extent of checking the flowers' names. Significantly, he refuses to reveal his motive for entertaining the children. Note his hedging:

> Then why the halfhearted magnanimity, the atypical gesture? Why this minor sacrifice, this exposure to boredom? . . . perhaps there was something more to my plan than deception, selfishness, showmanship. Perhaps I wanted to spare Catherine a moment or two, perhaps I wanted to ensure Hugh some time alone with my wife and his, perhaps I was simply inclined to amuse the twins for once and to appease Meredith in the process, show her my other side. . . . Perhaps I wanted to share my capacity for different games, for love on another plane. Who knows?
>
> (p. 158)

His refusal to tell forces us to interpret the statement, but he drops enough hints which give away his purpose. The mention of deception and selfishness intimates that he desires the appearance of appeasing Meredith when in reality he wishes her all the darkness and pain which his gift of flowers suggests. If this reading is acceptable, then Hawkes has deftly used a specific symbolic pattern to expose the narrator.

The difference between the symbolism of the goat deity and that of the flowers resides in Cyril's realization of what he is saying. While aware of the sexuality traditionally associated with goats and bulls, he seems ignorant of their associations with both fertility cults and self-destructive tendencies. Conversely, he consciously uses his knowledge of the Latin names for flowers, but he seems unaware that the names, once we bother to decipher them, expose his dislike of Meredith. In both cases the symbolic patterns boomerang against him ironically, revealing his meanness despite his insistence to the contrary. His consistent references to Illyria function the same way.

The name Illyria supports the original atmosphere, for its pastoral remoteness mellows the landscape's harshness. But the allusions go beyond those to a stagelike setting. Confident of their Shakespeare, Cyril and Fiona reveal their familiarity with *Twelfth Night* when they call Hugh "Malvolio." Fiona goes so far to claim that she "loves her Malvolio best." Though possibly another Hawkes red herring, this reference seems too pointed to ignore. Hardin Craig notes, "The name 'Malvolio' means 'evil desire, or ambition,' and he is a humor character whose peculiarity, or 'humor,' it is to attempt to climb impertinently above his own station." Professor Craig suggests that Malvolio "offers the most perplexing problem of interpretation to be found in the play." [16] We face a similar problem of interpretation when trying to understand Hugh. Cyril would have us believe that Hugh does indeed harbor both an "evil" desire to wreck his plans for polygamy and a humor or peculiar ambition to keep marriage chaste. In his eyes, this chastity amounts to a brand of puritanism indicative of Hugh's inability to adapt to an erotic Illyria. Cyril's interpretation of Hugh's actions reflects in part the characterization of Malvolio. In *Twelfth Night*, Maria calls Malvolio "a kind of Puritan," and the play clearly suggests Malvolio's failure to adjust to Sir

16. William Shakespeare, *The Complete Works*, ed. Hardin Craig (Chicago: Scott Foresman, 1951), p. 617.

Toby's festive life-style. Professor Craig writes that it was not Shakespeare's intention with Malvolio to encourage the impression that "a dangerous madman had been turned loose on the community." Malvolio is a responsible servant who is abused and humiliated by others. Yet acknowledging his virtues, we cannot overlook his aspirations to his mistress's hand, a hope which at the time was considered not only unnatural but also a grievous fault. Olivia, we remember, says, "O, you are sick of self-love, Malvolio, and taste with a distempered appetite" (I,v,98–99). And Maria calls him a "timepleaser; an affectioned ass" (II,iii,160). He acts as one convinced that all who see him must love him. Cyril wants us to accept the association of Hugh and Malvolio on a one-to-one basis. He seems blind to the possibility that he, not Hugh, is being criticized. Certainly Hugh hopes to protect the chastity of his marriage, but from our point of view his effort is far from a peculiar humor. His monogamy, although conventional, is one expression of love which Cyril cannot accept. Cyril is wrong to term as evil Hugh's distaste for sex-singing. The most ironic allusion is to Malvolio's error for anticipating his mistress's love. Unlike Olivia, Fiona would gladly accommodate Hugh if only he would accept her. Cyril considers Hugh's refusal abnormal, as unnatural as Malvolio's longing for Olivia. In *Twelfth Night* Malvolio gets pretty much what he deserves, but in *The Blood Oranges* Hugh's defeat has disastrous consequences.

Shakespeare's comedy illustrates many of the questions of love which would have fascinated seventeenth-century courtly gatherings: how love torments the lover, how concealed love never flourishes, how true love is jealous, and whether the man or the woman loves more deeply. Orsino, Duke of Illyria, argues, for example, that no woman can match "so strong a passion / As love doth give my heart" (II,iv,97–98). Cyril would agree. And Viola/Cesario instructs the Duke on the misfortunes of concealed love. When we recall her comparison of secrecy to a worm in the bud, we can easily think of Hugh's unfulfilled love for Fiona and the resulting suicide. Orsino, of course, is often a comic character in *Twelfth Night*, particularly in the beginning of the play. His first speech shows him to be in love with love, playing the role of a moody, love-struck aristocratic ruler. As self-proclaimed lord of his modern Illyria, Cyril suffers from a similar satirical laughter. He, too, acts out a role as chief lover. His consistent descriptions of himself in what he calls love's golden hues—gold glasses, watch chain, cuff links, hair, penknife, and even his cough—recall Orsino's metaphor for love as "the rich golden shaft." And the flower garland scene with Meredith ironically alludes to Orsino's thoughts: "Away before me to sweet bed of flowers / Love-thoughts lie rich when canopied with bowers" (I,i,40–41).

It is conceivable that in some instances Cyril resembles a twentieth-century Orsino—a man more in love with love's design than with Fiona, Catherine, or any particular woman. He loves Fiona and Catherine only because they so willingly add a new stitch to the tapestry. When Fiona leaves with the three girls, and when Catherine retires to mourn for Hugh, Cyril's first concern is not for Fiona's return or Catherine's recovery but to regain his lost position as love's chief disciple. He needs Catherine now that Fiona is gone because only with the help of a willing female versed in the strains of sex-singing can he begin to reassert the melodious sounds of sexual harmony. The allusions to *Twelfth Night* even invite a comparison between Catherine and Olivia. Catherine's mourning for Hugh, which cannot be taken too seriously because of the relative ease with which Cyril convinces her to accept him again, could suggest Olivia's extreme lamentations for her dead brother. Their mutually exaggerated grief calls attention to their comic roles. For once Catherine sees the female rabbits, just as Olivia sees Viola/Cesario, she realizes that she is bored and that she desires Cyril's companionship. The ironic difference between their mourning, of course, is that Hugh's suicide is a serious loss whereas very little is made of Olivia's dead brother. Though Cyril would argue differently, the happy ending in Orsino's Illyria is missing from his. At the end of the play love is multiplied. Instead of one pair of frustrated lovers (Orsino-Olivia), we have two contented couples (Orsino-Viola, Sebastian-Olivia) plus the promise of fertility and tranquillity. The reverse is true at the end of *The*

Blood Oranges. Two happy couples have been cut down to a frustrated twosome. But though love's tapestry is currently tattered in the novel, Cyril's final musings suggest that he is about to reestablish his erotic symmetry—a happy ending only as he defines it. Though writing of *The Lime Twig,* Leslie Fiedler's remark that love breeds terror in Hawkes' fiction applies readily to *The Blood Oranges.* The strange, menacing landscape of Cyril's Illyria makes a perfect setting for an investigation into the horrors of love.

Hawkes never insists on the allusions to the goat deity of fertility, the flowers, or *Twelfth Night.* We would misrepresent his art to dwell on them too extensively. The references are there for the alert reader to pick up. They add to the novel's mythic atmosphere and encourage the dominant metaphor of the tapestry. Yet caution must be exercised, for with these allusions Hawkes again clears the way for the unwary reader to trap himself, permitting the scent of the red herring to throw him off the trail. The allusions go on and on, developing into a labyrinth if the reader takes them too seriously. For example, Frazer writes of the legend of Talos, guardian of Crete, who was identified with both a bull and the sun. But we would be wrong to identify Cyril with Talos, just as we would err to insist on the relationships between Cyril and Dionysus, a flower god, or Duke Orsino. These associations are only suggested in the novel. The best bet is to comment on the allusions and to acknowledge their primary functions: the creation of irony and the support of an other-world setting.

Cyril's strange symbolic references and the novel's unusual setting result from Hawkes' detachment. Since Cyril's vision is ostensibly his alone, he remains free to violate our anticipations. He need rely on only his own authority as he tells the tale. This is why his Illyria is timeless and eerie, situated "beyond" the mountains, and full of symbolic goats, cypress trees, and a race of people who speak gutturally. The novel's setting becomes his private domain—surely it is strange to us—and the unfamiliarity persuades us to accept the peculiar shocks and jolts of his story. Cyril so completely commands the narrative that he might have successfully established himself as the kind of modern hero Skipper rightfully claims to be. But luckily his humorous theories, boastful arrogance, and designing manipulations eventually convey the truth. His unawareness of his own egotism finally moves us from contempt to sympathy. As one of the ruined members of our lot, Cyril becomes, as Hawkes has noted in another context, a creation of the author's "satiric and sympathetic impulses." [17]

Several commentators have complained that Cyril is too underdeveloped to carry the narration. It is true that Hawkes withholds concrete information about the characters' past. We never know where they come from, what they have done, or why they are here. Are they tourists; are they running away from something; did they plan to visit Cyril's Illyria? We have so little expository information of the kind most readers expect that their earlier lives cease to matter. Hawkes has no interest, and neither should we, in their childhoods or occupations, in how they met their spouses, or why they now live in a pastoral dreamland. The point is not that they are underdeveloped but that they are already in Illyria when we discover them. Their lives in this fantasylike world will reveal all we need to know.

In most of Hawkes' fictions the characters travel through the unique landscape, assuredly shaken by the terrors, but often confident that they can either extricate themselves from the nightmare or at least survive the violence. Skipper is the most developed of this particular Hawkesian character. His faith in his survival qualities and his belief in the power of love, indiscriminate though his application of it may be, mark him as the supremely confident man, the one Hawkes character who can declare, after outliving that long series of suicides and murder, that he is fifty-nine years old as he knew he would be. Michael and Margaret Banks, on the other hand, represent the other extreme. They are the Hawkesian characters who literally live out their fantasies, experiencing their dreams of love to the extent that the fantasies usurp their reality. Unable to awaken from the erotic nightmare, they perish within it. In both *Second Skin* and *The Lime Twig* the charac-

17. John Hawkes, "Flannery O'Connor's Devil," *Sewanee Review*, 70 (Summer 1962), 405.

ters acknowledge the nightmare. Skipper may survive while the Bankses are literally crushed, but both character-types know they have experienced horror. Not so with Cyril—he refuses to admit the possibility of terror, the nightmare which he himself has partly caused, or the necessity for grief when faced with tragedy. Obliviousness to pain and terror is usually unacceptable in Hawkes' fictions. Even Skipper recognizes the signs of evil. His problem is not unawareness of terror but inability to believe it can be used maliciously. Cyril's denial of the reality of pain or the necessity for grief finally damns him. Although he knows that love can be both gentle and painful, he insists that he is mild, a "steady, methodical, undesigning lover" (p. 11). The closest that he has come to suffering is his discovery that "most people detest a lover, no matter how modest" (p. 57). Unlike Hugh, or most of us for that matter, Cyril is not sexually possessive and thus he considers himself free from the pain of jealousy. He cannot grieve for Hugh because he believes that Hugh betrays the promise of love. Distinguishing between himself and conventional adults, he defines people like Hugh as those who think love a crime. Hugh may die for love, but not Cyril: "But it will take a dark mind to strip my vines, to destroy the last shreds of my tapestry, to choke off my song. It will take a lot to destroy Hugh's photographs or to gut the many bedrooms of the sleeping castle. I am a match, I hope, for the hatred of conventional enemies wherever they are" (p. 36). His serene confidence, comic and yet so much more maddening than Skipper's, is based not on faith in the ability to free himself from the nightmare but on refusal to admit that the nightmare exists: "The nausea, the red eyes, the lips white in blind grief and silent hate, these may have been the externals of a pain that belonged to Hugh but never once to me. Hugh's pain perhaps. Not mine" (p. 57).

Contrary to Mr. Beacham's complaint that the narrator is too underdeveloped to interest us, Cyril is one of Hawkes' most complex story tellers. He is so accomplished in sexual love and so sure of his bizarre theories that we are hard pressed to evaluate him when we finally suspect that he may not know what he is talking about. His tone may be infuriating, but his is the only account we have. Just as he manipulates the other characters, coercing them to accept his definitions of how their lives must be lived, so he controls the novel, narrating only those parts which he chooses to reveal. But if Fiona, Catherine, and Hugh succumb to his manipulations, we are not so unfortunate. They remain caught up in his passion for sex-singing, and thus, they cannot analyze the experience—they are too close to it. We, however, read of the erotic interlude after the fact as Cyril tries to exlain his current impoverished condition, and as a result we can detect holes in his narrative.

At one point he calls himself omniscient, but the irony of this claim never occurs to him. Unlike his confidence in matters of love, his narration is full of questions, fits and starts, musings. Far from omniscient, he must choose among possible motives for specific actions. His hesitancy and questioning in turn force us to challenge his reliability. Telling the story but never knowing answers, he has as much trouble with it as we do. He even wonders about the value of his tale—is it developing or is it now lifeless because love no longer favors him: "Am I embracing air? Could that be all?" Note his reaction, for example, when he recalls his removal of Fiona's bathing top:

> But had she wanted me to expose her breasts, I wondered, for Hugh's sake or mine? Or was the exposure purely my own idea and something that entered her consciousness and gave her pleasure only after I had touched her, untied the strings? I could not know. But I knew immediately that it was a good idea.   (p. 39)

Since Cyril does not know why he acts, we are left in the dark with only his assurance that it was a good idea. Should we believe him? His uncertainty is evident at the scene's conclusion when he waits for Hugh to reciprocate by unhooking Catherine's top:

> Was he then thoughtless? Selfish? Without even the crudest idea of simple reciprocity? . . . What was holding him back? Could he not see that Catherine herself was puzzled, uncomfortable? Could he deliberately mean to embarrass his wife and to tamper

with the obviously intended symmetry of our little scene on the
beach?   (pp. 42–43)

Not only is he blind to Hugh's modesty and unaware of Hugh's
motives, he also assumes that Catherine's breasts must be exposed
because the situation "obviously" demands symmetry.

Cyril's inability to determine the value of his narration or the
motives for various actions continues throughout the novel. Time
after time we are at a loss to explain why a particular scene takes
shape the way it does because he is uncertain too. Note, as he remembers his first seduction of Catherine, how he casts about for
interpretations of her replies until he finally chooses one: "Her
words alone, and they allowed me to choose between implied security or resignation or, finally, indignation at what she might have
taken to be the first signs of betrayal. I put the wine into her fingers and made my choice" (p. 102). He chooses what to discard
and what to believe, but he never tells us. How, then, can we trust
him? One more significant illustration should be noted. During
the burial of Meredith's dog, Cyril admits that he is assuming the
motives of others and selecting the interpretation he will accept:
"Yes, I thought, merely one more domestic incident for Catherine.
But as a matter of fact, perhaps she was just as susceptible to her
oldest daughter's grief and her husband's game as was Fiona. Why
not assume that she was moved somehow, and like me was quite
satisfied with her more pedestrian role in this makeshift ceremo-
nial affair?" (p. 215). When, at the end of the scene, he wonders if
his assumptions are valid, if his reading of the signs is correct, he
answers affirmatively. But we cannot share his assurance because
we have watched him pick and choose among possible interpretations until he finds one which suits his purpose. Like Skipper in
Second Skin, Cyril knows what has happened, but he does not
know why. He is a perfect example of what Hawkes calls his "increasing need" to parody the novelist's role. More importantly,
Cyril's uncertainty when narrating his tale conflicts with his confidence as a sex-singer, thus creating a fascinating though misguided character. Were it not for the holes in his narrative, we
might be tempted to consider his theories of love. His self-assurance

is often persuasive. But unawareness that the hesitancies undermine his assumptions often marks him as the butt of the joke. The
novel's tension—and fun—develop from two sources: the reactions
of the other characters to Cyril's dominance and the reader's reactions to his questionable reliability. If Fiona, Catherine, and
Hugh take themselves seriously, it is because they are forced to—
Cyril's plans threaten to snuff out their personalities, leaving them
as no more than subjects for his experiments. And if we experience
a combination of terror and amusement when reading *The Blood
Oranges*, it is because Cyril's challenge to chastity and conventional love is narrated in so humorous a manner.

He, of course, takes himself quite seriously. A good portion of
his tale is given over to explanation and defense of his ideas. So
pervasive are these discussions of love that the memories of his
life with Fiona, Hugh, and Catherine often appear significant
only as they illustrate his theories. Much more important than
their stories is the revelation of Cyril's personality. A summation
of his ideas about love helps explain why he is both culpable and
comic. As much as we despise his arrogance and self-righteousness,
we cannot help but laugh at both his idealistic beliefs and his
misconception of himself. Believing, for example, that his acts of
love are destined and that the gods direct him to "spread the legs
of women," he nevertheless insists that "fidelity is the most mascu-
line trait of all." Cyril has a private definition of fidelity—faithfulness to *all* the women he seduces. His unconsciously comic descriptions of himself as full of "aching candor" and "unlimited
gentleness" are thus justified in his mind because he retains love
for each mistress.

What makes Cyril so unusual is his belief in sex as an art form.
Defining himself as a "master" of the clandestine visit, he argues
that he never takes advantage of love because he is "the most dis-
criminating of sex-aestheticians." A serious reader of sex literature, he takes pains to communicate appropriate images of his
aesthetics. The most remarkable of these is the copulating birds
scene which is described early in the novel but late in the chronology, following Hugh's death and Catherine's illness. Returning

on his bicycle from a visit to Catherine, he comes upon "two enormous game birds locked in love." Fascinated and breathless, he stops to watch. Although this scene establishes the motif of physical love, it just as clearly points to Cyril as a comic character. For example, he identifies with the mating birds, but he nevertheless has only the bike to mount. This identification soon undercuts his role as sex-aesthetician: "Together we were two incongruous pairs frozen in one feeling, I astride the old bike and hardly breathing, the larger bird atop the smaller bird and already beginning to grow regal" (pp. 14–15). Later when the male bird flies away and its partner topples off the wall, Cyril rides off slowly on his now "humbled" bike. He glosses over the scene's humor, for he wants the mating birds to be a good omen, a positive symbol of his future as love's agent. But as he pedals back to the villa, he wonders if the omen might not be bad, the spirits of Hugh and Fiona clasping each other to fulfill what was denied them by the catastrophe of Hugh's death.

The mating birds are perhaps the most important image of Cyril's tale, for they foreshadow the ambiguity of an act which the birds can treat as purely physical but to which humans bring contradictory emotions. Cyril admits here love's contrasting forces: "Grace and chaos, control and helplessness, mastery and collapse—it was all there" (p. 15). One cause of the novel's tragedy is hinted at in this description. Perhaps Catherine but certainly Hugh cannot slough off the normal human feeling that a love partner is more than a physical object and that love itself transcends animal drive. Chaos and collapse consume Hugh. He believes in the ideals of total commitment to one's love, of monogamy, and of mutual trust. Though he is attracted to Fiona and nearly crazed by desire, he remains faithful to Catherine. Only when he discovers what he should have known all along—that Catherine has welcomed Cyril to her bed—does he sacrifice his ideals and take Fiona. Cyril scorns Hugh's modesty. Forgetting the comic parallel with the old bike, he likens himself to the copulating birds which, when finished, merely fly away. The sense of commitment which lingers over puritan Hugh remains foreign to both the birds and Cyril.

Cyril knows that he is vulnerable to criticism from conventional people like Hugh, and he admits that some may consider him a sex-offender: "There are those who in fact would like nothing better than to fill my large funnel-shaped white thighs with the fish hooks of their disapproval. . . . For some, love itself is a crime" (p. 36). Proud of his unconformity, he claims to be more than a match for the hatred of conservative enemies who include, presumably, his readers. Since he considers himself obedient to love's dictates, he can call himself a "quiet and agreeable" lover even though he wrecks lives. For him the essence of every love affair is purity. Making love to Catherine for the first time, he argues, egotistically, that his love restores innocence and virginity.

The Blood Oranges is full of Cyril's explanations and defenses, but the most significant of them occurs after Hugh finds the chastity belt. In what amounts to a two paragraph sermon, Cyril preaches in his most smug and arrogant manner. And yet for all our dislike of his condescending tone, he intends for the explanation to generate our sympathy. He wants us to understand, for example, that orgasm is not the only goal—love's lyrical song must also be played. Ideally he is correct, but he misinterprets the effect of his eroticism on others.[18] Attacking the inhibitions of jealousy,

18. Sometime after the manuscript of this study arrived at the press, John Hawkes and Robert Scholes published an interview: "A Conversation on *The Blood Oranges* Between John Hawkes and Robert Scholes," *Novel*, 5 (Spring 1972), pp. 197–207. In the interview, Hawkes reaffirms his need to balance lyricism and terror, and he defines *The Blood Oranges* as a novel about sexuality. But contrary to my reading of the novel, Hawkes declares that Cyril is "probably right" to brand monogamy the enemy. He argues that the word "adultery" and the phrase "wife-swapping" are vulgarities which should be dismissed, as far as this novel is concerned, in favor of Cyril's term "sexual extension." Rather than view Cyril as the victim of his own delusions, Hawkes calls him "a God-like man with infinite capacities for love" whose defiance of convention is only "modest." Hugh, on the other hand, is described as "remote" from love, the man who destroys the harmony between the characters. Thus while Hawkes admits that Cyril is "probably just as self-destructive as Hugh," he nevertheless conveys the impression that Cyril is right and Hugh is wrong: "I would rather have 'wife-swapping' than sterility." These are significant remarks, opinions which should be considered since they come from the author himself. Yet I do not believe that the novel supports all of the statements in this interview. It seems to me that the

he begins: "Need I insist that the only enemy of the mature marriage is monogamy? That anything less than sexual multiplicity
(body upon body, voice on voice) is naive? That our sexual selves
are merely idlers in a vast wood?" (p. 209). He goes on to explain
why he now expresses his philosophy so pointedly—to answer "nagging detractors" and to criticize the "soulless young" who abuse
the privilege of sex with love-ins and who allow orgasm to stifle
lyricism. "Old and wheezing detractors should curb their judgment of a man who knows, after all, what he is talking about. To
young detractors I will say only that if orgasm is the pit of the
fruit then lyricism is its flesh. Marriage, or at least the mature marriage, is the fold that gathers in all lovers nude and alone" (p. 210).
What is so outrageous about all this is his unwavering faith in what
he says. The absence of guilt encourages his self-righteousness.
There is a sense of mission about Cyril, a suspicion that he believes
his duty to be the restoration of virginity and innocence in all
women who will accept his mastery. In his mind adultery is elevated to an art form, illustrated by the tapestry and expressed by
sex-singing. Only Hugh's hanging rips the cloth and converts the
song into a dissonant wail.

It is significant that Cyril reserves his most complete defense
until after Hugh finds the chastity belt, for he is obviously trying
to counter Hugh's last effort to protect his marriage. One-armed,
handsome Hugh has been Cyril's antagonist all along. Agonized
while wrapped in love's tapestry, Hugh is, argues Cyril, better off
dead. Only Hugh feels embarrassed during the erotic sunbathing
scene. Only Hugh lacks an eye for what Cyril calls a "sex-tableau."
If we believe Cyril, Hugh's fatal weakness is his jealousy. Feeling

---

presence of Hugh's daughters shows that his love is not totally sterile. And
we recall that Fiona, a woman well-versed in the lyrics of sex-singing,
deserts Cyril following Hugh's suicide to care for the daughters, an act
which implies her criticism of Cyril's eroticism. Hugh wrongly attempts to
negate human sexuality, but surely Cyril's efforts to foster sexuality are
equally disastrous: Hugh's hanging, Catherine's illness, and Fiona's departure. Rather than illustrate a tension between right and wrong definitions of love, *The Blood Oranges* shows the flaws of both sexual freedom
and conventional marriage.

possessive toward his wife, he experiences pain when love dictates a new affair for him or Catherine. But once we see through Cyril's narrative, we understand that fidelity to Catherine is Hugh's only strength. Betrayal would ruin him. Cyril, of course, dismisses the idea as old-fashioned ignorance of love's true calling. He blames Hugh for ruining their idyl in Illyria, and he castigates him with words like "tormented, tempestuous, unreasonable." Incredulous that a married man could be capable of jealousy, Cyril frees himself of all blame and tries to shift responsibility to Hugh:

> When at last he allowed the true artistic nature of our design to seep into consciousness, for instance, he persecuted himself and begrudged me Catherine, tried to deny me Catherine at a time when I knew full well that, thanks to my unseen helping hand, he himself was finally about to lurch down his own peculiar road with Fiona. And yet Hugh was also a sex-singer of sorts. But in Hugh's dry mouth our lovely song became a shriek. (p. 58)

Perhaps Cyril interprets Hugh's missing arm as a symbol of sexual inferiority. Such an interpretation would account for his description of Hugh using the camera phallically when photographing the nude Rosella. It would also account for the curious scene, reminiscent of *The Beetle Leg*, in which Cyril spies on Hugh lying nude in the crab grass: "But what was he doing? Sunbathing? Embarking on some kind of freakish photographic experiment? Reading one of his faded erotic periodicals hidden from my sight in the crab grass? What?" (p. 84). Cyril cannot be sure, but when he notices the motion of Hugh's buttocks and shoulders intensifying, he decides that Hugh is substituting a lonely dream for sexual love of Fiona. He suspects that Hugh is masturbating, and he quickly interprets the scene as another sign of Hugh's inadequacy—with Fiona so beautiful and willing, why embrace crab grass? Hugh's onanism in this scene results as much from frustration and pain as from inferiority.

If we believe Cyril, Hugh turns out to be a potential sex-singer made humorously grotesque by conventional notions of jealousy and marriage. Cyril would like to laugh at his antagonist, incongruously associating him with Christ, St. Peter, and Malvolio. But as Hugh's frustration leads to suicide, Cyril finds himself at a loss to understand such a violent repudiation of love. He finally explains that Hugh suffers from the clutch of death's hand within his chest, exchanging a promised sex-song for "the rhythm of some dark death of his own." Hugh's search for the chastity belt in the medieval dungeon is by far the best illustration of his bewilderment. In direct contrast to the pastoral outings planned by Cyril and Fiona, full of nude bathing, mountain climbing, and the erotic grape-tasting game, Hugh's trek to the dungeon promises suspicion and pain. At first they do not know why he wants to explore this ugly place except that he intuitively believes he will find relief for his torment. Cyril makes sure while he narrates the scene that we see how Hugh's outing both violates the spirit of Illyria and illustrates the blackness of Hugh's heart. He contrasts the cold darkness of the narrow corridors with the pleasures of a blood orange sun, and the aroma of flowers and Fiona with the dungeon's unmistakable odor of excrement. Frustrated because he suspects Hugh's quest to be negative, yet unable to decipher what it means, he wonders if Hugh hopes to find a sexual totem that would excite them all or if Hugh wants to subject them to the "dead breath of denial. Who could tell?" (p. 186). Cyril's point is that he is as much out of place in the dungeon with its stink and darkness as Hugh seems to be in the arbors of love with their orange suns and flowers. But curiosity lures him on. Knowing that Hugh has not yet "shot his bolt of poison," he follows with the hope that whatever Hugh finds will "please Fiona and prove to be of interest, at least, to Catherine and me" (p. 195). This wish turns on him ironically, for the object of Hugh's search is the ancient, rusty chastity belt, surely of interest to all of them. After the belt's discovery, Hugh's plan could not be clearer. Cyril knows that they have reached a crisis because the chastity belt represents a "monstrous memento of Hugh's true attitude toward all of our well-intended loves" (p. 204).

Acting out of despair as much as determination to assert his right to Catherine, Hugh later locks this "artful relic of fear and jealousy" between his wife's thighs. Cyril removes it, sends Hugh to Fiona's bed, and then makes love to Catherine. He sees Hugh's rendezvous with Fiona as a victory, as the final completion of their harmony, but by now we know that Cyril has misinterpreted Hugh's personal needs all along. Rather than completion of the sexual symmetry, Hugh's night with Fiona signals his final defeat. He hangs himself, surrounded by his photographs of nude peasant girls. Despite Hugh's familiarity with Fiona's nakedness and the general pairing off of Fiona with Hugh and Catherine with Cyril, we must understand that Hugh never once sleeps with Fiona until Cyril outmaneuvers the chastity belt defense. For all of Cyril's efforts to achieve harmony in the group, Hugh balks. His refusal to accept Fiona, no matter how desperately he wants her, precipitates the break-up of Cyril's plans. It is true that Fiona seems more precious to Cyril once he willingly assigns her to Hugh, but to attribute traces of jealousy to Cyril, as Mr. De Feo does, is to overlook the fact that Hugh does not accept Fiona until the end and that Cyril refuses to experience an emotion as conventional as jealousy.

Cyril's observation that Hugh dies for love is meant to be disparaging, but we sympathize with the act. The suicide successfully ruins the tapestry, at least for the time being, and thus it can be seen as a sacrifice. If we have been unsure of the reliability of Cyril's narrative up to this point, Hugh's death should resolve some of the uncertainties. The tragedy forces us to look askance at Cyril's meditation on the purity of sexual multiplicity, for we know that Hugh has died to protest his act of adultery and to affirm his faith in monogamy. He may reject lyricism for convention, but his love is not sterile—he, not Cyril, has children. Cyril would have us believe that the death represents both a defeat and a manifestation of Hugh's unimaginative conventionality. But he protests so much that we are persuaded to reexamine his explanations. Indeed, the hanging, coming as it does at the end, should send us back to reread the novel, for this new information opens up a different point of view from which to evaluate Cyril's meditations.

The first-person narrative initially encourages sympathy for his ideas because we have only his point of view. But his seriousness is his undoing as far as final evaluation of him is concerned. Cyril describes games and rituals which are outrageous and comic, but he does so with such solemnity that we soon suspect Hawkes of undercutting reader identification. His proposals for sexual variety are nevertheless exciting, probably the stuff which most unadmitted erotic dreams are made of. He would like to transfer our fantasies into reality so that we would be free of all the guilt, fear, and uncertainty which usually attend these dreams. To complete the symmetry, he and Fiona need another couple. They are like spiders, ready to pounce on anyone who brushes their web. As the novel progresses, we suspect that Hugh and Catherine are no more than necessary threads for Cyril's tapestry—sacrificial victims to a bizarre idea of love rather than equal partners in a polygamous affair. Cyril does not want it to be this way, but his unsympathetic manipulation of the others unwittingly ruins his plan. Thinking that he has triumphed when he finally convinces Hugh to accept Fiona, he instead brings about his own loss. He would like to blame Hugh for poisoning their Illyria, but we know better. Thus as we get into the novel, we find our sympathies expanding to embrace Hugh. He needs our sympathy because of what happens to him while Cyril deserves it because of what he is. Hugh may be far from ideal—he is possessive, jealous and occasionally onanistic—but he also stands for stability, commitment, and a saner idea of love.

If Hugh is Cyril's unwanted victim, then surely Cyril is victimized by Hugh's death. Once the suicide is discovered, Fiona leaves Illyria to care for Hugh's daughters, Catherine falls ill, and Cyril finds the tapestry ruined. As a result of this defeat, his efforts in the novel's "present" are directed toward recovering his privileged position in the tapestry. Unable to continue his lyrical sex-singing, he must first convince Catherine to speak to him before he can resume his role as the white bull. The grotesque irony is that he will very likely succeed, for at the end of the novel he is once again celebrating harmony and his private concept of innocence. Calling the silent Catherine the "inert supine center of my life," he tells her that their love is fated and thus inevitable. Humorously enough, it is not his fidelity to what he calls their "sexless matrimony" which finally arouses her but a gift of female rabbits.

The strange boat-launching scene signals his recovery of the mended tapestry. While Cyril wonders how he can win her to his bed again, he and Catherine witness the natives' curious fertility ceremony. The white boat, guided by half-naked attendants, has a golden fish on its prow, a color of love in *The Blood Oranges*. A handful of *Lobularia maritima* is fastened to the boat which Cyril interprets as implying "fleeting tenderness on the part of even these boatbuilding villagers" (p. 124). But his interpretation is unconsciously ironic, for *Lobularia maritima* is traditionally used to cure hydrophobia and madness. As he watches the frenzied natives, Cyril reverts to his old tricks and begins to mold the ceremony to fit his own desires: "Priest, blood, *Lobularia maritima*, procession—how could it have been more plain? . . . Why not assume that a now invulnerable Catherine and reflective Cyril were starting over? Why not?" (p. 126). The word "assumes" gives him away, for the ritual is not at all "plain." Two consistent hints of sexuality, an orange sun and a man with the face of a goat, convince him that love with Catherine is about to be renewed. The goat-faced man, a satyr, strips—"his obviously unspent passion was hanging down and rotating loosely like a tongue of flame"—while the sun turns itself into a "diffusion of thick erotic color" (pp. 132–133). Now assured of Catherine's love, Cyril turns and murmurs, "Starting over." He lies to her that Hugh's death was accidental, he assures her of the essential virginity of their affair, and he celebrates his return to love's good graces. Noting three mementos from the immediate past, the flower crown, his shorts, and the chastity belt, he ends his memoirs by praising both his harmony and the timelessness of his special world: "Everything coheres, moves forward. I listen for footsteps. In Illyria there are no seasons" (p. 271).

With *The Blood Oranges* Hawkes extends the combination of terror and lyricism developed so beautifully in *Second Skin*. The humor is here, for Cyril's story is too preposterous to read with a straight face. Enough irony reflects on him to mark him a comic narrator. But the affirmation of Hawkes' two previous novels is qualified. For all of *The Lime Twig*'s pain and violence, Michael's sacrifice of his life to bring down Rock Castle constitutes a victory of sorts. And Skipper's escape from Miranda to celebrate the baby's birth in a graveyard suggests the strength of regenerative love in *Second Skin*. The love which triumphs in *The Blood Oranges*, however, remains sterile. Breeding nothing but fear and death, it is limited finally to lusty goats, erotic grape-tasting games, and chastity belts—suitable expressions of distorted love in a comic yet terrifying fiction.

A Few Remarks and Conclusions

THE task of expressing conclusions about a novelist as experimental as John Hawkes is made all the more difficult by the fact that he is at the moment alive and well, and, one hopes, working on a new novel. I dislike drawing conclusions about an artist who is still creating, as much as I fear making predictions about his future work. Conclusions at this stage of his career seem presumptuous, while predictions are just plain risky. A few remarks about the preceding chapters, however, are in order. The place to begin is perhaps with the observation made at the end of the previous chapter—that in *The Blood Oranges,* Hawkes extends the combination of dark comedy and lyricism which informs his earlier fiction. Cyril's renewed faith in the function of his tapestry may be a victory for him, but surely it is a defeat for the others involved. In terms of tone and vision, *The Blood Oranges* suggests that the affirmation in the Hawkes novels of the 1960s, hinted at in *The Lime Twig* and clearly revealed in *Second Skin,* has been modified in favor of the bleaker comedy associated with the fiction before *Second Skin.* This is not to remark that his fiction is regressing. *The*

241

Blood Oranges reveals a much more skillful handling of matters like narrative development and first person narration than, say, *The Owl.*

All of which is to say that Hawkes remains as unpredictable as he is experimental. His conscious goal is to disrupt the conventional forms of fiction—something we must keep in mind no matter which of his novels strikes our fancy. If he has a more specific target than traditional fictional forms, it would seem to be the unfortunate but persistent affiliation of the novel with realism. His distaste for verisimilitude and for all that a phrase like "the well-made novel" suggests is just as evident in *The Blood Oranges* as it is in *Charivari*, even though the former is "easier" to read in terms of what happens. Yet the author who hopes to break with realism must also reckon with an audience steeped in, and even demanding, conventional realistic fiction. Readers who look for a readily recognizable beginning, middle, and end, a sense of felt life, and an identification with the "good" characters are likely to be outraged, baffled, or both when a novelist refuses to meet their expectations. It is significant, then, that Hawkes' quarrel with realism is designed to free both author and reader. Violating traditional novelistic rules and reader expectations, Hawkes liberates himself to construct controlled imaginative visions, while he simultaneously delivers the reader from anticipated probability. The novel's "enemies," plot, character, setting, and theme, become secondary considerations in favor of totality of structure or "verbal and psychological coherence." The aim, insists Hawkes, is to create a world instead of to represent it. The difference is between the conventional novel with its structure based on logically developed meaning and the experimental fiction with its coherence based on imaginative vision.

Just as important as the break with realism is Hawkes' use of comedy. No one likes to overemphasize, but I believe that it is absolutely necessary for the reader to realize that he is reading comic fiction when he picks up a Hawkes novel. The union of experimental technique and nightmarish fantasy is intended to create a humorous effect. Those who ignore the humor can only misread the novels as grim experiments with terror, but those who accept Hawkes' membership in the so-called black humor movement are better able to read fictions like *The Cannibal* or *Second Skin* in the spirit in which they were written. Like Bruce Jay Friedman, who writes that it would be easier to define an elbow or a corned beef sandwich, I hesitate to pin down a term like "black humor." But if black humor means anything when applied to Hawkes, it suggests the comic treatment of violence and what Hawkes calls extreme fictive detachment—total narrative distance between the author and his materials. Neither characteristic by itself can lead to the kind of humor Hawkes writes. But when combined, his complete narrative uninvolvement with the truly violent, but nevertheless funny, fictional terrors creates a complex tone which the uninitiated reader may not know how to handle. Equally important is Hawkes' insistence that the combination of comedy and terror does not necessarily foster pessimistic novels. Contemporary fictional humor may deny the reality of stable norms and of verifiable moral values, but it maintains faith in the basic verities of love and sympathy. For all of the absurdity involved in his fiction, Hawkes relies on comic vision to suggest hope and to celebrate these permanent values. To oversimplify, his humor encourages sympathy while, at the same time, it exposes evil, a "pure" word which he means to preserve.

Neither Hawkes' break with the demands of conventional realism nor his use of comedy has hindered his development. The humor of *The Blood Oranges* differs from that of *The Lime Twig*, just as that novel is different from *Charivari*. If there has been a general direction in his fiction, it has been away from the militant experimentation of his earlier work. For all of the difficulties of his full length novels, the three novelettes remain his most aggressive experiments. They shock the reader with their challenge to his expectations. Atmosphere and imaginative vision are major concerns in all of his fiction. But in *Charivari*, *The Goose on the Grave*, and *The Owl*, they are so paramount that they all but dissuade the reader to explain, in the conventional sense, what is going on. Reality is subordinated to the needs of the imagination.

The characters are not meant to "live" because Hawkes is more interested in giving life to their fears, dreams, and longings. There is less narrative control and internal coherence in *Charivari* and *The Goose on the Grave*, and more of a tendency toward highly developed isolated scenes. No value judgment is implied here—the point is that the complex patterns of related action and recurring imagery are reserved for the longer novels.

The reader sympathy which Hawkes prizes so highly in his fiction varies in degree from novel to novel, but it seems lacking only in *Charivari*. Narrative detachment unites with reader concern in the majority of his novels with the result that we find ourselves involved. This combination of detachment and concern encourages the attraction-repulsion antithesis which forms our response to the major characters in, especially, his more recent work. For this reason, the tone of the later novels seems more complex. Our dislike, for example, of Michael Banks' appalling weaknesses is balanced by sympathy for his plight, whereas the sheriff in *The Beetle Leg* or the characters in *Charivari* seem to be continually repulsive. But while the later novels have a more varied tone, none is as difficult to read as the earlier work. Albert Guerard's prediction in the 1949 introduction to *The Cannibal*, that Hawkes would move toward realism, was prophetic if his use of the term realism is understood. In 1962 he explained his meaning—that the more recent novels are more orderly and "distinctly less difficult to read." This is certainly true, and it is doubtful that Hawkes' future fiction will be as perplexing as *The Beetle Leg*. Still, the suggestion that Hawkes has moved toward realism seems misleading. His more recent plot lines, for instance, may be easier to unravel, but they by no means resemble traditional plot development. The later novels do show a trend away from brilliantly controlled individual scenes in favor of more normal narrative flow, but their tones remain as complex as their experiments with technique. All of his novels, including probably those yet to be published, involve the reader in the creative process, as it were. The difficulties of his work make the reading of them an active experience, so that we cannot be passive recipients of what Hawkes puts in front of us. The scheme of related action and recurring image forces reader participation if the overall narrative coherence is to be grasped.

Although Hawkes is not moving toward realism in the traditional sense, Professor Guerard has been proved essentially correct —the later novels are clearer. This shift of emphasis began roughly in 1961 with the publication of *The Lime Twig*. Fantastic image patterns and nonrealistic style remain, but not in such liberal quantities. The result is a relative lucidity. "Relative" is the key word, for the later novels are rough going, just as his future work is likely to be. This toning down of visual power—of those incredible shots like the revolt in the asylum or Luke Lampson's shower—has been compensated by a more sharply focused narrative element. It is primarily for these two reasons, the more definite narrative line and the more sympathetic characters, that the reader of all of Hawkes' fiction feels a sense of relief when he reaches *The Lime Twig*, *Second Skin*, and *The Blood Oranges*. The difficulties are still formidable, but these novels seem more accessible. At the risk of sounding like a prophet, a dangerous role when writing about fiction as unexpectedly experimental as Hawkes', I believe that the novels to come will continue this direction toward relative lucidity, if only for the reason that he likes to parody novelistic conventions. The traditional rules and methods of novel writing are not as susceptible to parody in a militantly experimental fiction. Hawkes seems to have turned from the parody of genre, such as the western in *The Beetle Leg*, to a burlesque of the fictional process itself. Once again, *The Lime Twig* signals the change. The story of the Bankses' involvement with Larry and his gang of hoods is a parody of the hard-boiled detective thriller, but with the voices of Hencher and Sidney Slyter, Hawkes begins mocking the device of the first-person narrator. Always, though, the need to parody will remain a secondary function, for the primary aim will continue to be the violation of anticipated reality.

Another development in the various novels concerns the degree of fear felt by the reader. As the novels move away from the more obvious experimentation, the element of fear seems magnified. This may be because the characters' predicaments in the later fictions are recognizable enough to suggest the possibility of our identification with them. Not many readers have experienced the horrors of Germany during two world wars, but most can understand Skipper's anguished concern for his daughter or Cyril's pursuit of a perfect love. Because the situations are closer to home they seem designed to involve us. Skipper's snowball fight is not as removed from our world as the Duke's dissection of the boy. In the two most recent novels particularly, *Second Skin* and *The Blood Oranges*, Hawkes has encouraged a close relationship between the reader and the narrator. Yet the greater degree of experienced fears has been matched by a parallel increase in the comic element. These recent novels are also more obviously funny, and it seems safe to say that Hawkes will continue to emphasize humor. We remember that he has admitted his disappointment at the persistent misreadings of his earlier fiction as brilliant exercises in terror. Thus, one of his announced, and successfully realized, goals in *Second Skin* was to write a comic novel whose humor no one could miss. A similar, easily recognizable comedy informs *The Blood Oranges*. Because Hawkes considers himself a comic writer, it seems likely that in his future work he will continue to ease the difficulties associated with deciphering the function of comedy. This does not mean, of course, that his next novel will illustrate a corresponding increase in affirmation as the comic element is stressed. *Second Skin* is his most affirmative novel, but it is also the most violent in terms of sheer number of dire events. And that novel's emphasis on life's power to balance death seems to be neutralized in *The Blood Oranges*. Yet the comedy of both is a primary concern, a quality which must be recognized if Hawkes is finally to escape the criticism by negative readers who have eyes only for the terror.

Hopefully, this move toward both a more accessible reading experience and a more recognizable humor will encourage serious readers to sample the pleasures of John Hawkes. Though dismissing the notion that he might write for a particular group, Hawkes noted in the 1965 interview in *Wisconsin Studies in Contemporary Literature* that his books were finally gaining an audience. It is interesting to note that when he speaks of an audience, he seems to realize the boundaries of his potential appeal, for he mentions readers who are interested in the "limitless possibilities" of the novel. He continues, "I'm trying to write about large issues of human torments and aspirations, and I'm convinced that considerable numbers of people in this country must have imaginative needs quite similar to mine." His concern for the possibilities of the novel has enabled him to create the most imaginative fiction of any writer associated with the modern American comic novel. When reading John Hawkes, we know that the prophets of the novel's death are wrong.

Selected Checklist of John Hawkes

I. NOVELS

Charivari. New Directions 11 (1949), 365–436.
The Cannibal. Norfolk, Connecticut: New Directions, 1949.
The Beetle Leg. New York: New Directions, 1951.
The Goose on the Grave and *The Owl.* New York: New Directions, 1954.
The Lime Twig. New York: New Directions, 1961.
Second Skin. New York: New Directions, 1964.
The Blood Oranges. New York: New Directions, 1971.

II. SHORT FICTION

"Death of a Maiden," *Wake*, No. 6 (Spring 1948), 85–96.
"Death of an Airman," *New Directions 12* (1950), 261–266.
"The Courtier," *New Directions 13* (1951), 236–245.
"The Lay Brothers," *New Directions 14* (1953), 281–287.
"The Horse in a London Flat," *Accent*, 20 (Winter 1960), 3–19.
"The Lodging House Fires," *Audience*, 7 (Spring 1960), 61–77.
"The Grandmother," *New Directions 17* (1961), 51–64.
"The Traveler," *MSS*, 1 (Winter 1962), 166–175.
"A Little Bit of the Old Slap and Tickle," *The Noble Savage*, No. 5 (October 1962), 19–23.

"From *The Blood Oranges*," *TriQuarterly*, No. 20 (Winter 1971), 113–129.

"The Universal Fears," *American Review* (February 1973), 108–123.

III. COLLECTIONS

Lunar Landscapes. New York: New Directions, 1969.
    Includes: "The Traveler"
              "The Grandmother"
              "A Little Bit of the Old Slap and Tickle"
              "Death of an Airman"
              "A Song Outside"
              "The Nearest Cemetery"
              Charivari
              The Owl
              The Goose on the Grave

IV PLAYS

The Innocent Party. New York: New Directions, 1966.
    Includes: *The Innocent Party*
              The Wax Museum
              The Undertaker
              The Questions

V CRITICISM BY HAWKES

"Notes on Violence," *Audience*, 7 (Spring 1960), 60.

"The Voice of Edwin Honig," *Voices: A Journal of Poetry*, No. 174 (January–April 1961), 39–47.

"Flannery O'Connor's Devil," *Sewanee Review*, 70 (Summer 1962), 395–407.

"Notes on the Wild Goose Chase," *The Massachusetts Review*, 3 (Summer 1962), 784–788.

VI. INTERVIEWS

"John Hawkes: An Interview," *Wisconsin Studies in Contemporary Literature*, 6 (Summer 1965), 141–155.

"John Hawkes on His Novels: An Interview with John Graham," *The Massachusetts Review*, 7 (Summer 1966) , 449–461.

"A Conversation on *The Blood Oranges* Between John Hawkes and Robert Scholes," *Novel*, 5 (Spring 1972), 197–207.

"Talks with John Hawkes," *The Harvard Advocate*, 104 (October 1970) , 6, 34–35.

VII. BIBLIOGRAPHIES

Bryer, Jackson R. "Two Bibliographies" (John Hawkes and John Barth), *Critique*, 6 (Fall 1963), 86–94.

VIII. CRITICISM OF HAWKES AND SIGNIFICANT REVIEWS

Beacham, Walter. "Hawkes' New Novel Imparts Nagging Sense of Importance," *Richmond Times—Dispatch*, 5 December 1971, p. F–5, (review of *The Blood Oranges*).

Bishop, Tom. "Lunar Landscapes," *Saturday Review*, 9 August 1969, p. 31, (review of *Lunar Landscapes*).

Brooks, Peter. "John Hawkes," *Encounter*, 26 (June 1966), 68–72, (review of *Second Skin*).

Busch, Frederick. *Hawkes: A Guide to His Fictions*. Syracuse: Syracuse University Press, 1973.

Creeley, Robert. "How to Write a Novel," *New Mexico Quarterly*, 22 (Summer 1952), 239–241, (review of *The Beetle Leg*).

De Feo, Ronald. "*The Blood Oranges*," *Saturday Review*, 23 October 1971, pp. 92, 94.

Didion, Joan. "Notes from a Helpless Reader," *National Review*, 15 July 1961, pp. 21–22, (review of *The Lime Twig*).

Edenbaum, Robert I. "John Hawkes: *The Lime Twig* and Other Tenuous Horrors," *The Massachusetts Review*, 7 (Summer 1966), 462–475.

Fiedler, Leslie A. "The Pleasures of John Hawkes," in John Hawkes, *The Lime Twig*. New York: New Directions, 1961, pp. vii–xiv.

Flint, F. Cudworth. "Fiction Chronicle," *Sewanee Review*, 60 (Autumn 1952), 706–721, (review of *The Beetle Leg*).

Frohock, W. M. "John Hawkes's Vision of Violence," *Southwest Review*, 50 (Winter 1965), 69–79.

Frost, Lucy. "The Drowning of American Adam: Hawkes' *The Beetle Leg*," *Critique*, 14 (Summer 1973), 63–74.

Greiner, Donald J. "Strange Laughter: The Comedy of John Hawkes," *Southwest Review*, 56 (Autumn 1971), 318–328.

————. "The Thematic Use of Color in John Hawkes' *Second Skin*," *Contemporary Literature*, 11 (Summer 1970), 389–400.

Guerard, Albert J. "Introduction," in John Hawkes, *The Cannibal*. New York: New Directions Paperback, 1962, pp. ix–xx.

————. "Introduction to the Cambridge Anti-Realists," *Audience*, 7 (Spring 1960), 57–59.

————. "The Prose Style of John Hawkes," *Critique*, 6 (Fall 1963), 19–29.

_____. "Some Recent Novels," *Perspectives USA*, 1 (Fall 1952), 168–172, (review of *The Beetle Leg*).

_____. "The Illuminating Distortion," *Novel*, 5 (Winter 1972), 101–121.

_____. "John Hawkes in English J," *The Harvard Advocate*, 104 (October 1970), 10.

Hanzo, T. A. "The Two Faces of Matt Donelson," *Sewanee Review*, 73 (Winter 1965), 106–119, (review of *Second Skin*).

Lavers, Norman. "The Structure of *Second Skin*," *Novel*, 5 (Spring 1972), 208–214.

Littlejohn, David. "The Anti-Realists," *Daedalus*, 92 (Spring 1963), 250–264.

McGuane, Thomas. "*The Blood Oranges*," *New York Times Book Review*, Section 7, 19 September 1971, p. 1.

Malin, Irving. *New American Gothic*. Carbondale: Southern Illinois University Press, 1962.

Matthews, Charles. "The Destructive Vision of John Hawkes," *Critique*, 6 (Fall 1963), 38–52.

Moran, Charles. "John Hawkes: Paradise Gaining," *Massachusetts Review*, 12 (Autumn 1971), 840–845, (review of *The Blood Oranges*).

Oberbeck, S. K. "John Hawkes: The Smile Slashed by a Razor," in *Contemporary American Novelists*, ed. Harry T. Moore. Carbondale: Southern Illinois University Press, 1968, pp. 193–204.

Olderman, Raymond M. *Beyond the Waste Land: The American Novel in The Nineteen-Sixties*. New Haven: Yale University Press, 1972, especially pages 150–175.

Pearce, Richard. *Stages of the Clown: Perspectives on Modern Fiction from Dostoyevsky to Beckett*. Carbondale: Southern Illinois University Press, 1970.

Politzer, Heinz. "Five Novels," *Commentary*, 13 (May 1952), 510–512, (review of *The Beetle Leg*).

Redman, Ben Ray. "German Degeneration and Collapse," *Saturday Review of Literature*, 11 March 1950, pp. 16–17, (review of *The Cannibal*).

Reutlinger, D. P. "*The Cannibal*: 'The Reality of Victim'," *Critique*, 6 (Fall 1963), 30–37.

Ricks, Christopher. "Chamber of Horrors," *New Statesman*, 11 March 1966, pp. 339–340.

Rosenfield, Claire. "John Hawkes: Nightmares of the Real," *The Minnesota Review*, 2 (Winter 1962), 249–254, (review of *The Lime Twig*).

Rovit, Earl. "The Fiction of John Hawkes: An Introductory View," *Modern Fiction Studies*, 11 (Summer 1964), 150–162.

Sale, Roger. "*The Blood Oranges,*" *New York Review of Books,* 21 October 1971, pp. 2–6.

Scholes, Robert. *The Fabulators.* New York: Oxford University Press, 1967.

Schott, Webster. "John Hawkes, American Original," *New York Times Book Review,* 29 May 1966, pp. 4, 24–25.

Shepard, Allen. "Illumination through (Anti) Climax: John Hawkes' *The Lime Twig,*" *Notes on Contemporary Literature,* 2 (March 1972), 11–13.

Stone, Jerome. "Surrealistic Threesome," *Saturday Review,* 24 July 1954, pp. 35–36, (review of *Goose on the Grave* and *The Owl*).

Studies in Second Skin. Compiled by John Graham. Columbus: Charles E. Merrill, 1971.

"Surrealist Western," *Newsweek,* 31 December 1951, pp. 58–59, (review of *The Beetle Leg*).

Tanner, Tony. "Necessary Landscapes and Luminous Deteriorations: On Hawkes," *TriQuarterly,* No. 20 (Winter 1971), 145–179.

_____. *City of Words: American Fiction 1950–1970.* New York: Harper and Row, 1971, especially pp. 202–229.

"Teutonic Nightmare," *Time,* 6 February 1950, pp. 90, 92, (review of *The Cannibal*).

Trachtenberg, Alan. "Barth and Hawkes: Two Fabulists," *Critique,* 6 (Fall 1963), 4–18.

Index

Adeppi, *see* Chapter Two
Annie, *see* Chapter Five
Antonina, *see* Chapter Two
Archduke Ferdinand, *see* Chapter Three
Aristotle, 18, 19
Arsella, *see* Chapter Two
Artemis, *see* Chapter Five
artificial insemination, *see* Chapter Six
Ashley, Jack, 220fn
Austen, Jane: *Emma*, 20

Balamir, *see* Chapter Three
Banks, Margaret: xvi, 22, 201, 226–227, 245; *see* Chapter Five
Banks, Michael: xvi, 11, 170, 201, 226–227, 239, 244, 245; *see* Chapter Five
Barabo, *see* Chapter Two

Barnes, Djuna: 25, 26; *Nightwood*, 12, 18, 157
Barth, John: xiii, 1; *Giles Goat-Boy*, xiii
Baumbach, Jonathan: *The Landscape of Nightmare: Studies in the Contemporary American Novel*, xvii-xviii
Bayley, Harold, 141fn
Beacham, Walter: on *The Blood Oranges*, 206–207, 213, 214, 227
Beckett, Samuel, 129
Bergson, Henri: xix, 22; "Laughter," 20
Bishop, Tom: on John Hawkes, xvii
Black humor: compared with traditional humor, 16–28; defined by Bruce Jay Friedman, xii-xiii; definition of, xi-xvi, 243; et passim

Bohn, Harry, *see* Chapter Four
Bourjaily, Vance, xii
Brahms, Johannes, 178
Brooks, Peter: 121; on *The Beetle Leg*, 98–99; on *The Cannibal*, 70–71; on *The Lime Twig*, 160
Brother Bolo, *see* Chapter Two
Brother Dolce: 104; *see* Chapter Two
Bub, *see* Chapter Six
Busch, Frederick, 124fn

Camper, *see* Chapter Four
Camper, Lou, *see* Chapter Four
Capote, Truman: *Other Voices, Other Rooms*, xviii
Captain Red, *see* Chapter Six
Cassandra: 14, 15, 23; *see* Chapter Six
Catalina Kate: 10; *see* Chapter Six
Catherine, *see* Chapter Seven
Census Taker, *see* Chapter Three
Cervantes, 18
Cesario, 223–224
Christ, 235
Clytemnestra, 188
Coleridge, Samuel, 144
Cowles, *see* Chapter Five
Cox, Harvey, 17–18
Craig, Hardin, 222, 223
Crete, 225
Cromwell, *see* Chapter Three
Cyril: 9, 241, 246; *see* Chapter Seven

Daedalus, 63
De Feo, Ronald: on *The Blood Oranges*, 206, 236
Diana, 142
Dionysus, 216, 225
Donleavy, J. P.: xii, xiii; *The Ginger Man*, xii, xvi
Donne, John, 144

Dora, *see* Chapter Five
The Duke: 10, 22, 23, 104, 246; as a cannibal, 94–95; *see* Chapter Three

Edouard, *see* Chapter Two
England; *see* Chapter Five; *see also* London

Faulkner, William, xiv, 123
Fernandez, *see* Chapter Six
Fiedler, Leslie: on John Hawkes, xvi, 61, 129, 139, 151, 225
Fiona, *see* Chapter Seven
Fitzgerald, F. Scott, xiv
Flint, F. Cudworth: on *The Beetle Leg*, 120
Ford, Ford Madox: *The Good Soldier*, 202
Franco-Prussian War, *see* Chapter Three
Fraser, John, 167, 168, 169, 171
Frazer, James George: *The Golden Bough*, 216, 217, 218, 219, 225
Freud, Sigmund, 17
Friedman, Bruce Jay: *The Dick*, xiii; *Stern*, xiii; defines black humor, xii-xiii, 243
Frohock, W. M.: on John Hawkes, 97–98, 170–171; on *The Lime Twig*, 127
Frost, Lucy: on *The Beetle Leg*, 124fn
Frye, Northrop, 23

Gaylor, *see* Chapter Two
Germany: 130, 215, 246; *see* Chapter Three; *see also* Nazism
Gertrude, *see* Chapter Six
the Great Slide, *see* Chapter Four
Greene, Graham, 130
Grimm's Fairy Tales, 59
Guerard, Albert J.: on John

Hawkes, 126, 130, 244–245; on *The Beetle Leg*, 107, 119, 121–122; on *The Cannibal*, 68, 69, 84, 86, 90, 96

Il Gufo: 167, 184; *see* Chapter Two

Hamlet, 188

Hanzo, T. A.: on *Second Skin*, 182, 186

Hawkes, John: affinity with experimental poetry, 11–15; comic technique, 16–28, 242–243, 246; development of, 244–247; fictional technique, 1–16, 242–245; parody of novelistic conventions, 7–9, 245–246; place in American fiction, xi-xix; reaction against traditional comedy, 21–28; visual sense, 9–11

ARTICLES

"Flannery O'Connor's Devil," 3, 4, 177, 226

"Notes on Violence," 11, 12, 96

"Notes on the Wild Goose Chase," 3, 12, 13, 26, 157, 167, 208

"The Voice of Edwin Honig," 13, 15, 26, 177, 182

INTERVIEWS

"A Conversation on *The Blood Oranges* Between John Hawkes and Robert Scholes," 232–233fn

"John Hawkes: An Interview," 5, 6, 7, 8–9, 10, 25, 27, 87, 100, 126, 131, 134, 137, 139, 156, 160, 170, 189, 209–210, 247

"John Hawkes on His Novels: An Interview with John Graham," 7, 10, 25, 70, 74, 142, 148, 157, 161, 162, 176, 210

NOVELS

The Beetle Leg: 7, 8, 125, 159, 160, 170, 205, 234, 244, 245; arid landscape in, 104–105; critical reaction to, 98–99; mixture of humor and violence in, 101–104, 111–112, 116–119; parody of the Western in, 97, 100–101, 106–107, 109–113, 117–118, 122; potential for violence in, 105–107, 110–111, 116; style and structure in, 121–124; uses of myth in, 113–115, 119–120; *see* Chapter Four

The Blood Oranges: 9, 241–242, 243, 245, 246; compared with *Second Skin*, 201–203, 226–227, 229; critical reaction to, 205–209; distortion of love in, 203, 222–227; effect of Hugh's death in, 204–205, 233–237; humor in, 209–212, 230–231, 238–239; narration in, 207–210, 215, 227–230, 232–233, 236–237; recurring images (animals, flowers, Shakespeare) in, 214–226, 238; setting in, 213–214, 225; theories of love in, passim; *see* Chapter Seven

The Cannibal: 5, 8, 9, 10, 12, 22, 27, 52, 54, 65, 97, 104, 105, 126, 127, 130, 147, 159, 160, 177, 205, 214, 243, 244; animal imagery in, 89–94; cannibalism in, 73–75; experimental narration in, 8, 84–85; isolated scenes in, 70–73; recurring images in, 5, 87–94; uses of history in, 68–70, 75–80; *see* Chapter Three

Charivari: 6, 71, 205, 242, 243, 244; anti-realism in, 34–37; comedy and violence in, 37–40; flaws in, 42–43; structure of, 40–42; *see* Chapter Two

The Goose on the Grave: 67, 71, 104, 243, 244; sterile traditions in, 44, 50–53; unexplained events in, 53–55; victim-victimizer theme in, 53; *see* Chapter Two

The Lime Twig: xvi, 7, 10, 11, 22, 40, 52, 61, 70, 71, 97, 159, 160, 201, 203, 206, 225, 226, 239, 241, 243, 245; affirmation in, 155–157; as more accessible fiction, 125–126; critical reaction to, 126–127, 129–130; experimental narration in, 8–9, 130–133; loneliness in, 134–138; parody of detective thriller in, 125, 126–127, 147, 158; recurring images in, 157–158; sexual frustration and love and terror in, 128, 135–136, 138–142, 144–148, 150–153; theme of liming in, 138, 144, 147–150, 151, 158; use of dreams in, 127–129, et passim; victim-victimizer theme in, 152–153; violation of innocence in, 146–147, 152–155; *see* Chapter Five

The Owl: 67, 106, 177, 242, 243; combination of love and terror in, 61–62; language and form in, 64–66; narrative method in, 65; sterile traditions in, 56–61, 62–63; *see* Chapter Two

Second Skin: xiii, xvi, 6, 7–8, 9, 10, 14, 15, 23–25, 26, 27, 40, 43, 48, 70, 71, 119, 147, 201, 203, 205, 206, 215, 226, 229, 238, 239, 241, 243, 245; 246; affirmation in, 162, 176–178, 183, 185, 198; as more accessible fiction, 159–160; color imagery and recurring image in, 189–199; heroism in, 161, 171–176, 182–183; 187; language and poetic technique in, 14–15, 168, 183, 185–187, 199; life versus death in, 176–183, 185, 198; parody of first-person narrator in, 7–8, 160–161, 162–163, 183–185, 187–189; reader reaction to Skipper, 161–167, 171–173, 179–180, 185, 187; victimization in, 163, 164–167, 171, 181; violence in, 167–173, 176–179; *see* Chapter Six

Helen of Troy, 188

Heller, Joseph: 25; *Catch-22*, xii, xiii, xvi

Hemingway, Ernest: xiv; *A Farewell to Arms*, xvi

Hencher, William: 8–9, 160, 184, 203, 245; *see* Chapter Five

High Noon, 100

Honig, Edwin, 13, 26, 177, 182

Horst-Wessel Leid, 84

Hugh, *see* Chapter Seven

Icarus, 63

Illyria, *see* Chapter Seven

Iphigenia, 188

Italy: 213; *see* Chapter Two

Jacopo, *see* Chapter Two

James, Henry: *What Maisie Knew*, xvi

Jomo, *see* Chapter Six

Jutta: 22, 104; *see* Chapter Three

Kennedy, John, 16

Kesey, Ken, xiii

Knickerbocker, Conrad, xii, xv

Kostelanetz, Richard, xii

Kronenberger, Louis, 19–20, 21

Lampson, Hattie, *see* Chapter Four

Lampson, Luke: 170, 245; *see* Chapter Four

Lampson, Ma, *see* Chapter Four

Lampson, Mulge, *see* Chapter Four

Larry: 245; *see* Chapter Five

Laughlin, James, 130

Laval, Sybilline, *see* Chapter Five

Leech, Cap: 167, 170; *see* Chapter Four

Leevey, *see* Chapter Three

Lehner, Ernst and Johanna, 218fn

Levine, Paul: on John Hawkes, xvi-xvii

Lewis, Sinclair: *Babbitt*, 16

Littlejohn, David: on *The Beetle Leg*, 99; on *The Cannibal*, 71; on *The Lime Twig*, 129, 130

London: *see* Chapter Five; *see also* England

McGuane, Thomas: on *The Blood Oranges*, 205–206

Maddocks, Melvin, 16–17

Malvolio, 222–223, 235

Mary, Virgin, *see* Chapters Two and Six

M*A*S*H, 17

Matthews, Charles: on *The Lime Twig*, 156

Menelaus, 188

Mephistopheles, 88

Meredith, *see* Chapter Seven

Meredith, George: xix, 22, 158; "On Comedy and the Uses of the Comic Spirit," 19

Miranda: 23, 147, 239; *see* Chapter Six

Monica: 10, 52; *see* Chapter Five

The Naked and the Dead, 67

Nazism: *see* Chapter Three; *see also* Germany

Nino, see Chapter Two

Nixon, Richard, 17

Oberbeck, S. K.: on John Hawkes, 128

O'Connor, Flannery: xviii, 4, 25, 26, 177; *The Violent Bear It Away*, 14

Olivia, 223–224

Duke Orsino, 223–224, 225

Pan, 216

Pascal, 194

Plato, 141fn

Poirier, Richard: *A World Elsewhere*, xii

Politzer, Heinz: on *The Beetle Leg*, 123–124

Pope, Alexander, xiv

Poppins, Mary, 139

Prince Paris, 188

Princip, Gavrilo, *see* Chapter Three

Pucento, *see* Chapter Two

Purdy, James, xiii

Pynchon, Thomas, xiii

Red Devils, *see* Chapter Four

Reutlinger, D. P.: on *The Cannibal*, 75

Robbe-Grillet, Alain, xviii

Rock Castle: 239; *see* Chapter Five

Rosella, *see* Chapter Seven

Rosenfield, Claire: on *The Beetle Leg*, 118

Rovit, Earl: on John Hawkes, 53, 130, 158; on *The Beetle Leg*, 99; on *The Cannibal*, 73; on *The Lime Twig*, 126, 136, 139

St. George, 175

St. Peter, 235

Sale, Roger: on *The Blood Oranges*, 207–208, 209

Sarajevo, *see* Chapter Three

Sarraute, Nathalie, xviii

Sasso Fetore, *see* Chapter Two

Satyrs, the, 216

Scholes, Robert: 11, 16; *The Fabulators*, xiv, 2–3; on *The Blood Oranges*, 232fn; on *Charivari*, 6, 30, 43; on fabulation, xii, xv; on *The Lime Twig*, 152

Sebastian, 224

Selvaggia: 52; *see* Chapter Three

Shakespeare, William: 214, 215, 222, 223; *Twelfth Night*, 144; *see* Chapter Seven

Shane, 117

sheriff (*The Beetle Leg*): 8, 184, 244; *see* Chapter Four

Silenus, 216

Sister Josie, *see* Chapter Six

Skipper: xvi, 9, 14–15, 23–25, 26, 43, 48, 119, 201, 215, 226–227, 239, 246; as narrator, 7–8; compared with Cyril, 202–204, 225–226, 229; in belly bumping contest, 14; in snowball fight, 24–25; *see* Chapter Six

Slyter, Sidney: 245; *see* Chapter Five

Snow, Ernst: 102; *see* Chapter Three

Snow, Stella: 5, 102; *see* Chapter Three

Some Like It Hot, 17

Sonny, *see* Chapter Six

Sorrentino, Gilbert: on *The Blood Oranges*, 207–208

Sparrow, *see* Chapter Five

Spitzen-on-the-Dein, *see* Chapter Three

Sterne, Laurence, xiv, 18

Stewart, Jerrie Ashmore, 141fn

Herr Stinz, *see* Chapter Three

Stone, Jerome: on *The Goose on the Grave*, 44

Swift, Jonathan, xiv, 18

Talos, 225

Tanner, Tony: on *Second Skin*, 187

Thegna, *see* Chapter Four

Thick, *see* Chapter Five

Thor, 188

Three Soldiers, 67

Sir Toby, 222–223

Tremlow, *see* Chapter Six

Troilus and Criseyde, 144

Uncle Billy, 14

Van, Emily, *see* Chapter Two

Van, Henry, *see* Chapter Two

Venus, 188

Viola, 223–224

The Virginian, 100

Vonnegut, Kurt: xii, xiii, 1; *Cat's Cradle*, xii; *Mother Night*, 16

Wain, John: on John Hawkes, xvii

West, Nathanael: xii, 4, 25, 26; *Miss Lonelyhearts*, 18

Wordsworth, William, 144

World War I, *see* Chapter Three

World War II: 132, 134, 139; *see* Chapter Three

Wyatt, Sir Thomas, 144

Zizendorf: 5, 8, 65, 147, 167, 183; *see* Chapter Three